Janet Walton is the mother of the world's first all-female sextuplets. With her husband Graham, she had been trying to have children for a number of years when she finally fell pregnant after her thirteenth fertility treatment. Janet still lives in Wallasey, Liverpool, and is glad that at least one daughter — Hannah — still lives at home. She was the administrator of the Newborn Appeal at Liverpool Women's NHS Foundation Trust for over twenty years.

SIX LITTLE MIRACLES

Janet had been told she couldn't have children, so she and her husband Graham were overjoyed to find out she was pregnant. Then they told her it was not just one baby, but six! On 18 November 1983, Janet gave birth to the world's first all-female sextuplets: Hannah, Lucy, Ruth, Sarah, Kate and Jenny. Janet takes us through the reality of parenting six children of the same age — the extreme sleep deprivation, the bottle-feeding, and later the chaotic routine of getting the six of them to school on time. As they grew up, Janet kept a sense of humour through the teenage tantrums and boy trouble, and she watched her little girls blossom into individual, confident young women. She has loved every minute.

JANET WALTON
with Robert Ettinger

◆

SIX LITTLE MIRACLES

The heartwarming true story of raising
the world's first sextuplet girls

Complete and Unabridged

CHARNWOOD
Leicester

First published in Great Britain in 2015 by
Ebury Press
an imprint of Ebury Publishing
London

First Charnwood Edition
published 2016
by arrangement with
Ebury Publishing
London

Plate section credits:
Page 6 (bottom) © Alistair Morrison; page 4
(bottom) and page 7 (top and bottom) © Mirrorpix.

A catalogue record for this book is available
from the British Library.

ISBN 978–1–4448–2785–9

Published by
F. A. Thorpe (Publishing)
Anstey, Leicestershire

Set by Words & Graphics Ltd.
Anstey, Leicestershire
Printed and bound in Great Britain by
T. J. International Ltd., Padstow, Cornwall

This book is printed on acid-free paper

To Graham, the love of my life
and my best friend

Contents

Prologue

I lay in the room with Illa, who was overseeing the scan. I had been told as a teenager that I wouldn't be able to have children, and I had only found out that morning that I really was pregnant. My head was still spinning from the shock and my emotions were all over the place.

Illa had a wonderfully expressive smile and her joy at my news was clear. She began her work and her hand moved across me time and again. I waited for her to speak. More hand movement — and then I detected a slight change in her face. She was looking quite intensely at the screen. I couldn't wait any longer for her to speak.

'What can you see, Illa?' I asked, almost apologetically, not wanting to disturb her concentration. 'Is everything alright?'

'Well, Janet,' her voice hadn't altered; the joy of the pregnancy still seemed there, 'it looks like you may be carrying more than one.'

'Do you mean we are having twins?'

'Well, it does look like a multiple birth,' she said cautiously, 'but I need to go and get somebody else to look at the scan.'

Illa told me to wait outside with my husband Graham, while she went to get the doctor in charge of the department that afternoon. More waiting time — but double the joy! To me, this couldn't have been better news. Not only was I finally pregnant, after all the years of heartache and pain, but the reward was more than I could ever have hoped.

The word 'multiple' didn't really register as meaning anything other than the possibility of twins at that stage. I was pregnant, perhaps with twins! It sounded the most wonderful thing I'd ever heard, and I now moved up to cloud ten. I was absolutely as high as a kite.

I went to find Graham. He could see that the smile on my face was even bigger; I was beaming from ear to ear. I grabbed hold of him and gave him the biggest hug ever.

'It might be twins!'

I was shaking, and tears of happiness began to flow. We had talked about twins when the adoption society had said we might be eligible to adopt more than one baby. Graham was both bemused and shocked by the unexpected news, but no less joyous at the possibility.

Before long, I was called back into the room, where I was given a second scan, this time in the presence of the doctor in charge on the day, Adrian Murray. After a while, though, the mood in the room seemed to change. For a start, there were a lot more people in the room.

The scanning went on. It began to feel like things were taking a little too long. I began to notice that the familiar faces around me weren't as joyful as they had been a little earlier. Eyes around me seemed to narrow and brows dropped.

My patience disintegrated in a flood of emotion, fuelled by a sudden belief that

2

something was seriously wrong. I raised my voice above the murmurs of incredulity around the scanning equipment.

'Will you please let me know what's going on!'

The doctor looked at me with a face that wasn't delivering happy news of a baby.

'It looks as if it might be a multiple birth,' he said.

I knew this. This was why Graham and I had felt so good not so long ago.

But Dr Murray now delivered a bombshell.

'It appears that you are expecting six babies.'

Instantly, I felt an explosion of emotion. I was surrounded by people, but I had never felt more alone. It was as though the huge number of nurses and doctors disappeared and I wasn't aware of any of them. Graham was ushered into the room to be by my side, more bewildered than ever, and I started crying again. This time, though, they weren't tears of joy.

It was impossible to take in this kind of information. One minute we were possibly having twins; the next it was a major multiple birth and the doctors were not smiling. Wherever my eyes focused in that room there were only concerned, anxious faces. No one in the room had ever experienced a multiple birth of this size.

No one knew whether I would be able to have the babies or not.

Yet, despite all the anxiety in the room, I was suddenly overcome with a sense of calm. I made a promise to myself. I was going to do everything I was told. I was going to be the best patient ever.

I was going to make sure I had these babies.

1

Bedtime Stories

One of the most endearing and enduring memories of my childhood is a simple ritual that almost everyone experiences during the first precious years of life. It brings with it feelings of security and warmth, of adventure, excitement and vivid colours. Sometimes it would bring with it laughter and sometimes tears. There seemed no limit to these escapades and my little heart would beat faster than I could ever have imagined possible. There were occasions when I giggled so much it hurt and there were just as many times when I was plunged into darkness as I pretended to hide, finding protection under the soft blankets of my bed.

Each night, at almost the same time, I would lie with my head on the pillow, face scrubbed, teeth and hair brushed as I waited patiently for Mum to come and sit on the edge of the bed. The place was a tiny bedroom in Smithy Close, a tiny cul-de-sac in the village of Ness. It was the first home of my mum and dad, Peter and Nancy Leadbetter, nestling in the heart of the Wirral peninsular, a finger of rolling green countryside overlooking the Welsh hills. With the tidal waters of the River Dee on one side and the River Mersey lapping away on the other, it points directly towards the Irish Emerald Isle.

The ritual was the bedtime story. It could be a traditional fairy tale from Hans Christian Andersen or the Brothers Grimm: 'The Princess and the Pea', 'Hansel and Gretel' or 'Sleeping Beauty'. Although I had my favourites, in truth it didn't matter which it was because what I really wanted was to have my mum to myself for a little bit each night before I fell asleep.

She told the stories to me in her very best pretend voices, making sounds in the way she spoke that I would never hear during the day. She had a voice for being happy, a voice for being annoyed, a voice for being kind, an angry voice and one for crying and being terribly upset. When she sounded worried, I was worried; when she sounded upset, I was upset; and when she hid her eyes or pretended to cry, I always lifted my little fingers from where they were clutching the edge of the blanket that was already halfway up my face and pulled at her fingers to see if there were real tears, and when there weren't we would laugh together.

It took me many years to realise what the meaning really was of those precious moments. Over thirty years later I would sit in a semicircle of six children using the same intonations I had heard as a child from my mother. I, too, was now a mother and nothing in the world has ever given me the same thrill as when I sat among my children reading the same stories, with the same pretend voices. And also new characters, such as Enid Blyton's *Noddy and Big Ears* or Roald Dahl's *Fantastic Mr Fox*, created by more modern imagination.

The fundamental act of telling a story to a child is one of the simplest things we have to pass on from one generation to another. Without either of us knowing it at the time, Mum taught me, by example, everything I needed to know about raising children before I even went to school. No lesson outside the house could have prepared me better for what chance brought to me many years later.

It would be just another evening and our six four-year-old girls' favourite time of the day. Each had her own favourite story and each had learnt the important lessons of patience and sharing. There was, in truth, little choice. They would sit and listen intently, all together, each responding in her own different way. Ruth might pretend to sneeze or Lucy might cry out 'No-o-o!' in a ridiculously extended manner that would have all the others in pleats of laughter. Sarah would be very quiet, taking it all in, and Hannah also would never miss a trick; Kate would impersonate a character from one of the stories; and then Jenny would get the biggest laugh of all by pretending to be me by saying a phrase I might use that was totally familiar to the girls.

So whether it was my mum reading to me, me reading to my little sister when I was sixteen, or, years later, me telling similar bedtime tales to my six daughters, sitting in that semicircle on the landing between the bedrooms, it was all about the story. Although each has its reason for being written in the first place, each has its moral lesson of the battle between good and evil, the importance to me is the passing on of the ritual. A special moment between parent and child, an everyday tradition, passed on unwittingly from Mum to me, that I could also have with me and my girls.

2

The Bowling Green

Uncle Humphrey was a bachelor who lived with his sister Molly on the other side of the village. One of my earliest memories is of walking, one fresh summer's day, hand in hand with my Auntie Molly through our little country village of Neston. The fragrance of the azaleas and rhododendrons followed us and lingered along the road as we made our way from my Nanny Fox's emporium of knitting and wool to where Molly and Humphrey lived. It was only around the corner, not too far for my little legs to manage. To combat the boredom and restlessness of a six-year-old I was taken there for a cup of tea and, if I'd been good, a slice of cake. The tea walk would happen a few times each summer and I was always in awe of the house as it was crammed to the ceiling with all sorts of bits and pieces.

In the corner of the parlour there was a brown leather tube-shaped satchel with the initials 'H' and 'L' for Humphrey Leadbetter embossed above the brass lock. On occasion the lock wasn't clasped shut and the bag was left partially open. Inside I could see three large, perfectly formed, shiny black balls with rings etched into them. Each one had a bright yellow dot in the middle of the ring. I wasn't sure at that age what they were but they were bright and shiny and of interest to a curious child — especially as we had the same in our house, except the ones at home had a red dot.

'You can't play with those balls, Janet!' Auntie Molly would say, every time she closed the front door behind us. 'Your Uncle Humphrey would have a fit! Besides, they are far too heavy for a little girl to pick up.'

'But we have the same in our house,' I would reply, having watched in wonderment as my dad spent ages polishing his pride and joys. The only difference, besides the colour of the dot, was that my dad's leather bag required a 'P' for Peter embossed alongside the 'L'.

Once I was old enough, I used to go and watch my dad play bowls with Humphrey. I'm not sure whether he had to get special permission to allow me to keep score but because I was so quick at adding up and calculating he encouraged me to mark his card. There must have been a few raised eyebrows as all the other players used to have older members marking their cards. But I sat in the sunshine on the wooden benches on the border of the huge undulating green square, breathing in the smell of cut grass and focusing with all my young powers of concentration on the shouts of 'one-up . . . two up!' and carefully noting down the score as the bowls chased the jack.

To make ends meet, my mum and dad both worked full time. Dad at first was at the Shotton Steelworks, about ten miles from where we lived. Besides the enjoyment he got from playing bowls, he also loved sketching and was quite a good portrait artist. Years later, when he retired from the steelworks, he was happy selling picture frames and prints on the local markets.

Mum worked in her mother-in-law's shop, which she had acquired after having built up a small knitting and wool business.

3

Nanny Fox

Each time the door opened in the little wool shop a bell would ring. The tone was clear and resounded through the air just long enough to allow the proprietor to stand and straighten her skirt, put a hand to her hair and present herself to the customer. She was an imposing figure but with rosy cheeks, a kind face and smile. The customer was always right. There was a skill in caring for the customer, a skill that was handled as softly as the stock on display on the shelves and in the wooden and glass cabinets, but as sharp as a whaler's harpoon in order to catch a sale. 'People skills' she called them, time and again reminding her young granddaughter and pretend sales assistant that they had served her well. I always listened. I loved to give her my full attention although as a ten-year-old I had little real idea of what she was on about, I just loved the feel of the wool, the smell of the shop, sorting the strands and being a helper.

Nanny Fox was first and foremost a businesswoman. It didn't matter a jot that her empire was no bigger than the cottage-sized shop she stood in day after day. It was cash that counted and that kept trouble away and food on the plate. Officially I was 'assistant number two', listening and taking instruction both from her and from the first assistant, my mum, as three generations sorted out all the wool and knitting needs for Neston. It was a village famous for Nelson's liaisons with his Lady Hamilton, its horticultural gardens and an annual Ladies' Day, the latter connected — perhaps appropriately in my case — to female-friendly societies. Mum had also by then added to the female ranks in the village, having given birth to my baby sister Alison.

By the time I was twelve my responsibilities had grown. I was now serving customers and selling the wool by the ounce and it was never one single ball of wool, always multiples. Mental arithmetic became a game as I calculated the cost of a customer's order faster than Nanny Fox's ready reckoner.

Although the wool was the main product, throughout the year other things would appear on the counters for sale. In line with half the other traders in the village, toys were sold in the run-up to Christmas; but her diversification into fireworks might have caused a couple of health-and-safety concerns nowadays . . .

One day, Mum arrived home, nerves on edge and looking pale. She was never comfortable with Bonfire Night and was clearly recovering from a traumatic experience.

'You will never believe what happened today,' she exclaimed.

I could see a cup of tea was necessary.

'Sit down,' I said, playing mum. 'I'll put the kettle on. What's Nanny Fox been up to now?'

'It's the blinking fireworks!'

Quick thought — I hadn't *heard* any explosions. I was finding it hard to keep a straight face.

'It wasn't funny!'

'What wasn't?'

'A man was choosing his own fireworks — ' she was still pulsating ' — picking them up one after another and putting them in the back near the wool.'

There were a few really big ones; they weren't in boxes and were sold individually. Nanny Fox also used to sell penny bangers and sparklers; a whole selection lay with their blue touchpaper nakedly displayed. As far as I recall, she didn't sell matches, although what use would one be without the other? And I can hear Nanny Fox saying, 'Every penny counts.'

'He was getting some fireworks,' my mum continued, 'and he leaned into the big cabinet with them all in . . . with a cigarette in his mouth!' The tea in her second cup was gently slopping over the edge into the saucer as her hands carried on shaking, some ten minutes after telling of the troubling occurrence.

In the early 1960s a cigarette hanging loosely between a man's lips as he chatted away was as common as the flat cap on his head. The only place you might just see a no-smoking sign was at a petrol station. You'd lose customers if you stopped people smoking in your shop — at least, according to Nanny Fox's rules for her emporium.

★ ★ ★

Every Saturday morning my nan used to send me to the local cake shop to get the bread for lunch and buy butter on the way back. The cake shop had a counter that was filled in, like a desk, and it had glass coverings and all the fancy cakes were on shelves. My eyes grew bigger and my taste buds danced every time I watched the assistant delicately use prongs to pick up the cakes.

It wasn't a big shop; there was barely room for the staff, let alone the customers, but it was always busy. The owner and his wife were caricatures from a jolly seaside picture postcard, blusteringly big, bright and colourful, keeping their customers content. When stocks were running low, he would shout an order to the kitchen for more meringues or sausage rolls to accommodate what always seemed a never-ending queue.

One Saturday, to the slight annoyance of the baker, a queue of people began to form behind me as I stood in the shop, distracted by an advert for someone to work on a Saturday. It was as if the wonderful aromas of pork pies and freshly baked bread had sent me into a trance. Somehow, they lured me into a new confidence and a desire to tackle the world outside the safe confines of the family business. (There was also the small matter of the family business not paying me, while this job would give me some money.) I ran back to the wool shop and before the bell had even finished its ring I was talking too fast for Mum's ears.

'There's a notice, Mum, a notice, in the shop.

I think it's just right. Do you think anyone would mind if I worked there instead of helping here?'

'Slow down, Janet.' She could see my excitement but I wasn't making any sense. 'What notice?'

I went around the counter and gave the bread and butter to Nanny Fox.

'There's an advert in the cake shop for someone to work on a Saturday.'

'Well, what about it?' She was testing me — this was a growing-up moment.

My excitement had been pegged back, but only a little. 'They want a Saturday girl and it could be absolutely right for me.'

'And what do you want me to do about it?'

'Well, will you ask about it for me?'

'No.' She said the word with so much finality, I was momentarily stunned. All that excitement and good feeling seemed to unravel quicker than a ball of wool. But she hadn't quite finished. 'If you want the job, you go and ask about it for yourself!'

Her tactic worked. I walked back to the cake shop, waited until a customer had been served, and then took a deep breath and asked about the job.

The baker was of a similar age to my nan. He had always seemed friendly, but asking for a job was different to ordering a loaf of bread: this was an interview. His cheeks seemed to take on a more serious tone of red and the tip of his nose seemed a touch more purple than usual. I suddenly felt a little intimidated.

He took his time answering me. I mentally

15

issued myself instructions: *deep breath, assert yourself.* I was standing businesslike, upright, to attention, just as I'd observed Nan do over the years.

'What makes you think you can do the job?' he said at last.

'Well, I've always helped in the wool shop.'

'Yes, but this is a bakery. There's a big difference between wool and bread, young lady. What skills have you got?'

This interview business was a little more difficult than I'd expected.

'Skills?' I hesitated as my brain clicked away, looking for the right thing to say.

'That's right, skills.'

Then Nanny Fox came to the rescue.

I looked him straight in the eye and said, 'People skills. I have people skills!'

He smiled, the familiar smile I'd seen on so many Saturday mornings. 'Oh well, you're a big girl. I'm sure you'll be able to do it!'

So I worked there every Saturday. I got ten shillings for the morning — a ten-bob note — and then I was promoted to working all day, Saturday afternoons as well. I had to make all the cake boxes up for the rest of the week and fill up the shelves with them, as well as serve in the shop, and for all of that I earned the grand total of sixteen shillings.

I could eat anything that I wanted, which — for the first couple of weeks — was absolute heaven: free cakes, free biscuits . . . For about two weeks it was 'just another' shortbread out of the jar, and then 'just another', until I hit the 'wall'. By this time I'd served the biscuits so many times and nibbled away at them in between customers so much that I became that sick of them I began putting extra effort into selling them, in order to get them away from the shop and temptation! The biscuits were only about a penny each; there were custard creams and chocolate fingers, and three different types of shortbread: plain ones, some with chocolate in and others with currants.

When people needed serving quickly, I was always ready for the next maths challenge. Whether it was six pork pies or seven sausage rolls, there was lots of adding up to do and to the delight of the boss that was one of my 'people skills'. I even got promoted to putting the jelly in the pork pies with an old teapot. Now I was going places!

And, on top of the excellent salary, there were the 'pork pie perks'. Anything that wasn't sold that would not last till Monday in the shop — like cream cakes, trifles and steak and kidney pies — was a bonus and would be put in boxes for me to take home. So it was an absolute thrill at first that our family could enjoy all these fabulous treats. At home we were eating them on Saturday night, all day Sunday and sometimes through till Monday. Then, after a while, my mum used to say, 'Please don't bring any more pastries home.' We ran out of people to give them to!

Mum and Dad had very little money, and absolutely no savings at all, and so I decided I would try to save. I opened an account at the local Trustee Savings Bank opposite my nan's shop and I used to take my wages over the road to pay them in. I also had a piggy bank supplied by the bank, which could only be opened by them, and so any other money I was given for birthdays or treats went into the pig and that helped to build up my savings there too.

The whole thing made me feel very important. It was a good feeling going in, and an even better one coming out with my book signed by the cashier, who always had a friendly word for an important young saver. Some impression must have been stamped on me as well as my savings book as, although I didn't know it at the time, direction signs to a career were being pointed.

4

Grammar School

The benchmark of my school career came in 1963 when, along with thousands of other children around the country, I sat the II-plus exam.

Arithmetic was an integral part of the exam, while much of the other two parts needed practicality and common sense. It must have been due in part to some of my earlier everyday experiences of life — calculating the change for customers in the wool shop, or working out the scores for my dad's bowls team — but as I tackled the paper, lights seemed to go on in all the right places. When we were told to put our pens down at the end of the exam, I felt quite pleased with my efforts.

The odds, however, were stacked against my chances of success. Most of the children who found their way into the grammar schools were from middle-class families; not only that, but with my birthday being in June, I was one of the youngest in my year, and statistics showed a higher pass rate from the older children. But they hadn't sold balls of wool and added the figures on the bowling scorecard.

A few weeks later, already changed out of my school uniform, I was conscientiously sitting at the kitchen table, toiling over some homework concerning long division calculations. Dad was home from work, also sitting at the table, drinking a cup of tea and reading the evening paper. Mum came over with a plate of Nanny Fox's home-made biscuits on a tray. This was before my job at the bakery, and biscuits still smelled wonderful, Nanny Fox's in particular. Together with a glass of juice they helped sharpen concentration and the thinking process. Usually, the biscuits would sit in a colourful tin on the kitchen surface, and either there would be a gentle motherly tap on the back of the hand if I went to grab one (and I'd be told to wait for tea) or I would be the one asking before Mum had a chance to offer, but today she was in rewarding mood. Also on the tray, leaning against the glass of juice, was a very official-looking letter.

'You received a letter this morning, Janet.' There was an emphasis on the 'you' because, besides birthday cards and the one time I wrote to a pen friend in a Scandinavian country and got a reply in a language I couldn't understand, I didn't receive mail. Council rent and rates or notification of works to be done, along with utility bills was about as exciting as things got through the letterbox, so the importance of the letter had the full attention of both Mum and Dad.

I stared at it for a few moments. It looked very official and on the pristine white envelope, embossed as if stressing its importance, was the name of the sender: Wirral Education Authority.

'Well, aren't you going to open it?' my mum

said, encouraging me. There was an excitement in her voice that raised my hopes. All of a sudden I felt a new sensation: I was nervous. I thought I didn't care what the result was, that it didn't really matter, and more importantly I had my little group of friends and as long as we all stuck together then life would be good.

'They'll have finished building that submarine at Camel Lairds by the time you open it.' The moment wouldn't be the same without a quip from Dad. In his own way, he was just as excited about the prospect of his daughter's grammar school education and had folded away the paper with its story of the local shipbuilder.

I reached past the biscuits and took the letter. A small gap on the triangle of gum that sealed the letter invited my slender finger to slide in and with only a little pressure the envelope sprang open. I pulled out the paper and as I did so it unfolded in my hand.

'Well?' Mum couldn't bear the tension any longer.

'I did it!'

'You did it?'

'Yes, I passed. I *passed*. I can't believe it!' This was a good feeling.

'Oh my goodness, that's wonderful! I knew you would. I don't know where you get the brains from but I knew you would pass.'

'They must have taken pity on your marks!'

Dad had to say it his way, but I'd never seen a bigger smile and his face was full of pride.

'It's a long way to the grammar school, you know.' Mum was suddenly struck by the realisation that her little girl was going to have to make a long bus journey every morning and evening. She was used to the comfort blanket of me having always been only just around the corner since I started my school life.

'I'm not worried!' I said this with an extra element of confidence — firstly because, for some strange reason, I felt this was only the beginning of my travels from the sleepy village I'd been brought up in; and secondly, I could sense her concern and wanted her to know that I thought I was going to be perfectly safe. 'The walk to the bus stop every morning will be good exercise and the bus journey will be fun!'

It worked — Mum smiled and Dad gave me a familiar wink that said, 'That's my girl!'

Mum's delight was not diminished by the concerns she must have harboured about how they were going to pay for the new school uniform. There was no way she and Dad could afford the expense of the brand-new blazers, skirts, sweaters and ties that adorned the hangers and shelves in the official stockist shop, but they certainly hid those worries from me.

Yet Mum was nothing if not incredibly resourceful and while almost all the uniform — except for the horrendous obligatory navy blue gym knickers — was second-hand, somehow when the time came for the new term to begin everything looked absolutely pristine. All dressed up in my new kit, I looked at myself in the mirror. I pulled at the cuffs of my jumper so that the stripes at the ends of the sleeves balanced on either side, straightened my skirt and then my tie. Finally, as if the moment needed the seriousness of a coronation, I lifted the school hat and, closing my eyes just for a second, placed it gently on my head.

I looked again and what I saw was a different girl. This was the first time I had looked in the mirror and not seen a child. As I looked, I felt a wave of confidence flush through me; there was nothing second-hand about the experience. It was all absolutely brand new to me and it felt good.

The passing of the 11-plus had meant change in other ways too. My group of friends at school was breaking up; only one of the other girls had passed and was going on to the same grammar school. But I convinced myself that change was good.

★ ★ ★

Wirral Grammar School for Girls was a whole new world for me. Firstly, there was lots of travelling. My new daily place of learning was miles away in the comparatively big town of Bebington.

Not being the only one from Neston to win a place at the grammar school, at times there would be a whole bunch of us running to catch the bus service in the morning to get to school, and legging it for the bus at the end of the day; then it required some quickstepping skill to outmanoeuvre the lads from the 'famous' Wirral Grammar School for Boys next door. While some of the boys may have been chasing the girls for other reasons, most of them just wanted to ensure a seat on the bus home. If you weren't quick enough there were times you couldn't get on the bus, meaning an hour's wait for the next one.

The 'fame' tag for the boys' school was not just for its good performance in educating the young bucks of Bebington. It only needs one pupil to take a school from relative obscurity to national notoriety. Within a year of my joining Wirral Grammar School, Harold Wilson, an alumni of the boys' school, became Prime Minister and went on to win four elections. Whatever your politics, that's not bad to have on your CV!

At the same time as Wilson's first successful election, there was a huge furore at his old school, prompting excitement among both the girls and boys at Wirral Grammar. By the wisdom of the governors, the two prestigious schools, each housed in impressive historic architecture of its own, were joined by modern extensions. This served to bring the two institutions to a closer relationship and one or two couples among the students even closer too . . .

With the two schools being adjacent, they were not surprisingly each harbouring huge amounts of hormones ready for the new world discovered by teenagers in every generation.

I soon settled into the Wirral Grammar way of life, and it wasn't long before I made lots of new friends. One lesson flowed into another and in between the girls' entertainment was usually watching the boys play football on the muddy winter pitches and cricket in the summer across the green playing fields.

I was never a super academic nor had aspirations to become one. The end-of-year reports never pointed to a glorious university and professional career but instead seemed to see where my strengths lay, detecting the ordinary, logical and practical girl just trying to be as organised as possible, trying to use common sense and doing her best to stay ahead of the game. It was always: 'Janet does well. Janet worked well in class. Janet gets on with it.' It was never: 'Janet is top of the class.'

For the next five years, more than anything else I exercised my conscientious muscles, always too scared not to do the right thing. Nevertheless, I still found things within myself that would prove so important later in life. I continually discovered a deep-rooted determination to achieve the very best I could. I think that came from both my parents who each, in their own admirable way, would stubbornly stick to their principles.

There were times when I wondered whether I had made the right choice to go to the Grammar. Only about a third of children had the advantage of a grammar school education, but the choice wasn't necessarily the best one for everyone. I was just the student in the middle, Miss Average at everything, often thinking what might have been had I chosen the path more travelled. Perhaps there I may have acquired different skills.

But my life was busy. As well as working at the bakery on Saturdays, I was soon charged with the responsibility of taking the Sunday-school class while the main service was conducted in our local church.

Thereafter, there was something special about Sundays for me. The sound of music filled the room as I sat in the centre of a necklace of smiling faces. I'd sussed out by the second week that singing was the answer when the children's interest in the stories I was telling had waned and one or two of the boys, who always seemed then to have a mischievous twinkle in their eye, were starting to become a distraction.

I also had a spy in the camp in the form of my sister Alison, who thought herself elevated in importance now that I was the teacher. Feeling she had to set an example for good behaviour, she would sit cross-legged with a straight back, awaiting the teacher's next instruction.

'Right, children, listen!' I was only just into my teens, so it felt strange talking to the little ones with such authority.

'Get out your songbooks. You can choose your favourite song — so which one do you want to sing first?'

It was always the same song. Ambition or perhaps it is hope is drilled into us at an early age and these children wanted 'The Whole World in His Hands'.

The boys, between five and eight years old, were at an age where, as long as they knew the words, they loved to sing their hearts out as much as the girls. Invariably, though, it became a game to see who could sing the loudest. Sometimes things would get a little out of hand and one of the church wardens would appear around the corner of the door, asking for a little less enthusiasm.

'Perhaps 'The Lord Is My Shepherd?'' he would suggest, knowing that it was expected the children should sing the hymn each week — and that it would dampen the over-excitement a little.

If I hadn't spent time carefully preparing the stories, songs and activities for the class, the legion of boys in the Sunday school might have ganged up on me and tied me to a post, or at least made life difficult and uncomfortable for me. But not preparing was unnatural to me. I was probably driven by the same fear that drove me in school to make sure I did my homework. I wasn't a worrier as such, I was just always concerned to make sure I got on with it or I was prepared and ahead of the game.

In the end, I think I probably learned more than the children, not so much through Bible study, but in the practical lessons of caring for and looking after little ones.

5

The Problem

I have always been a very private person and, especially as a teenager, I never talked openly to anyone, not even best friends, about anything that was remotely personal. The best use I found for my school hat was what I could keep under it! If something was nobody's business then sharing it, as far as I was concerned, could only lead to trouble — or at the very least unwelcome embarrassment.

There is a kind of taboo that surrounds menstruation. Talking periods is not for discussion at the kitchen table; well, it certainly wasn't in Rose Gardens when Dad was around. I was, however, aware of what to expect — around the time I started at grammar school Mum gently prepared me for the event. In those days, however, sometimes the language of 'hint' was used, which wasn't necessarily that easy to decipher, but there was enough in what she said for me to be prepared for something, even if I didn't totally understand.

Some of the less discreet girls at school talked about experiences a little too graphically, but in the main the subject was personal and private and only shared if a first experience was impossible to hide. The consequences could be, on a horror scale of 'Oh no!', anything from mildly uncomfortable to positively embarrassing to blind panic if you hadn't been pre-warned and genuinely had absolutely no idea of what was going on.

The concept of anytime from 'now' until the age of fourteen or fifteen is a long time to wait when you've just taken the 11-plus. There were other things going on in my world like netball, homework and watching the boys at the bus stop, so eventually the maternal forewarning floated into the distance.

But as each girl around me started her period, and being prepared for it each month became as much a part of a teenage girl's school requirement as sandwich boxes, lacrosse sticks and navy blue knickers, slowly the subject appeared more and more in my thoughts. None of my friends noticed, none was aware or bothered. The subject was of no interest because everyone had settled into her own cycle, but it began to feel as if I had been the only one left without a bike!

When I had first mentioned my worries to Mum, around the age of fourteen, she said it would happen anytime over the next few years. She showed no concern whatsoever. When she had given me the original 'talk' I had thought it must be something that was going to happen within weeks; by then, it had been more than a couple of years. But we left it at that and nothing else was said for almost another year.

But the next time I brought the subject up, Mum knew I was a bit bothered.

'Well, look, I'm sure there's nothing to worry about.'

'Yes, but Mum, it really feels now like every single other girl has already started.'

'Well, somebody always has to be first and somebody always has to be last. And it doesn't really matter if you're the last one, does it?'

As usual, that sounded very sensible, but I had to tell her how I was feeling. If I couldn't tell Mum, there was no one else.

'I'm still a bit bothered, though. I feel different.' It had started to become one of those things that had settled in my mind and wouldn't go away.

Mum didn't like me saying that I felt different. No mother wants her daughter to be an odd one out among her friends.

'Now, you listen to me. You are absolutely just like everybody else. The only thing that makes you different is that you are the most sensible young girl in the world. If you never worry about anything, you can deal with anything!'

There's nothing like a good pep talk from the one person in the world you know you can always love and trust.

'Thanks, Mum', was all I could say, but I felt a little better.

Yet she looked at me and decided I needed a little more.

'I'll tell you what we'll do,' she said, purposely sounding upbeat and positive in order not to alarm me. 'I'll make an appointment with Dr Simpson and we will get his opinion to put your mind at rest. OK?'

I suppose that was what I had been fishing for. There was something not right, I felt it. I needed to know why I hadn't started having periods when it seemed it had happened for every other girl on the planet, or at least in my year at school.

★ ★ ★

The waiting room in Dr Simpson's surgery seemed quite small but it was warm compared to the cold outside that had arrived in the last days of autumn. I followed Mum in and was so close behind her that the cloth of our coats blended and folded together.

'Good morning, Mrs Leadbetter.' The receptionist's eyes blinked heavily together as a red-nosed patient sneezed just as she spoke.

'Good morning,' Mum said, ignoring the interruption. 'We have an appointment with Dr Simpson.'

Not wanting to show me that, by this stage, even she was a bit concerned, Mum's voice was very upbeat. There was a tiny alteration in her accent. A visit to the doctor's was not like going to the shops. Dr Simpson was a little bit posh and very 'middle class' and you always dressed up a bit for an appointment in those days.

'Please, Mrs Leadbetter, take a seat.' The receptionist, knowing who the appointment was for, smiled at me. 'You too, Janet. Doctor will be with you in a minute.'

We sat on the front row of chairs near the receptionist's window, as far from the cold as possible. I glanced at the noticeboard on the wall

31

at the end of the row. A large poster was giving advice on how to prevent colds in the winter. There was another sneeze. This time it was even louder. The receptionist slid her window closed.

'I hope we get called in before that other man,' I whispered to Mum. 'It's enough worrying about my non-existent periods without getting a cold as well!'

The window slid open as quickly as it had shut. There was a shining smile from the receptionist. 'Janet Leadbetter,' she announced, as if presenting me on stage in front of an audience. The man sneezed in protest as he had been waiting longer. I stood to attention at the sound of my name and looked at Mum.

'Come on, I'm not going in alone.'

'Of course I'm coming,' she said, getting up, 'and don't worry, it will be alright.' As she turned the handle of the doctor's door, I could hear the window slide shut behind us again — and another sneeze from the man.

After listening to Mum and asking me a few questions, Dr Simpson began talking in another language altogether. At least he might as well have done, as I hardly understood a word he was saying.

'Amenorrhea,' he said, quite suddenly. It sounded like another sneeze!

Mum moved a little uncomfortably in her chair. 'Sorry, could you repeat that, Doctor?'

'Amenorrhea.' This time the word came across the desk with an air of confidence borne from his knowledge of the uncommon. 'It is the absence of menstruation. The hypothalamus triggers the

32

pituitary gland to send hormones . . . '

After a few more long medical terms, Mum asked him to write down the diagnosis. She knew my curiosity would want to know the exact terms used.

The doctor then changed gear and gave a more simplified explanation. It became clear that this wasn't going to end with the perfect prescription to produce any periods. He thought I had best see someone more qualified in that particular area of medicine.

'I think it would be altogether better if I make a referral on your behalf for you to take Janet to see a specialist,' he said now. 'There is a clinic in a Liverpool hospital that deals with patients who have an absence of periods. There will be someone there who specialises in this area of medicine so you'll be in good hands.'

I felt a cold shiver run through me.

He went on. 'And they have experts who will be able to give Janet some tests and hopefully find an answer to the problem.'

The 'problem'. The word underlined my fears of being the odd one out. From the girls in my class at school, from my other friends, family, in fact everyone — because none of them knew there was anything wrong. That day the number of people 'in the know' had just increased by a third.

I didn't like the sound of what I was hearing at all, and he must have detected my discomfort. Softening the blow, he looked at Mum and said, 'Although you shouldn't leave it too long, there is no harm in Janet waiting a little longer before attending the appointment because lots of girls do begin their periods late.'

★ ★ ★

Hormones are all over the place for most of us when we are at that age, and there is too much going on to worry about whether they are going in the right direction. There is a special vibrancy, thanks to which worries are distant clouds and cares mostly wash away like soapsuds in a bath. The most awkward and difficult things seem surmountable and no mountain is too high to climb. Fuelled by ambition and aspiration, toil and trouble is left to the adults.

There were moments when I did stop and think about the consequences of the confirmation I had received from the doctor. I think most teenagers expect to have children later in life and until then I was no exception. Now, I believed that this wasn't going to happen for me.

But even though I thought I understood this, I decided it was something I could shelve. I would file the problem away for another day and I would neither dwell upon nor fret about something I couldn't do anything about. At least, that was my theory under the cloak of being fearlessly positive. Was I kidding myself? Even now, when I look back, I'm not sure.

It didn't happen often but there were also times when I would fall into a bit of a world of my own. I would think about the meaning of being different to the other girls at school. Now and again, I would think: why me and not her?

Was I betraying close friendships by not saying anything to my closest friends? Well, I never thought so.

This was a secret too personal to share. I was always a very private person and that was over small matters, so the barriers immediately went up and — somewhat ironically — I built an impregnable wall of protection around myself. No one was going to enter this part of my world. I decided that the only people who were *ever* going to know about this, besides me, were my mum and the doctor.

6

The Bank

With a little trepidation, at the age of sixteen I left the sleepy village of Neston and made the journey to work in Birkenhead, and more precisely to the heart of the town (or at least the originally intended heart of the town), Hamilton Square. Almost 200 years old, the importance of the square is underlined by the fact that only Trafalgar Square has more Grade I-listed buildings in one place. As I was just a little country bumpkin, it definitely made an impression on me, one mixed with a touch of awe and excitement.

Much of Birkenhead was controlled or owned in the late eighteenth and nineteenth century by the Lairds, the Scottish family famous for building some of the world's biggest ships. They commissioned one of the leading Edinburgh architects to design the square and surrounding area as a layout for a new town. Not surprisingly, the imposing Georgian terraces that surround Hamilton Square are consequently similar to much architecture in Edinburgh. Even the stones used to build the town hall originated in Scotland. And at the top of the town hall, in the centre of its imposing tower, was a clock, of which I was acutely aware. As I turned the corner into the square, I glanced up towards the blue-green roof of the tower where the clock face showed the large hand just slightly inclined to the left. Chop, chop! I simply hated being late.

One of the impressive buildings just off the other side of the square was the bank. Its large door seemed huge to the nervous sixteen-year-old standing before it. Nevertheless, I bolstered my courage, straightened my dress and coat, made sure that my hair hadn't blown all over the place and then pointed my finger at the pale green doorbell that sat with a white surround in its socket.

I stood on the steps of the bank, slightly raised above the pavement, and glanced over my shoulder to see waves of hats and heads bobbing up and down as the growing throngs of commuters rushed past in both directions. It was the summer of 1968 and mingling among the miniskirted and fashionably Mary Quant coiffured secretaries were stiff-collared pinstriped bosses with black bowlers, sideburns and a 'dab' of Brylcreem. It was a time when, in almost an act of defiance, some men still wore trilbies and fedoras, covering their heads as if in protest against the new mop-haired generation of the Beatles and Mick Jagger and his Rolling Stones.

This was a whole new world for me, a long way from the classroom in Wirral Grammar School, and I was more than a little apprehensive. Anticipation, especially when peppered with fear, always makes time seem longer. As I waited for someone to let me in, I could feel the nervous twitching in my knees.

Eventually, I decided that no one was going to

respond to the bell and so I thought I should knock. I looked up again at the huge door. At eye level, right in the middle of the door, there was a brass letterbox polished so thoroughly that I could see a reflection of my coat, people moving and even the buildings behind me on the other side of the road. Above it was an equally shiny brass knocker. First day at work dilemma: to knock or not to knock — that was the question. My mind was made up as the great clock in Hamilton Square struck the first of the nine o'clock chimes.

At the exact moment my hand rose towards the brass handle of the knocker, I heard the metallic sound of a lock being turned, then another, then another, followed by more metal sliding as security bars were released on the other side of the door. The clock gave another chime. *If he doesn't hurry up, I am going to be late*, I thought. Then I asserted myself, thinking: *I definitely rang the bell before nine o'clock.*

Finally, the door opened and a friendly face appeared from behind the enormous wood panelling.

'You haven't rung the bell, have you?' The smile remained but it felt like a sting and, feeling reprimanded, I could sense my cheeks burning with embarrassment.

'Yes,' I said. 'I'm starting today.'

'Oh no!' he said. 'You're not supposed to come into work this way. You're supposed to go around the back!'

Everything around me seemed to grow a little

bigger. This, of course, made complete sense for a bank that size, with all those locks and bars and security at the front.

So there I was on my first day at work and look what I'd done — my first mistake and I wasn't even in the building yet! Luckily, I did just manage to get inside before the last of the Hamilton Square clock chimes.

I resolved to make that my first and last mistake at work. Sweet thoughts for a fresh-faced sixteen-year-old. Eventually, you come to realise that without mistakes you learn nothing, and life is a constant journey where quite often mistakes are the best guidelines to success.

Summoning every ounce of the conscientiousness noted in all my school reports, I did my best to do all I was told as efficiently as possible in the first few weeks of my new career in banking. I soon discovered that as long as I could count and knew the alphabet then common sense did the rest. Cheques had to be sorted into alphabetical order and other administrative and simple secretarial jobs were allotted to me as the junior of all juniors.

Although at times I felt that I was thrown in at the deep end with the minimum of instruction, all that was part of learning how to deal with the adult world. I had left the protected environment of school far behind me now.

And I was soon to learn that working in the big world of banking sometimes brings with it big decisions — though most of them, especially when you are a new junior, you don't make yourself. Just as I was getting used to a life of commuting and the busy big town of Birkenhead, I was reminded of my country-girl roots sooner than I had expected.

One day, I was engineering my way through endless piles of cheques, happily settled into the routines within the grandeur of the head office at Hamilton Square, when one of the managers came over to my desk. My mental arithmetic was in full flow and I was halfway down a long column of figures.

'Janet?'

Not a great moment to be disturbed. I squeezed my eyes together for a split second to try to memorise the subtotal, then looked up and smiled.

'Janet, the Neston branch is short-staffed and we've had a chat and you are the obvious candidate for the job.'

OK, I thought, *not expected and not necessarily part of the life plan. But no choice: wages are too important to ask questions or debate, so go with it and look at the positives.*

'Oh, that's great!' I said. Then: 'Fantastic!', finding a few extra bubbles of enthusiasm. 'I'll be able to have an extra hour in bed in the morning. When do I start?'

I smiled sweetly to make sure my real thoughts were kept to myself and tried to rescue the subtotal — to no avail. My eye and my pencil went back to the top of the column.

7

Meeting Graham

The prominent oak doorway, and subtle signs of security woven within its architecture, imposed the bank's authority on Neston High Street. And while all the other places of business along the street enterprisingly opened their doors a touch earlier or a little later to catch an extra sprat of cash, opening and closing time at the bank was as precise as the finest of Swiss watches in the jeweller's further up the road. Opening on the dot at ten o'clock, traditionally the bank closed its doors to the public as the clock in the local church struck three each day.

The manager, my boss, was Fred Barnett, a genial gentleman with a kind face, silver-fox hair and an air of authority accented by a raised eyebrow. As with most bank managers at that time, he commanded respect both within and without his place of work. He was, after all, a very important man.

A couple of the faces were familiar, but it wasn't long before I knew everyone who worked at the Neston branch. I missed the excitement and importance of the head office, but everything was more compact and quicker and, besides, my favourite cake shop was just over the road!

The smaller branch also gave me a greater

opportunity to blossom. I was good at organising and calculating; columns of figures may not be the most exciting things in the world, but it is always a good feeling when they add up. At first I was working at the back of the bank, out of the sight or at least out of the line of fire of the customer. But eventually, after six months, I worked my way up to the responsibility of the counter and that was a different world.

Now I was in direct contact with the customer and suddenly this little bank, which had been there for as long as I could remember, was busier than I could ever have imagined. I thought I was leaving behind pressure when I left Hamilton Square but here the work was non-stop. I could also feel the adrenalin flow as my personal responsibility grew with handling cash at the front desk.

★　★　★

One of the freedoms work gave me was to experience my first big holiday with a friend. Holidays had been scarce growing up, and I had spent most of my summers going on days out with Mum and Alison. The longest time away from home had been in a caravan on the North Wales coast. With my own money from working, the world was now my oyster and with my 'pearls', in the form of pounds from the bank, I could choose to go wherever I wanted. Together with my friend Eileen, we daringly booked a boarding house in Douglas on the Isle of Man. We quickly settled into our new and

42

temporary surroundings, not least due to the kindness of the landlady, who, realising our adventure into adulthood and responsibility, went out of her way to make us feel at home. She gave us daily dollops of extra helpings of food and friendly gossip about the town and island, coupled with advice on where to go and what to do, which all helped to settle us and remove any undue nerves about being away from home.

Within the first day Eileen and I had worked out our plans for the first week, what to do and where to visit. The sunshine that had guided the boat from Liverpool to the little island seventy miles off the coast looked like it would stay with us for our two weeks, so sand, sea and swimming was on our agenda.

I felt very grown-up. Just the experience of travelling had been exciting. I was looking forward to exploring the island, making new friends and enjoying my new-found freedom. It felt a long way from the local table-tennis tables in Neston, where much of my recreational time had been spent so far that summer. I was just eighteen: experienced, practical and sensible in many things, but still at heart an innocent country girl, naïve in other matters. The last thing on my mind was boys and I genuinely wasn't expecting that to be one of the highlights of the holiday.

In between our sunbathing stints every day we would find other things to do. The crowds were huge and it was exhilarating just to be a part of the great swathes of people that had flocked to the island. The colours were vivid and ever changing, moment by moment, as holiday-maker after holiday-maker appeared before us along the promenade. Accents broke out into the air momentarily and then dispersed, blending into another. First, a broad Scottish drawl, which then suddenly became the sound of Ireland, with a lilt of blarney. It was traditional each year that there would be a mass exodus across borders and seas, as Celts from both countries took their traditional holidays in the Isle of Man in the days before the package holiday to the Mediterranean became affordable.

Everywhere I looked there were excited children brimming with pure joy: young boys jumping about with new wooden yachts with white sails and colourful bows; little girls with pigtails and ponytails tied with ribbons to match their costumes as they walked along the beach barefoot; or teenagers chatting in flip-flops. Everyone was in flip-flops — except the grandparents, who were much more conserva-tively dressed in sandals, long trousers and the occasional straw fedora. Some elderly jokers wore boater hats with a band saying 'Kiss Me Quick'. In among the gaiety there was the occasional child who pulled on a patient parent's hand, crying out for some lost treasure he or she wasn't allowed to have at a bypassed shop, walking a couple of paces behind, with disappointment written all over a tearful face: yet another child facing the fact that they weren't going to get the ice cream or toy that had looked so tempting. Overall, though, the air was full of laughter and the happiness that always helps create the atmosphere of a holiday.

I loved stopping at the souvenir stands along the promenade at the front. Alongside the multicoloured confectionery, in which pink, white and bright yellow always seemed to be the dominant sunshine colours, plastic windmills on sticks and buckets and spades were piled high, stacked according to size and price.

A couple of days into the holiday we were both feeling peckish after a relaxing morning on the beach. I had been writing a few postcards and slowly reading a book, turning myself over as often as the page to get an all-round front-and-back tan. We made ourselves respectable for the high street and followed our noses to get a bag of chips each, which would see us through to one of the landlady's 'specials' that evening.

We meandered our way in our miniskirts along the busy promenade, heading back towards our spot on the beach and picking at our food, when suddenly I got the feeling a group of lads ahead were looking at us. I gave a quick gentle nudge to Eileen.

'I think we are being watched,' I said out of the corner of my mouth, like a spy in a Hollywood crime drama, and casually placed another chip between my lips, intent on not showing any interest.

They were in and out of sight as a wave of people in a haze of heat weaved and bobbed along the front of the resort.

'No, over there. Look to the left, ahead. Those boys leaning on the railings.' We were getting closer and my voice had become a strained whisper. I couldn't help laughing and almost choked on a vinegar-soaked chip. They were now within hearing distance.

There was a group of them, four or five, all around our age, each with a cheeky smile on his face, laughing and chatting. They were posing, perched on the railings of the sea wall that overlooked the beach.

'They've got local accents,' Eileen said as we drew near. 'I wonder if any of them live on the Wirral.'

It came as a pleasant surprise to hear the Scouse accent among all the others we had become accustomed to hearing. 'Looks like we'll soon find out,' I said. That was all I could think of saying. The closer we got, the less comfortable I had become; it was clear they were going to say something to us. One directed his attention to Eileen.

'Those chips smell good.'

Eileen stopped and at the same time the other boy turned around.

'Not enough for two.' She wasn't going to encourage him.

Those of the boys facing us sniggered, enjoying their friend falling at the first fence. One of them was slightly hidden behind and was looking out to sea so I couldn't see him properly.

'How about if I buy you some more tomorrow?' said the cocky lad.

The other boy turned around at that, as though thinking he'd better take a closer look at what was going on. He had a cheeky, confident look about him, with an engaging smile, and he looked straight at me as if I was the only person on the promenade.

'Give us a chip!' he said, smiling at me.

I hadn't realised my hand holding the chips had moved enough for him to think I was offering him one. I wasn't, but didn't care that he'd taken one.

'My name's Graham.'

I hesitated a beat too long.

'It's usual to tell the other person your name . . .'

'Oh, yes. Janet. It's Janet,' I said, a little nervously.

'We're here for the fortnight camping. There are three of us in a two-man tent. It's a bit of a squeeze but we're having a great time. Where you from?'

'Don't be so cheeky!' I was trying to hide the fact I liked his confidence. He obviously had a sense of humour as well. 'If you must know, Neston, and we are staying in a bed and breakfast. You sound like you've got a local accent.'

'Very posh!' A second chip disappeared and I laughed. 'I'm from Wallasey, but,' he went on, 'my sister lives in Neston. How about that for a coincidence?'

In the distance, a steamboat's sharp whistle announced its intention to dock. The shrill sound scattered a flock of seagulls hovering on its bow. The sound cut through the crowd and heads raised and eyes were directed across the bay. And yet, somehow, I only had eyes for Graham.

★　★　★

It was more than anything a meeting of friends, and we became a group in the days following. Graham went back to his campsite and he and his friends would do their own thing during the day, while Eileen and I explored the island. We mainly met up in the evenings at the Theatre Bar on the front of the prom, having a laugh, a drink and a singsong, then some of the group would carry on and go to watch the live acts at the Lido. The cabaret room was brilliant. What was so fabulous was that if you were there for two weeks you'd see all the acts. Different people were coming every week but it was brilliant in the seventies because Scottish Week and Irish Week created a fabulous atmosphere. On stage there was Ronnie Dukes, and Rickie Lee with the mother-in-law who used to play the piano; also the Dallas Boys and Liverpool comedian Sonny Jones.

It wasn't long before I found myself talking to Graham more than any of the other boys and then the walks became a touch more romantic as we held hands walking along the promenade at night.

Towards the end of the holiday, Graham decided the time had come for him to impress me and demonstrate some of his attributes and skills. He had a girl on his arm — what more masterful way of showing manliness to her than to captain a ship and sail her into the sunset?

His vessel took the form of a rowboat for two on the boating lake on Douglas promenade. We paid for our hour and with a shove from the man in charge we drifted towards the middle of the lake. It wasn't long before it became apparent we weren't going very far. The oars span around in the metal sockets on the side of the boat, and the paddle end of each one flapped about — more successfully spraying me with water than guiding the boat in any particular direction.

It was the first time Graham had ever attempted rowing a boat and he was losing the struggle. As good as he was at going around in circles, that was *all* we were doing. We were, however, attracting the attention of all the others in the group, who found our antics hilarious, and a rather worrying gathering of seagulls, who were flying in circles overhead like hungry birds of prey.

It was an idyllic evening nonetheless. The sun was setting over the town and the silhouettes of our friends lined the jetty, where all the other rowboats nestled next to each other, bobbing up and down, safely moored for the night. Our hour of questionable prowess had run out — along with the boat-keeper's patience.

'Come in, number twenty-seven. Your time is up!'

'I can't come in! I've got problems with me oars!'

'What's the matt-tt-er?' His voice was amplified but breaking up behind a misfiring Bullhorn.

'They won't work!'

Belly laughter on the landing stage.

'Help! We can't get back to the shore!' I

decided to add to the drama in damsel-in-distress fashion.

'Do you need a t-t-tow tow?'

There were no sails on Captain Graham's boat for the wind to be taken. So I decided we had to take the offer, whatever the embarrassment.

'Yes, we're stranded!'

'Stand by-by!'

As the words bellowed across the lake, he set out to rescue us. The streetlights of the promenade reflected our path home on the water as we were slowly towed back to the giggling group on the jetty. It was Graham's first chance of impressing me, and he fell at the first hurdle.

So, the man had to come out and tow us back that evening on the boating lake on the Douglas promenade. And boat twenty-seven, with its bow between its oars, finally took its overnight berth next to all the other numbers.

★   ★   ★

Although we had paired off in the group by the time the holiday came to an end, there was no serious side to any of the romances. I never thought about it really because we weren't looking ahead and I wasn't looking for a relationship. It had just been a lovely holiday and we'd made a lot of new friends.

That said, I was half hoping that Graham might ask me out again, but it seemed less and less likely right up to the very last moment. He was either not interested or he was being extremely cool about it.

We came home from the Isle of Man on the same ferry. Huddled together, we sat cuddling on the boxes that stored the ropes all the way home from Douglas. As the steamship slowly sailed into Liverpool Bay, I knew that it was the closest we had been and so, by the time the boat had docked, my hopes of seeing Graham again were even higher. But still there was no mention of another date. I began to think nothing more was going to happen. I tried to brace myself for the disappointment.

He should next have taken the ferry across the Mersey to Seacombe, which is what his friend Kenny did, but instead he did the chivalrous thing and took the Woodside ferry, the one Eileen and I were sailing. From there we were to catch the bus at the terminal to Neston.

I don't think there was a specific moment it clicked with Gray — as his mates, and now I, called him — to ask me out again. For even though we didn't live that far from each other, meaning there was at least the geographical potential to maintain our blossoming friendship, Graham had said very little on the way back. He was still acting very cool. He gave even less of a clue to the future as he did the gentlemanly thing of seeing me to my bus once we'd crossed the Mersey.

And then, just as I got on the bus, right at the last possible moment, as it was pulling away, he shouted, 'I'll see you again. I'll be in touch to make the arrangement!'

And my heart pounded away for the whole six miles from the bus terminal to my front door in

51

Neston where, as soon as Mum opened it, I said, 'I met this really nice lad, who lives in Wallasey, and his sister only lives up the road, and we are going to go out.'

She was pleased — although there was a little explaining to do when the holiday snaps finally came through with a photo of Graham and me taken in one of the theatre clubs . . . with a long line of empty beer glasses in the background.

The first thing Graham did when he got home was to find one of his most prized possessions: a perfectly-kept, boxed, pristine-condition train set. Within a few days he had sold it to fund the travel costs of a new venture.

Courting a girl from out of town.

8

The Gazelle

It was the spring of 1971, the snowdrops had made way for the bluebells and the ten-shilling note was becoming an extinct species, in favour of the new decimalised coinage in the form of a hexagonal piece of metal: the fifty-pence piece. The bank had become the most important place in town, with everyone in a state of confusion over the decimalisation. Day after day people were bringing in bags of old money to exchange for the new coins, to a soundtrack of complaints from the senior citizens of Neston that were equal to the expressions of interest and support from the younger generations. The staff at the bank probably had most reason to complain — for all the extra work and sore fingers from counting so much money.

At the end of one particularly exhausting day, I picked up a batch of files from the front desk and once again found myself staring at a circular looking for staff interested in doing relief work. This time it wasn't for London but was instead offering opportunities to be on call to go to branches anywhere in the region. The area included the surrounding counties of Merseyside and — rather exotically to a teenager in the early seventies, well, at least to me — it included the Isle of Man. That meant a flight from Liverpool

53

Airport. The whole idea of the relief work suddenly catapulted my job into the category of an exciting career; it would be like being an air hostess, travelling all the time and not knowing where you were going to be sent next. At the bottom of the circular, however, there was a condition: applicants must have a driving licence and their own car.

Well, I had a car, but it was far from reliable. I had used some of my savings to buy a rather basic and elderly Hillman Imp. It only cost seventy pounds, and it served its purpose in getting me through my test and meeting up with Graham, but it didn't really know if it was coming or going. It was one of the few vehicles with its engine — confusingly — in the boot at the back and it had a choke lever whose handle often came off in my hand. I had to make an apology every time I pulled the choke because if the passengers in the back didn't lift their feet they were in danger of receiving a sharp rap on the ankle.

A plan began to formulate inside my head. My manager, Mr Barnett, had suggested I take out a loan for a car. I'd dismissed the idea of borrowing money at the time, but now I needed a vehicle that was more reliable. And there was only one way to get it. The loan was definitely my route to relief work.

I waited that night for Mum and Dad to get home from work, building up the courage to tell them of my decision to borrow the money. Over tea, I broke the news, expecting words of advice and warning.

'Brilliant!' Dad's voice lit up the room.

I couldn't believe his reaction. He was totally excited about the prospect of his daughter being in the market for a 'new' car.

'But, Dad, it's £350!' Even though I'd made the decision to take out the loan, I was still very concerned about such a big risk, and in truth I was probably petrified at the cost of the monthly repayments.

'Well, it's your decision. Just make sure you think it through.' Mum was, as usual, reading my mind and being cautious. Yet she knew how much I wanted to apply for the new position, and the fact that I was getting beneficial rates for being an employee at the bank made it feasible.

'OK, I'm going to do it,' I said.

'Fantastic!' Dad was really happy for me. His eyes were shining and I think he was already behind the wheel out for a Sunday run.

'I think I'm going to need a bit of help finding the right car, Dad.' I'd prepared that part of my speech beforehand, thinking it would soften the blow of the loan. How wrong had I been? He was firing on all cylinders.

'Don't you worry about a thing. My friend Norman's a mechanic, he'll have a look out for you. He'll have you another car in no time!'

The Hillman Imp was always going to be a temporary measure. It had taken such a battering in seeing me through my test and my early months of driving that now it sadly passed on, suffering from something terminal that neither Dad nor Norman could repair. I was looking forward to getting the new vehicle.

Within a couple of weeks of the loan money being sorted out, Norman called me one morning at work with the news that he had found a bargain.

'I'm not sure I can talk . . . ' I was making a strange, strained whispering sound. 'Really . . . really . . . that sounds great!' I didn't want the others to overhear what I was talking about.

'Well, it is. I've found the perfect car. It's a beauty and it's only three fifty.'

'That's the whole loan and I haven't sold the Imp yet.'

'It's worth every penny. It's a Singer Gazelle with walnut fascia all round. It's a beauty.' He was clearly already in love with it.

He was right. Even though it was the cost of the full loan, it was a snip at £350. And it was the perfect car for my new role. I was now on standby at the bank and awaiting orders to appear at different branches away from Neston.

One evening, shortly after I got the relief job, I came home from work to find a package wrapped in brown paper on the kitchen table. Mum, Dad, Alison and I each had our places at the table and the package had been carefully placed in front of my chair.

'Hi, Dad.' I was looking at the blue ballpoint ink that had clearly been quickly scribbled on the paper bag. It was Dad's writing and my name. 'Is that for me?' Dad really wasn't one for presents and I wasn't used to surprises.

'Got your name on it, hasn't it?' He was being nonchalant, trying to appear not interested, but I could tell it was an act. If it was to build up my curiosity, it worked. He was reading the evening paper using his reading glasses and his eyes rose above them now, waiting for my reaction. At least in the early seventies cars were still more of a man's thing, and Dad was discovering all sorts of new ways of giving advice and reaching out to his eldest daughter.

I quickly opened the package and was absolutely thrilled; it was a huge and detailed premium-edition, all-singing and dancing A-to-Z street directory of all the towns in the areas in which I would be working in my new job.

'I thought it might be a bit useful for you going off in all directions,' he casually commented, as I started flicking through the pages, 'we can plan out your routes in advance. It'll make it a lot easier when you're on the road.'

The book was useful, very useful, and I was made up — but what made me even happier was his thinking. He wanted to reach out to me and he had done it in such a thoughtful way. He knew that the last thing I wanted to be doing was asking directions wherever I went, which had all the potential for — even worse — making me late for work. In addition, this was something we could work on together. So whenever I was told where I would be going next, the map would come out.

Dad's help was also invaluable because as well as knowing the roads, he also knew the landmarks and signs I could look out for (which, invariably, I'd never see until the third or fourth journey, but they would always be there and he was always right). I didn't realise it at the time, but it was all part of the guidance of being pointed in the right direction in life, so that you know what must be done later. It was the little things like that that meant such a lot.

Mum played her role as well. Now and again we would do a 'dummy' run on a Sunday, discovering exactly where the branch was and where I could park and what I could do at lunchtime. This proved very useful when on one occasion the old Gazelle wouldn't start as I tried to make my way home, deciding to stand its ground like a stubborn mule right outside the bank I was working in, in Frodsham. At least I was a little familiar with the high street I was being pushed both up and down by my boss — much to the locals' delight! There was at least a little laughter as we made our slow way uphill.

Despite that false start, though, the Gazelle to my girls in today's language would probably have been referred to as 'well good'; it was totally cool. I absolutely loved driving it, even though it was probably too big and possibly a bit posh for such a young girl to be driving around in, but I was seduced by the absolute freedom it gave me — I was literally going places! For as well as the travelling I was doing with work, my new car opened up the geographical world of my social life too.

In the summer evenings I headed off with Graham or friends or family to the riverside resorts along the southern Wirral peninsular. Sometimes it would be a pub at Parkgate, where we would sit on the old sea wall that held back a sea of reeds that had sprung from the marsh; it was once an important harbour on the River Dee. Another time we might head through the country lanes to Thurstaston Hill, from where there would be a stunning silhouette of Wales in the distant sunset, evoking memories of childhood holidays; or to West Kirby, where the sand seemed to stretch forever.

Now and again, the country lanes were so narrow that if the farmer hadn't already been down the lane with his tractor and hedge cutter, I'd worry the sides of the car would be scratched by protruding twigs. In the summer, nature always played tricks with the country car owners as hazy dust clouds from farmers' fields powdered the windscreen and speckled the paintwork as if casting some sort of spell.

Then the accidents began to happen.

★ ★ ★

I'd had one accident in the Imp — not my fault, I hasten to add — but I thought driving would be a lot safer once I got used to the larger Singer Gazelle. That was until the day I was doing my best to be a conscientious, considerate and courteous car owner and road user. As I approached a zebra crossing in the centre of Neston village, I saw a lady waiting on the edge of the pavement, her hand gripping the black-and-white pole of the Belisha beacon and her face intermittently lit up by the flashing amber globe above. I took another glance in the mirror. The car behind was a safe distance away.

I slowed down, came to a smooth stop,

glanced across at the lady. Remembered not to give any hand signals to tell her to walk . . . waited . . . and . . . BANG! My eyes squeezed tightly closed, the car jolted forward and the distance between the car behind and mine no longer existed. Luckily, the seat belt did its job.

I forced myself to peek and see where the lady was. I searched to the left and right. Nothing! Though I hadn't seen or felt any impact at the front, I thought the worst; where was she? I got out, but she'd disappeared. The zebra had bitten my Gazelle and it had a stinging rear!

After that, I had a series of misfortunes in that car. It became 'the Gazelle with the spell'. There were so many accidents and dints and dents that the whole family felt that the car was jinxed and it seemed to spend as much time being repaired as on the road. Dad used to say that, with the roof being the only metal panel not to have a dent or scratch in it, he fully expected a helicopter to land on it one night.

$$\star \quad \star \quad \star$$

But, accidents or not, I was at least on the road and life working for the bank was improving all the time. I loved being on relief and it wasn't long before I was flying off in all directions. My base branch was in Neston but I didn't know where I would be working from one day to the next. I'd report in to work, do some clearing and sorting, and then a call would come in and it would be, 'Could you just ask Janet to go to the Allerton Road branch?' or 'Please could Janet go

60

to the Smithdown Road branch?' Both of those branches were situated on the outskirts of Liverpool.

One afternoon, I was at the Liverpool University branch. It was a Friday and I thought I had a quiet weekend ahead. I'd only been there a few minutes when the accountant came over to me.

'Staff department have just been on, Janet.'

There was no clue of anything special in his voice: just another job, another request, another staff placement. No big deal. For some reason, the one or two branches on the dodgy side of town that had been firmly placed at the foot of my favourites' list were at the forefront of my mind for next week's location. There was even one where a madam used to parade in with her girls to pay in, all while pouting her lips, and promptly parade out again, leaving a dusting of compact powder over the banking hall floor. Girls were not supposed to be sent to that branch. I tried not to let my worries show.

'That's good,' I said cheerfully, 'where to next?'

'They want you to go to Douglas in the Isle of Man on Monday. It's short notice, I know, but Head Office obviously think you're up to it.'

Bingo! Brilliant. I couldn't believe my luck. The one job I'd been hoping for since the first time I'd seen the fliers about working on relief in the first place — and now my chance had come. My smile was so glued to my face I couldn't answer.

'Do you want to go?'

I was thinking: *Is that a serious question? Of course I want to go!*

I heard myself saying as nonchalantly as possible, 'OK . . . '

'There's no time to get tickets sorted before Monday,' my colleague then said.

In the pre-Internet age, there was of course no way to do anything online because online didn't exist. The accountant explained that I would be travelling with another member of the bank and that he would have the documents.

I'd never been to an airport before, let alone flown, and now I was like a character in a spy novel, meeting a man I'd never met before at an airport.

'His name is Cliff Goldsmith and he'll have your ticket and hand you the travel documents.'

It was my dad who took me over to the airport that first time. So with Dad in the background, I went over to a likely-looking man and said, 'Excuse me, are you travelling to the Isle of Man with a young lady?'

Luckily, it was him, and so we travelled together from there.

The Isle of Man was brilliant. Not only was it where I met Graham for the first time, so I loved it for that special, personal reason, it was also the height of summer and the high street in Douglas, the island's capital, was bursting with holiday-makers. This was such a contrast from the quiet village of Neston. People practically in their swimwear would walk into the branch to cash cheques. The cashiers' desks held a vista of long lines of bright red, blue, green and yellow costumes; the customers carried straw bags with sandwiches and flasks for lunch on the beach. The bank was full of flip-flops flapping on the floor, each slap echoing amid the sound of happy holiday voices. I always had to take a little extra care with and pay a little more attention to my calculations, with such distractions when I looked through the cashier's glass dividing panel as an octogenarian with a kiss-me-quick hat.

I was booked into a hotel at the other end of the high street from the bank, and when work finished for the day there was nothing to do but enjoy the holiday atmosphere. And the great thing was they asked for me again and again. It was brilliant because I used to fly over on a Monday morning, work there all week, fly home on a Friday night, give my mum all my washing and it would be ready for the Monday morning! Mum was a star. I would sometimes go for two weeks. It was generally in the summer months because that is when people went on their holidays and the branch was too busy to cope without relief workers. It was really great, and became a regular jaunt for me each summer.

Eventually, as Graham's and my relationship blossomed, he used to take me to the airport. I would be in the Isle of Man before he got back from dropping me off. By the time they'd served the coffee they were collecting the cups up, because we were landing. The speed of the journey always amazed me.

Being on relief for the bank was in a way like being a member of an exclusive club. There were not many of us at the time. Nowadays, they just seem to close the tills if there are not enough staff. In banks where there used to be eight tills, now there are two. They want you to bank online or use a machine these days — it's not like it used to be.

9

Telling Graham

What Graham didn't bargain for when we began dating was that at times it felt like my little eight-year-old sister came as part of the package. Wherever we went, Alison came too. On the one hand, it was a good excuse for Graham and me to see more of each other and to get away from the ever-watchful parental eyes, but she was part of the picnic when she was eight and still at the zoo with us when she was nine.

The new face around the house was an important change for Alison. We soon settled into a regular routine. I'd drive once a week over to Wallasey and Graham would come over to Neston every Sunday for lunch and also on a Thursday evening; because that was the night Dad went to the British Legion and Mum went to bingo. Our job officially, therefore, was to 'baby-sit'.

I'd spend ages on a Sunday morning getting ready, listening to favourite records on the radio, always excited and looking forward to my boyfriend ringing the doorbell. I'd choose one of my best outfits and make sure of any finishing touches sitting at my dressing table in the bedroom.

For the first few weeks, Alison sat on the bed watching me get ready. I would see her little eyes in my mirror bright and wide open in excited anticipation of the day ahead. Then one Sunday I was brushing my hair while answering at length one of her usual questions about how long I thought it would be before Graham arrived.

'Well, you know he has to first walk *all* the way from his house in Wallasey to the station. Then he has to buy his ticket and then he has to wait for the train that comes at *exactly* eleven o'clock.' It was like a story and she giggled whenever I lengthened a word, especially the same word each week. This time there was no giggle.

I looked in the mirror and there was no Alison sitting on the bed. I turned to be sure but she had left the room. I shrugged, thinking the novelty had worn off, and carried on brushing my hair. I was still trying to work out which style was Graham's favourite.

I glanced at the clock on the bedside table. He would arrive soon so I made my way to the landing to go downstairs. I almost walked straight into Alison. She had been in her own room, having decided to take a lesson from her big sister. With such an important guest — after all, it was her big sister's *boyfriend* — now regularly coming to our house she determined it was only right that she should put on her best dress too. She only had the one and from then on, more often than not, a white dress with red polka dots picnicked with us in the park. By the time she had outgrown the dress, we had progressed to ice-skating and the zoo.

The Thursday nights were, in our minds at

least, different. This was 'Jan and Gray' time. Courting in our teens and early twenties became a sweetheart thing, a kiss and cuddle on the settee, secure in the knowledge Mum and Dad were calling 'house' and a couple of pints away. But it never quite seemed to work out, as no sooner had we settled down than a tiny voice would call from above, bursting our bubble of passion.

'Janet!'

'Was that Alison?' Graham would always say the same thing each week. It was never easy to hear the first call.

'Here we go. I'm not going up; she's doing it on purpose.'

'You'll have to go, luv. It's what we're supposed to be here for, isn't it?'

'Janet!' This time she was shouting. The wait had been long enough.

'She just wants to spoil our fun.'

'Janet! I want a drink of water.' The volume was rising each time she called.

'She wants a drink of water. Do you want me to get it for her?'

I told her to go back to bed and took her up the water and tucked the cheeky face back under the covers. It was the same routine each week. We could almost count the minutes between that and the next call. Another brief encounter and then . . .

'Janet!'

We were the ones dreaming if we thought it would end there.

'Alison, it's past your bedtime. Mum is not

going to be pleased. You've got to go to sleep.'

A slight case of exasperation usually settled in at this point. I knew what was next. I used to read her a book — the same book every week: *Touché Turtle*. Every week! Every week it was 'Touché was a turtle, he had a sword in his hand and a feather in his hat and he had a friend who used to love to go to sleep . . . ' I used to try and turn over two pages at once to get back downstairs to Gray as quickly as possible, before my mum came in.

And Alison would say, 'Oh, you've missed a page out — what about his friend?'

★   ★   ★

It was on one of our Thursday night dates that I decided to tell Graham about my secret. After seeing Dr Simpson, I had eventually gone to see a specialist in Liverpool. As my GP had warned, there were some basic tests, but the results only confirmed my absence of periods. They asked me to return twelve months later and it became an annual pilgrimage always, though, with the same outcome. By now I was convinced I wouldn't be able to have children. It was something I had to talk to him about and it wouldn't wait any longer. I didn't have to get too graphic and it didn't have to be embarrassing, but the truth must be told and he had to know. I talked to Mum about it and as usual her advice was right.

'It is best for him to find out now.' Mum's voice was strong and resolute but at the same time gentle and caring, as only a mum's can be.

'If Graham wanted children,' she continued, 'and you simply cannot fulfil his dream then it is better to give him the opportunity to end the relationship.'

I listened to Mum. She was right.

'I'm just so afraid of losing him, Mum.' I said it as clearly as I could, but it wasn't easy to be strong.

'You have to give him the choice, to be free to go and find someone else if that is what he wants.'

'I know you're right but . . . ' I couldn't bring myself to finish the sentence. I would be devastated if that happened, but it would only be fair to him. Mum gave me a hug.

'I think Graham is strong and I think life is full of surprises. Just be what you always are.'

'What?'

'Be positive and strong and do the right thing and things will always work out in the end! Also, if you stick together, there will always be the possibility of adoption.'

The future was impossible to see. One thing I did know was that, if he stayed, from that moment on the bond between us would be unbreakable.

★　★　★

Graham arrived a little late that Thursday night, and I had somehow managed to get Alison off to sleep after reading the same story three times. Touché! She must have done a lot of running about the playground that day. I was relieved when the doorbell rang that it didn't wake her up.

Graham and I both knew our relationship was serious and neither of us wanted anything other than to spend more time together. He had to know about my problem. It was only fair. However confident I may have been of his feelings towards me, it would have been perfectly understandable if, once he knew I wasn't able to have babies of my own, he wanted to end things.

By the time Graham arrived, Mum had long gone to her bingo and Dad was at the British Legion. The smell of fish and chips flowed through the air as he pecked me on the cheek and hurried in to get the meal as quickly as possible into the oven.

He'd had a good day working outdoors on a large detached property. Graham was a painter and decorator. He loved climbing the ladders and working high off the ground, working high in the air on top of the drainpipes, the eaves and the gutters. Sometimes the views were wonderful around the coastline of the Wirral, with so much sea to look out on. The fresh air from the light breezes at that height on summer days was exhilarating and he was in a particularly good mood.

As he came through the door, I raised a finger to my lips and pointed upstairs to Alison's room. He understood and we went straight to the kitchen, where we didn't waste any time eating supper. As we swallowed down our meal, everything tasted of cardboard to me. I knew I couldn't put it off any longer.

'There's something I've got to tell you.'

'Well, go on.'

I bottled it. 'Not now, after supper, when we settle down.'

He didn't argue, but I could tell there was some apprehension in the atmosphere. His mood had taken a slightly downcast turn. Yet that was nothing compared to the turmoil I was feeling. Was I about to lose the man I loved?

We cleared away the supper plates and eventually sat down on the settee. With Alison not likely to intervene, Graham snuggled up close.

Not now.

Groan.

I shifted slightly away from him, so I could look him in the eye. 'I told you I've got something to say.' I was in serious tone.

He sat back on the settee. There was a resigned look of failure in his face, as if he had done something wrong. Without me realising, there was a reversal of roles.

'OK. There is something wrong, isn't there? What have I done? You want to finish with me, don't you?' He was genuinely hurt and my confidence about telling him my secret grew a little.

'No. No, it's not that *at all.*'

Graham had surprised me with how open he was about how he felt. I knew our relationship was good, but this was more than I had expected. He deserved the same from me. Somehow, I gathered my courage and, with my nerves bolstered by my pep talk with Mum, I

71

told him everything. Afterwards, I held my breath, waiting for his reaction.

I can still remember his response. He was stronger than I'd ever seen him. He was absolutely positive and was clear.

'It's you I want to be with, luv. I'm not interested in being with anyone else and if we can't have kids, then that's the way it will be.'

10

The Wedding

After our heart-to-heart, it was never a matter of *whether* Graham was going to pop the question. It was just a question of when. It had been half a dozen years since we'd met in the Isle of Man and we knew almost from the start that we wanted to spend the rest of our lives together. Following Graham's commitment to be with me no matter what, it became even more of an inevitability. The marriage date was set for 12 August 1976.

But my dreams of walking up the aisle that summer were shattered when Graham unexpectedly became redundant. He didn't want to get married while he wasn't working. I understood and I knew the postponement was temporary, but that did little to soften the sore feeling. I was miserable, fed up and feeling for once that maybe practicality and common sense weren't so great, especially when sitting in the kitchen of Rose Gardens listening to my little sister bawling away in the other room. No wedding meant no flowers, no bells, no reception and no bridesmaid's dress. It was a disaster, the worst thing that could possibly happen, and Alison thought the wedding was never going to take place. I knew better — but felt worse.

My friend Sue Jones, a girl I had grown up

with and who was also going to be one of my bridesmaids, was there for me when I broke the news. But she, along with our other friends, had booked to go abroad on holiday days after the wedding. I was going to be even more alone at a time when I needed the support of my friends the most.

'Why don't you come on holiday with us?' Sue was speaking for all of them, suggesting I should go along. They didn't want me to be left alone to mope.

It sounded a lot better than any alternative but it was the middle of summer already and the chance, I thought, of getting extra tickets was remote. 'OK,' I agreed, not holding out much hope, 'if you can get me a place, I'll go.'

It was Sue's mum, Sylv, who took the initiative and went to the travel agent. The next day, she appeared at the front door with the tickets. She was straightforward, to the point and didn't dwell on disappointment.

'Right, Janet. Here you go. I've sorted the tickets out with the travel agent. Here is everything you need. This is what you owe and you're going!'

So my friends did what true friends do and cushioned the blow. In the meantime, Graham had managed to get temporary work. It wasn't a job that would last forever but he became a bit more confident that he would somehow be able to get another post after that; after all, he was a painter and decorator and they were often in demand. So, having talked it over, we decided not to be so sensible for once about whether or not he was working full-time. While we would now have to wait a couple of months, we would get married in the autumn — whatever Graham was doing workwise then. So by the time I was on the plane, although the disappointment lingered, the hurt had disappeared altogether.

Once I got back, we wanted to marry as soon as possible but met another stumbling block. There was no available Saturday for a wedding at the church right the way through to the end of the year. Most weddings in the village in those days took place on a Saturday so to suggest another day of the week was unusual, to say the least, but when the vicar at St Mary and St Helen's Church in Neston saw our faces he took the rather 'go-ahead' decision to allow us to marry on a Thursday. A new date was set: 25 November 1976.

★ ★ ★

My big day arrived. The dress looked perfect and I felt like a princess. Its traditional sheer pleated sleeves and high neckline complemented the flowing skirt, which spilled out at the hem into the train that would follow me up the aisle. When Mum and the bridesmaids had gone off to the wedding, I was left in the house with my dad, waiting for the wedding car to arrive. Dad was a little bit on edge. It was something new for me, because I had never seen my dad anxious or nervous about anything before and there he was, as he stood before his daughter on her wedding day, in need of calming down.

'Don't worry, Dad,' I said, trying to understand his emotions. 'You know Gray is the right one for me.'

'You look absolutely gorgeous! I can't believe my little daughter is getting married.' Just for a moment, no quips or jokes to cover his emotions: he just spoke as he felt.

He looked at me in all my glorious white and smiled. I could feel the pride beaming from his face but it was mixed with some jitters.

'Are you alright?' I asked, a bit concerned. Then I joked: 'It's me who should have the butterflies!' Dad still didn't seem reassured. I thought a job might help. 'Can you do me a favour?'

'Of course I will — anything for the girl of the moment.'

I proffered my arm in his direction and pointed to the sleeve. The only part of the dress I couldn't fasten were tiny buttons hidden inside the cuffs; always easier for someone else to do as long as all their fingers are moving in the right direction.

I had never known my dad be so nervous about anything. He tried and tried, yet no matter what he told his fingers to do they wouldn't obey. He was shaking like a leaf and trembling so much that in the end I had to get the steady hand of one Henry Norman, local wedding limousine driver and funeral director, to take on a new job of button fastener.

A wedding in Neston during the week was rare so there was an air of excitement and the streets were lined with people watching. As the car wound its way along the high street of the village up to St Mary and St Helen's, the church bells rang out and I couldn't stop smiling and waving. Shopkeepers and shoppers alike looked as happy as I was feeling. The bank was open, and members of staff were standing outside the entrance or behind the window, waving to me as the limousine went past. I even caught a glimpse of the bank manager, Fred Barnett, in the street, tipping his hat to me as he returned to work.

My sister Alison, Sue, and Graham's niece, Karen, were all waiting at the church, shivering in the navy-blue and white patterned summer dresses that had been bought for a hot summer August wedding. Dad, on the other hand, had stopped shaking. His smile and pride had won the battle over his nerves, he gave me a wink, and before I had time to think he took my arm as the organ sounded the famous first bars of the 'Wedding March', and he led me down the aisle towards my husband-to-be.

The bells of the church drew out more of the villagers, curious as to why they were ringing for a wedding on a Thursday. And so, as we made our way outside after the service, newly married, there were even more people outside the church as we emerged under showers of confetti and good wishes.

★ ★ ★

Later that night, when all the celebrations were over, the cold November air was filled with rain. A little rain certainly wasn't going to spoil such a wonderful day. We had both had enough champagne to last till spring, but as we sat in the back of the minibus that was taking us and our friends who lived in Wallasey home from the evening reception, we were just another content and happy newly married couple. Although, as the journey progressed, Graham had a storm brewing of his own.

'What's the matter?' I asked, sitting back slightly from my new husband and watching him go through each pocket of his suit time and time again.

'It's the keys, luv. I can't find the keys.'

The worn-out windscreen wiper screeched, echoing both our worst nightmares. We were almost home, on our own now, as we had dropped off our friends on the way to Browning Road. It was absolutely throwing it down and there was no way to get into the house. The warmth indoors suddenly seemed a million miles away.

'I put them in my jacket pocket and they've gone!' Graham cried. 'Someone is having us on!'

'But we changed — remember?' I couldn't believe it; the keys were nestling in the pocket of Graham's other suit, which was now in the boot of his brother Dave's car, all the way back at the reception. Maybe it was the champagne or the sheer joy of the day, but we both couldn't help laughing.

The minibus had driven away and we faced this dilemma alone. Thankfully, the cavalry arrived, in the form of one of Graham's friends, Jimmy MacKinnon, who had been with us that evening and was passing our house as he drove home. He stopped to help and I got into Jimmy's car to shelter from the rain.

'Just stay dry, wait there in the carriage, Mrs Walton. Just wait a few minutes while I sort the problem,' my new husband said.

My brain paused a split second as I took in my new surname. I liked it. But suddenly, it seemed, I was married to action man.

'What are you going to do?'

Before I had even finished the question, Graham was disappearing down the side of the house, the back of his shirt already sticking to the skin of his back from the downpour. Within minutes he returned, carrying one of his longer decorator ladders, which he propped up against the front of the house. My eyes followed the ladder all the way to the top, where a small transom window was slightly ajar.

Graham shouted to Jimmy: 'Could you give me a hand here, mate? Just hold the ladder while I get up there.'

With the ladder securely in place, he began his ascent to save the day. I winced at a couple of slips of his soles on the rungs as he climbed. The next time I dared to look up, all I could see was Graham's rear end wriggling through the gap.

There was a clatter as he clearly crashed to the floor in the room above . . . and then nothing. Only the rain splashing on the pavement below broke the silence. The time I thought it might take him to get down to the front door passed. He'd been much, much longer than he should have been. Just as I began to worry if I was a wife or a widow, the hall light went on, the front door burst open and there was my new husband and hero: in the doorway, taking a bow. Then, in true gallant-knight style, I was whisked out of the car and carried across the threshold!

Graham thanked Jimmy for his help and very kindly asked him in for a cup of tea.

Common sense prevailed . . . and he refused.

11

The Annual Check-Up

The annual check-ups and tests that I had endured throughout my teenage and courting years had sadly only seemed to confirm my infertility. But my resolve to be a mother one day had, if anything, become stronger. Whatever hormonal messages were lacking from my pituitary gland to my womb were made up for in reminders from elsewhere in my brain that I still very much wanted children.

I was now a Wallasey housewife — although I was also still working at the bank — living away from my roots in Neston. I had chosen to live in Wallasey as Graham had been brought up there, but I had the best of both worlds in having good reason to return to see my family regularly. Alison, lured by my enthusiastic attempts at cooking with a touch of the exotic, would come to stay every so often, or just pop over for tea; the distance in a way brought us a little closer and made the difference in years seem less of an issue.

Mum, influenced by her job as a school cook, was very practical and basic when it came to meals at home. A lot of that was probably to do with making the most she could with what little money she had. It was about making ends meet. There was cooked ham, boiled potatoes and

81

carrots and turnips. There was one neighbour who, whenever they happened to be near our kitchen when dinner was being laid out, would always take a rather huge, deep intake of breath through two oversized nostrils and declare, 'Ah . . . war food!' Meat and potatoes may not have been the most exciting menu, but it was always nourishing, satisfying and tasty.

In my own kitchen, and as a new housewife, I wanted to experiment and impress and so the menu at Browning Road was constantly changing. This was a revelation for Alison, who was fascinated by Scotch eggs. It was not exactly exotic by today's standards but a move away from school dinners, at least. After supper, we would give her a lift back to Neston, in our minivan. Alison would be perched on a stool in the back, hanging on for dear life every time we went round a corner and trying to avoid kicking over a pot of paint.

Graham and I settled into married life, working hard and cementing old and creating new friendships. The Browning Road house was small but was all we needed and we kept it neat and tidy. Having started a new business working for himself, Graham was busy, but whenever he had time between jobs he would redecorate a room or add a fresh coat of paint to a ceiling or skirting board. I had become accustomed to both the pleasant and the not-so-pleasant smells that came with the work of a painter and decorator. Turpentine moments were mixed with the odd whiff of glue and paste, especially when we had to use the van to travel. Sometimes they were so strong I thought the van could float on fumes alone.

Once we were married, to bring an extra element of stability I decided to apply to work full-time in one branch of the bank rather than be available on relief to travel. No more summer days in the busy Isle of Man, no more variety in different places, no more 'madams' with their entourage. As it turned out, though, it was a promotion. I was made chief cashier in the Moreton branch on the Wirral. I couldn't have been happier.

* * *

On my first visit to the clinic after we were married, Graham took time off work to come with me to see the specialist. We were happy and content in the knowledge that when we decided we wanted to start a family we were going to apply for adoption. We both knew there was no guarantee, and that there was a possibility we may not be deemed a suitable couple, but it seemed to offer the best chance of parenthood.

My annual health check was, as far as I was concerned, mainly for the specialist to see whether my symptoms had developed in any other direction. The total absence of a menstrual flow isn't that common, and I'd wondered how much these annual visits were simply a case of the doctors monitoring rare problems, of me contributing to medical knowledge. I also wondered how much longer I would have to be bothered with them.

When the doctor, who I'd met before, opened the door for us, he seemed slightly taken aback I wasn't alone. 'Good morning, Janet.' He glanced at Graham, curiosity written clearly across his face. 'It's nice to see you again.' There was a second glance at Graham. This time it seemed a knowing look, but he asked the question anyway. 'And who do we have here?'

As the doctor brought an extra chair across the room and placed it alongside the one already there, Graham automatically extended a nervous hand, which the doctor firmly shook.

'I'm Graham, Graham Walton. I'm Janet's husband. How do you do?'

After all the years I'd been doing this, it felt so good no longer to have to go through it alone.

He smiled. 'Well, the first thing I need to do is adjust your file.'

I looked at him with a slightly puzzled expression. 'Sorry?'

'Congratulations. It's nice to see you're now married. The name on the file needs changing.'

Of course! I was still getting used to the fact that I was no longer Janet Leadbetter.

'Thank you.' Graham and I answered in harmony the same words at the same time, as if rehearsed. And then it was straight to business; we weren't the only patients the doctor was seeing that morning.

He sat on the other side of the desk, looking over my file. Silence. A page was turned. Then another. Silence. That word then returned as if to haunt me. 'Amenorrhea . . . ' It was almost a whisper, slow and deliberate. My moment of meditation in Greek was disturbed by a prolonged humming noise coming from the doctor, who was deep in contemplation, considering all the facts in front of him.

'Well, Janet,' a turn of the head and a nod of acknowledgement to Graham, 'we've had a look at the results of the latest tests and I'm afraid there is no change.'

This wasn't going to be a long appointment. It was an annual ritual. It seemed as if it was the same thing each year. No change and that was that; see you next year. There was, though, a touch of hesitation in his voice this time.

'You see the thing is, this absence of periods, this . . . ' He spared us the complex words. 'The point is, besides that, there is nothing really wrong with you. You see, that is the *good* news about the various tests you've had over the years. All the trouble is caused by a gland the size of a pea that sits in the middle of your brain.'

'The pituitary gland?' After so many years, the main players on this stage of mine had become familiar. The hypothalamus was the other but I wasn't going to go there; after that I was lost anyway.

'That's right.' Encouraged by my depth of medical knowledge he continued. 'The hypothalamus fuels the pituitary gland and that sends the messages in the form of hormones to the ovaries.'

This was all new to Graham but I had heard this before and so, although I didn't take my eye off the doctor as he spoke, my mind began to think about what time I'd be back at work and what else I had to do that day.

The doctor, however, went on.

'So what we really need to do is to stimulate your ovaries into producing an egg.'

12

Early Treatment

Like all young couples, once we married Graham and I would spend much time dreaming and planning for our future together. Not just for now or the next week or for the next five or ten years, but for the rest of our lives. We had been open and honest with each other from the beginning. No secrets meant everything we did was either with each other or for each other. The fact we knew where we stood as far as the possibilities of having a family were concerned meant that at least that issue would not be something that would come between us in the future.

When the time was right, we decided we would look at adoption if necessary, but in the meantime it was a happy surprise to be able to go through the fertility treatment. A number of different methods were being tried at that time; some were quite experimental. Early on, one of the doctors asked me to try some treatment which entailed securing a needle to my body by means of a rather large oblong box that mechanically ensured the injection of a drug at regular intervals. It was hoped that a menstrual cycle might be 'kick-started' — a phrase quite often used at the clinic.

It wasn't so much embarrassing, because it

was nearly totally hidden beneath clothing, as awkward — to say the least, it being a bulky, burdensome, unwieldy piece of equipment that made its presence known with an intermittent 'whoosh' each time it carried out its duty of injection. The box was experimental and I was a kind of guinea pig. It was holstered to my body with belts and the needle was in a permanent position in my hip. This became a part of me for a number of months. Mum came up trumps with a number of quite fashionable waistcoats adapted to hide the box. Another gold star in that direction!

On occasion when I woke at night, the regular 'whoosh' sound it made as the drug passed through the needle into my body would seem louder because of the silence and stillness of the hour. There was even one night when either the air must have been particularly still or perhaps Graham and I were both sleeping very lightly, and we were woken by the 'whoosh' at the same instant. The bedside-table lamps were flicked on; we took in the surreal moment. Nothing was said. We realised what had woken us and, as if to add insult to injury, it repeated itself.

Graham and I, with the same 'we must be mad' look on our faces, switched off the lamps, turned over and went back to sleep.

★   ★   ★

Even with the little extra money from my promotion and Graham doing well with his decorating business, we still wanted to try to do

88

something that would give us a little more independence in the long run.

A market stall was the answer and, with Mum knitting away ferociously, making as many baby clothes for sale as she could, and Graham and I stuffing the trunks of cuddly elephants with the aid of sometime assistant Alison, we would pitch our goods on painter's pasteboards every Sunday in Coed Mawr market on the North Wales coast. Often we would work late into the night on our stock, until the stuffing had been tightly packed into enough pink elephants and bears to fill our trestle tables.

In the pitch black of the early hours of one winter Sunday morning, Graham drove the Sherpa van slowly along an icy road towards the market. The black box had been a part of me for a couple of months at that time and it was starting to take its toll.

Halfway through the day at the market — having successfully snagged a pitch — I began to feel even more weary. I was wearing one of the specially adapted outfits Mum had made, with a holster to hold the machine. She had even made a matching skirt for the padded waistcoat. Good old Mum! But as comfortable as she had hoped it would be for me, nothing that day was helping. I had never been so tired and fed up in my life.

Whatever the pump was doing, it was becoming more and more obvious that I was reacting to it in a negative way. I became increasingly faint and nauseous and had to go back to the van in the end. While Graham and Alison worked the stall, I was asleep all day in the market car park.

Needless to say, I was 'needle-less' not long after that and the treatment moved on to a more conventional fertility treatment.

Yet the treatments didn't seem to be working. Our initial hope and optimism was soon dampened as one treatment after another failed to work. The more sessions I went through, the more stress and tension there was; not just for me but for Graham also.

It had been made clear to us right from the beginning by our specialists that there would only be so many times that they could justify allowing any patient to go through the courses of treatment. Firstly, they were expensive drugs to administer, and the clinic could only allow each patient a limited number of injections. Secondly, there is only so much a body can take of this kind of treatment. Thirdly, as well as the physical stress, there was the psychological stress. In time, all treatment would have to stop.

All we could do was hope that my body might start to respond to the treatment before that cut-off point came.

13

The Fertility Clinic

One by one, our friends began family life. We had never felt different to them before, but we couldn't help but do so now. Nonetheless, we kept the fertility problems to ourselves. Even after so many years, besides talking to the various doctors over the years, I hadn't told a soul. Only the very closest members of the family besides Mum and Graham were aware of something, but it wasn't a subject for anyone to dwell on.

I was twenty-seven and Graham was almost thirty now; we had been married for three years. When the possibility of different treatment came along, it just didn't make sense to wait. We were given a referral to the Liverpool University Fertility Clinic, which was based at the Liverpool Women's Hospital.

It felt as if the air was charged with optimism the day we went for the first appointment. It was spring and a perfect pale blue sky was scattered with cotton-wool clouds. Seagulls that normally hovered over the ferries as they crossed the Mersey flew a little inland and circled above us, cawing out a seeming celebration as they ducked and dived between the two great cathedrals that dominated the skyline near to where the hospital stood. The huge sandstone Anglican edifice and

91

the more modern Catholic Metropolitan, a giant crown of coloured glass, both stood guard magnificently in all their glorious grandeur. They seemed two symbols of harmony facing each other at either end of a street called, appropriately enough, Hope.

The referral letter had confirmed an appointment with Mr Usama Abdulla, consultant obstetrician and gynaecologist. He was a member of the staff working under Professor John Beazley at the university department of Obstetrics and a consultant working at the Liverpool Oxford Street Maternity Hospital.

A multitude of different little things have to happen to make one big event occur in life. Chance and timing are beyond our control. To have Mr Abdulla working in Liverpool at all was about to play a huge role in my life. He was recognised throughout the medical profession as an expert in the field of infertility and was the main reason that Liverpool had become an important centre for research into and treatment of that area of medicine.

And he more than lived up to his reputation. From the moment he introduced himself to Graham and me on that day, every perception I had about being able to have children seemed to change. It was as if a dark cloud had been lifted and the future held some sort of hope and belief that made the impossible possible.

In a quiet and calm manner, he took us through the basic methods of a treatment that he felt was appropriate in my case. There were to be courses of injections of a drug called HCG, which stood for Human Chorionic Gonadotro-pin, known by its trade name of Pregnyl. It was this that would, if all went well, stimulate the ovary into producing an egg. Then, if successful, there would be a second stage in the treatment, when I would have to come to the hospital for another injection.

His clear bright eyes were engaging and enquiring at the same time and when he had your attention it was difficult not to listen. From what I'd seen on popular medical dramas on television, there is often a hospital hierarchy that creates an aura around the consultants at the top, especially around those involved in surgery and performing the more serious operations, to the extent that it is rare for anyone else's ideas or views to be aired. Sam Abdulla couldn't have been further away from this stereotypical image. Given his position within the profession I had expected a powerful personality, but that was completely at odds with his bedside manner. He was so soft in the way he spoke; the effect would always calm you down. Everyone I got to know who also knew him said the same thing: that if the word 'gentleman' ever needed an example of its true meaning, then Usama Abdulla was the perfect illustration.

Other methods of infertility treatment had been pioneered through the sixties and seventies, including IVF, but many of the major teaching hospitals were concentrating on the drug-injection method. All the check-ups and tests I'd had over the years had established this as the best course of treatment for me.

The medication was powerful. Patients had to be warned about what could happen. By the time our hour was up, at the end of the appointment, Mr Abdulla had laid all the dangers, potential side effects and pitfalls before me. It was proper to have a short period to think things over, but I think he knew I had already made up my mind. I was a suitable candidate and there was no way I was going to turn down this chance.

After that first consultation there was nothing that Mr Abdulla could ask me to go through that I would not be prepared to go along with; it was the beginning of a relationship of absolute trust and belief. We all have questions and doubts over major decisions and some may well have lurked somewhere in the back of my mind, but to me this was the best and only opportunity of physically having children. I was prepared to have as much treatment as I could to see if it worked and all I could think was that the decision was simple and straightforward. It was as if I'd been given a second chance. I wasn't going to put anything in the way of having a baby.

I began the course of treatments and soon realised that the process, even if successful, was going to take time. Patience would play an important part. In all we went through thirteen treatments over a period of three years.

There were timings to consider; weeks, days and even hours could be critical. I kept a diary marking down the days on which I had the initial course of injections. It would read 'injection' on a certain day or 'final injection' on another, or note that I couldn't have the final injection that time, and from that I would know what followed next.

I'd go through a waiting period of between ten and fourteen days after the first injection and then it was all down to a call to the ward to see if I could have that final injection. If I couldn't have it, there would be a break in the treatment and I would have to wait two or three months before I could start again. It meant the treatment had failed that time; my ovary had failed to release an egg. The waiting period was frustrating while the Pregnyl went out of my system. As the second, third and fourth treatments failed, the frustration grew.

We would always start again, and each time we would have to wait for a call from the hospital to say yes or no as to whether the Pregnyl had worked. If the first injection brought a positive response from the hospital, we had to drop everything and go to the ward in order to have the next one. Because I was working in the bank, I had to try to juggle times and schedules. Sometimes I couldn't get time off so we would try to get to the hospital in my lunch hour, and so there were times I was going into work and then nipping over to Liverpool for an injection.

Graham would also have to be available at short notice; it was my body that was going to be at the brute end of the treatment, but this was something we had to face together. And after that final injection, at which point it was theoretically possible for me to conceive, the nurses would wave us off with a cheery smile, telling Graham to do his best!

It was tiring. The 'going over' — the travelling from Wallasey to Liverpool — sometimes through heavy traffic, stuck in endless queues, feeling exhausted and all the time thinking about the importance of what we were doing, took its toll. And then the hospital would sometimes ask us to come back a second time.

Half a dozen times or more they said no, I couldn't have the final injection. That meant I had to wait for the next course, which might be two or three months later. The memory of the negative phone calls still leaves a haunting feeling. I'm normally a totally together person, but each time it was 'no' I felt the failure hard and burst into tears. We kept the phone on top of the cupboard at the bottom of the stairs. There was no phone seat or anything, and so I used to sit on the bottom stair and brace myself to phone up. That image never goes away: me sitting on the stairs, crying my eyes out on the phone.

Each failure meant going back to the drawing board and an already long process extended yet further into a seemingly endless tunnel of despair. But the period of time had to be that way because each time my body had to put itself back into its original state before they could start again.

Those in the family who knew what I was putting myself through thought it took courage to persevere, but I never looked at it as being brave. I just looked at it as something that I had to do for the end result. Although it might have appeared like a sacrifice of some sort, I didn't feel that way. I just felt that it was what I had to do. The potential of that end result made it something worth fighting for.

As ever, I was really just trying to do everything to the best of my ability; everything. But one thing became clear to me: unless you were in an absolutely stable relationship, you couldn't go through all that. I felt luckier than ever to have Graham by my side.

★ ★ ★

Three years passed, and even with all our efforts at remaining positive, my journey of infertility had eaten away at the confidence I'd felt at the beginning when I had first met Sam Abdulla.

And now there was nowhere left to turn. The clinic had been gentle and understanding but unyieldingly firm about the decision to make this our last treatment. It would now be a case, if it didn't work out, of them saying, 'Sorry, we've done all we can.' I tried to prepare myself to accept that situation.

But all of a sudden, the knowledge that I would have done everything I could didn't feel like any kind of consolation. The dozen failures had taken their toll, and the tears I'd shed were the testament. At least the sadness at the bottom of the stairs would be over.

My thinking had always been that I would go on until I was told by the doctors to stop. It had caused strain and tension and tested our relationship. Graham had wanted me to give up before now; it wasn't just the physical pain, he hated seeing me so upset each time there was a negative response from the hospital. The psychological pressures were just as hard to bear and he couldn't stand the mental anguish it caused.

Somehow, I had recovered each time, taken the punishment of the waiting period till the next treatment began and moved on positively and calmly. Until now. This time there was no more.

If it failed, this time it would be the end of the line.

14

Adoption

Although I was aware that we had one final chance to conceive ourselves, my new resolve — partly to save my sanity — was to concentrate and focus all my efforts on adoption. It was something we'd been looking into for a while. In fact, for two whole years we'd been investigating that option. It helped to soften the blow each time there was a negative phone call from the hospital, or when it became clear that I hadn't fallen pregnant on those occasions when my body had behaved and done what the injections had intended.

And once we'd made that decision to explore adoption, we quickly realised that it was a whole new saga. There were questions to be answered and a host of practical things to be done.

The first issue we had to deal with was to answer the question: under what conditions did we intend to bring up children? The moment you begin to take adoption seriously you realise the decision isn't the same at all as deciding to have a child. Having a baby, or at least trying to have a baby, is a decision that only two people need be involved in, whereas adoption is no longer a decision for just the potential parents.

I discovered quickly that there was a lot to learn. The child's interests are paramount and the whole process of adoption is carefully controlled, in that everything being done is with the welfare of the baby coming first. Suddenly, Graham and I were under the spotlight, being the subjects of an assessment. Like many couples, we would readily have accepted any child, whatever race or creed, but that wasn't the way it worked. It was thirty years ago and things were very different. The people in charge said that if we were considered acceptable, it would depend on how many similar children were in the community as to whether we could take a particular child; they looked at whether or not the child might be too isolated.

It was much more of a serious matchmaking process and we were merely applicants whose suitability was scrutinised. The choice of the child was never ours and it wasn't just a case of whether you had a nice, tidy home. Nor did it feel as if it was about our bank account. The agency looked at our family background and history and it was always about our suitability.

Although being married helped our case, it wasn't necessarily a guarantee for approval for adoption, depending on which route we chose to go down. Thirty years ago there were choices as to where you adopted from, although not as many as there are today. Catholic Societies in particular had a strict policy with regards to suitability; even today there is much controversy within the Catholic groups regarding new laws dealing with couples' different relationships. With Graham's family having strong Catholic roots and me having a Protestant upbringing, a further decision needed to be made. Would the Catholic Society give us a green light, given my religious background?

My world was now in Wallasey and by the time we had settled down to married life in Browning Road, we were firmly planted in the Diocese of the English Martyrs, the Roman Catholic Church to which Graham, his mum and dad and all the family were members. Over time, I'd also come to know the priest at the local church, Canon Martin Kehoe. The more we talked, the more it became clear to me that — in our case — this Church would be in our best interests and those of our future children. So it was I who made the change and made the journey from Sunday-school teacher at St Michael's Church in little Neston across to a different set of Christian beliefs.

I began taking lessons under the instruction of Canon Kehoe almost immediately after we made the decision to adopt. Week in, week out, I attended classes and, of course, became a regular member of the weekly Sunday congregation attending mass. I was definitely on a route less travelled; at the time I was the only student convert. Ever more a practical person than a lover of theory, I did my best to learn as much as possible but understood that in order to be received fully and be welcomed into the Catholic Church, it was going to take time.

As it happened, Canon Kehoe was also an enthusiastic golfer, and with no one else in his class to talk to about his hobby, as he walked me to the door at the end of our lessons I invariably

101

learned almost as much about pars, birdies, eagles, the rules of golf and how to get out of a bunker as I did about the Catholic faith!

Adopting a child is a whole new way of thinking and a whole new kind of love. Rather than making love to make babies, you find a different and equal love for each other. Sometimes, when I think back to the chats and discussions Graham and I had, as all the thoughts about the idea of adopting ran and sometimes raced through my head, I think that the experience of making such a hugely responsible decision, as a couple, brings you even closer than those fortunate enough to have their own children.

The process is hard and common sense tells you it should be difficult. We didn't mind being asked awkward personal questions. I found a similarity in many ways to my mental approach to the fertility treatment. With that, I always used to think to myself how much it was worth going through all the heartache and pain, time and time again, because I always believed it was ultimately worth the struggle in the end if it was going to work.

The same applied to adoption. Everything involved in the process was worth doing if the end result was that we would be given the gift of becoming parents. It's the same thing — there's nothing you wouldn't do, until somebody says you are not suitable.

It was the same as we neared the end of the fertility treatment. If someone had said to us, 'Sorry, but we've done all we can,' I would have accepted it; I would have said, 'OK, that's it.'

As it was, we had one last roll of the dice to throw.

* * *

In the spring of 1983, I was as close as I had ever been to moving on from the idea of fertility treatment being the route to motherhood. The one last chance we had been given was something I was grateful for, but life would have come to a standstill if we hadn't taken the parallel route of adoption. It had been two years since we had first met with the adoption agency and we were almost there; all we were waiting for was a letter of confirmation regarding our approved suitability — if, indeed, we had passed all their tests.

The months of March and April 1983 proved both difficult and busy. Difficult because the final course of fertility treatment began and I had to fit the injections into my work schedule. Busy because, besides the obvious challenge of having to deal with both work and other commitments and the hospital appointments, it always took a huge amount of time to get to the ward through the rush-hour traffic. I never knew whether I was coming or going and was forever seemingly rushed off my feet, going from one place to the next. But to me there was no choice: I was going to see this through to the end.

The first injection of this last-ever course of treatment was on 29 March at 5 p.m., in ward 3B at the Royal Liverpool Hospital. Joan

Warburton, the nurse who had lived through the pain and the hope and the disappointment of the treatments of the past three years with me, was there as usual and ready with a familiar smile. She would always say the same thing at the end of each visit. 'Good luck,' she would say, 'good luck . . . ' She was always warm and genuine in her wishes, but it must have been hard for her dealing all the time with so much disappointment; not just mine, but that of all the other hopeful mothers for whom the treatment didn't work too.

Within two days, more traffic, same time of day, and I was back for a second injection. I knew all too well what lay ahead for the next couple of weeks, and so resigned my body to becoming a pincushion once again. A week passed. On Friday 8 April, Joan phoned — another injection, this time at 7.30 p.m. that same evening; followed by others on Sunday 10 April and Tuesday 12 April. In between the injections there was scan after scan, and also the ever-awkward, never-ending request for urine samples that, in clinical terms, had to be 'collected' by the patient. With the best will in the world, wee on demand does not flow easily.

There were times when, instead of driving to the hospital, I found myself sitting exhausted on the commuter train, clinging to a carrier bag containing my 'collection' for the day. If I ever nodded off, a jolt from another passenger would invariably stir me and there'd be an uncomfortable beat of a moment when I'd slowly look

104

down at the bag to make sure there was nothing embarrassing on the floor!

On it went through the middle of April, day after day, one injection after another, followed by more scans. The same discretion that Graham and I had always maintained meant that no one at work knew what I was going through at the time. It always seemed so private and the workplace felt no different to me than the schoolroom. I wasn't asking for any time off, so I wasn't causing any disruption. As far as I was concerned, there was no need to make any excuses other than for an uncommonly high number of toilet breaks, each time the treatment required me to add to my 'collection'.

★ ★ ★

One day during this final round of the 'first' injections in the cycle, as Graham and I crossed our fingers and hoped that they would work, that we would later receive a positive summons from the hospital for the — at last aptly named — 'final' injection, a telephone call came through for me at work. The receptionist had answered it.

'Janet!' She had been looking for me. 'There's a telephone call for you. It's Graham, I think.' She was right and he sounded a little nervous.

'What's the matter?' I said at once.

'Nothing, luv, it's just that the post has arrived and it's here.'

'What's here?'

There was only one letter we were waiting for, but I needed to hear him tell me.

105

'I've got the letter from the adoption agency in my hand.'

The anticipation was infused with a touch of excitement. My heart began to beat faster.

'Should I open it?' Graham continued. 'It's just that I thought you might want me to wait until later, so we can open it together.'

It seemed reasonable and the best thing to do; after all, it was just as important to both of us, so if it was good news we could celebrate the moment together.

'OK, Gray, good idea. We'll open it later. See you. Love you. Bye!'

'OK, luv, see you later.'

Two minutes later, I rang him back. 'I can't wait!'

'Neither can I, I'm so glad you called back! I would have been thinking of nothing else all day.'

'Well?' Now we'd agreed to open it, I couldn't wait a moment longer to find out what it said.

'Just a min.' Graham began to unseal the envelope one-handed, as he held the phone with his other hand. There was a fumble, a rustle and a sharp knock. The phone had slipped from his hand and the hard plastic of the receiver had hit the banister.

'Gray?' I exclaimed.

'Hang on, nearly there,' he said, recovering, and then he withdrew the letter from the envelope. It had one fold across the middle and he slowly lifted one side to make sure it was the right way up. He wanted to try to read it so that we would hear the news together.

He succeeded . . . and so had we. It was

fantastic news. The letter was a confirmation that we'd been accepted for adoption and, to add to the excitement, it even talked of a possibility of twins!

It was the best feeling ever. The next stage in our life plan could now be put into action: put the house on the market, focus more on our weekend soft toy market-stall business to boost our family funds — and book a holiday. We'd gone to Malta the year before and enjoyed it so much that we'd decided to return this summer.

Happy as I was, though, I was suddenly reminded of one other thing to consider as I glanced down to my bag, at the bottom of which the latest sample sat. There was to be another injection to endure that night.

It would prove to be one of the last I would ever have.

★　★　★

Even though I arrived home early from work on the allotted day for the call to the hospital, and had plenty of time to prepare, my nerves were already on edge. I walked slowly from my car to our front door. The few yards felt like a mile.

Operating on autopilot, I opened my bag and reached inside for my house keys. I flicked a couple of the keys along the ring until I held the front-door key in my hand. But instead of it sliding effortlessly into its slot, the tip of the metal scraped the surface, moving from side to side over the hole, again and again. There was no hiding from the call I was going to have to make and my hand was shaking, betraying any attempt I was making to kid myself confident.

Finally, the door opened for me. Graham had heard the unusual metallic scratching and undid the latch. I walked into the hall at Browning Road. All I could say was: 'Coffee. I need a strong black coffee.'

But after we'd both had a cup, there was no putting it off any longer. For three years I'd been making this phone call — the phone call that would determine whether or not we had a chance of conceiving ourselves. Would the injections have worked? Would we have a green light for the last-ever 'final' injection? Or would we have fallen at the first hurdle? There was only one way to find out.

I dialled the familiar number with a shaking hand. The hallway was bright in the spring sunshine but I felt nothing but cold. I traced the carpet's pattern with my shoe, seeing the well-worn tread of the bottom step, where I'd sat and cried my eyes out so many times after a negative response to this very same phone call. Would there be tears today?

There weren't. It was good news. I couldn't quite believe it, but we had received a stay of execution. Our dreams of conceiving were kept alive for one more stage of the process at least. And so Gray and I returned to the hospital for the last time. I had the very last injection. Gray was instructed, with the usual cheeky nudge and wink, to 'do his best'. And then all we could do was wait. The treatment was at an end.

And, somehow, I knew I was going to be OK.

I was going to be OK about it not working because I was totally sure I had given it everything I could. I hadn't given up. I'd always promised myself I would wait until the doctors said 'no more'.

That day was now closer than ever. After this, there would be no more injections, nor scans. No more hospital appointments. No more hope about ever conceiving a baby.

Yet any slight sadness that there may have been that the treatment likely hadn't worked was countered by the fact that — through the adoption process — Graham and I now knew that at long last we were going to fulfil our dreams of becoming parents.

15

Sickness

As the spring of 1983 merged into the heat of the early summer months, Graham and I looked forward to our much-anticipated return trip to Malta. We had holidayed there the year before, when I was two-thirds of the way through the fertility treatment. It had been the perfect antidote to the drugs and all the negativity of the failed cycles. We enjoyed it so much that we were determined to return as soon as possible.

Purely by coincidence, on an excursion to Gozo during our first trip, we had discovered the ancient temple of Ggantija. It is regarded by many as the site of a fertility cult; from above it takes the appearance of a womb with multiple chambers. In one of these, an oblong boulder acts as a form of seat. There was a legend that sitting on it could have pretty powerful consequences. Of course, I'd sat on that boulder as long as I comfortably could, but it seemed its spell wasn't cast for me.

Every time Graham and I had ever been on holiday since we'd been together I was always organised, prepared and packed in good time, sometimes even a week ahead of our departure. The house would be left in a perfect state and I would have cleaned everywhere . . . but not this time. I was really lethargic; I just couldn't be bothered. I didn't know what was wrong with me.

I came home from work the night before we were due to fly feeling awful. I had been sick several times and was only interested in sitting down.

'I'm sorry, Gray, I'm not feeling very well.'

'Look, luv, we don't have to go if you're not feeling well. We'll just cancel.'

'But the flight is tomorrow and the hotel is booked.' In between what I hoped might be undetectable gulps of an uncomfortable throat that, in truth, I had very little control over, I tried to sound as strong as I could. 'We can't just cancel like that. It's too late, we'll have to go.'

I was acting totally out of character and, of course, Graham knew it.

'We don't have to do anything. Your health comes first. I'll ring the company and see if we can get another date. We can leave it this year.'

That sounded drastic action. Neither of us really wanted to cancel and we certainly couldn't afford to lose the money. On top of this, if we didn't go, I felt I would be the one spoiling the holiday and I didn't want to let Graham down. So cancelling wasn't something I wanted even to contemplate. I figured that I'd feel better within a couple of days . . .

'I'll be OK. I think a holiday is exactly what I need, the way I feel.'

'I'm sure it's all those drugs you've been taking.'

Without realising it, Graham was right — but for the wrong reason. In fact, he had never

111

spoken a truer word. But the moment passed us by as we concluded our debate. We agreed to carry on with the holiday, but Graham wasn't happy.

Many times I could see in his eyes that he was really worried about me. The strain we had felt over the past three years, especially once he began wanting me to stop the treatment, had, at times, been very testing for us. We both knew that the last fertility treatment I had been through was the final one. That choice had now been taken from us and the only route to parenthood, in our minds, was adoption. That was what the holiday was about: to have a break as we prepared for the wonderful change in our lives that our anticipated adopted baby was going to bring.

We had both gone through a lot over the last few months. We had each been working as hard as we could and although I was the one who had been taking the injections and the drugs, both of us had gone through the anguish and pain of the disappointments and the stress that fertility treatment brought. We both needed the break.

★　★　★

That holiday proved to be unforgettable. It felt as if I was practising the bilious business of regurgitation from the moment we left the house until we returned a fortnight later.

It wasn't that I had anything against any of the food put in front of me, but it was rejection and ejection most of the time. What I needed was a bowl against my pillow. I was ill on the plane going out; I was ill on the plane coming back. Every single morning, a retching ritual dismissed anything I may have managed to eat the night before. Whenever I dared to leave the hotel room, it was never without a good supply of polythene bags.

There are, of course, many reasons why someone might have a feeling of nausea, and as many for severe vomiting. Was it something I ate? I didn't think so; it had gone on too long for that. But, still, it was almost too much even to consider the other possibility.

As the days went queasily by, there was little to do. I was stranded like a shipwreck in a hotel bedroom in St Paul's Bay, with brilliant sunshine merely visiting me in my sick state as it burst through the windows each day. It seemed that thinking about swimming pools, beaches and sunbeds was the nearest I was getting to a holiday; I could have done that at home. I felt dreadful.

Determined to get some sort of tan, I did eventually get to the sands to sunbathe, but I wasn't any better. I remember even being ill on the beach. I was so tired and so fed up of being sick, which by that stage was more like bile; I did what I needed to do as discreetly as possible. It was as if my sunbed was a boat on choppy waters and I was intermittently leaning over the edge, heaving on the sand and quickly covering it up, murmuring to myself that a bucket and spade would have been handy!

Before we came home, we did go for a walk. It

was brute determination that got me through it because I really wasn't any better. By now, I was starting to look forward to getting home.

About ten miles from St Paul's Bay is the capital of Malta, Valletta, where there are loads of churches. It's beautiful there, it really is, and we would go in a church to look around and soak up the wonderfully peaceful atmosphere. Then I would come out and I would have to sneak up a little side street and be sick, and then I would walk on and go on to the next one. It was awful, absolutely awful. But with fertility temples and so much sacramental meaning in Malta, maybe mumbling a little prayer wasn't out of place.

But the people who happened to be walking past as I was ill just gave me a pitiful look, a disdainful glance and uttered a few 'tut-tuts', perhaps thinking I was a little worse for wear, having had a touch too much wine or whisky in the Maltese sunshine. They stared at me as if I was hungover. Enough was enough.

By this time, my suspicions about what was going on were growing inside me. There really was only one explanation, but I barely dared hope. Yet by the end of the two weeks I admitted it to myself.

I thought that I might be pregnant.

★ ★ ★

Martin, Graham's brother-in-law, picked us up from the airport. He told us of various bits of family news, including the fact that one of

114

Graham's nieces was pregnant, adding to my growing belief that I could be too.

We didn't say anything about how ill I'd been, for the same reason that I had never spoken to anyone before about anything to do with my problems. It was too private. The same feeling that had applied all through school, with the period problem, had been perpetuated with all my friends throughout the last three years while we were going through the fertility treatment.

I was now an expert at avoiding conversations about anything awkward, side-stepping issues even with our closest friends, John and Lynn. We used to go out a lot together and often Lynn's mum would say, 'Are you thinking of having children?'

I always used to avoid answering the question. I never told anybody anything, except for the people who we wanted to know, like my mum and Graham's mum, Betty. But perhaps now we would finally be able to engage in those awkward conversations.

The day after we got back from Malta we went to the hospital. The more hours that passed, the more convinced I was becoming that I was pregnant. There was something inside me that was telling me — in more ways than one. I couldn't think of any other rational explanation for why I had been so ill and so sick so many times.

But the ounce of common sense still inside me said I wasn't absolutely sure. I needed 100 per cent confirmation and the only way to get that was to go to the most informed place about pregnancy I knew: the place where Sam and his team would be able to witness — hopefully — the success of all their work.

The staff in ward 3B were aware of my case and it was not long after we arrived that a nurse carried out a simple pregnancy test. Although she was new to the job the test was straightforward, and all the indications were giving a positive result. I was, though, a patient who had just gone through three years of unsuccessful fertility treatment; enough for anyone to want a more senior nurse to double-check. She told me she would arrange for a second opinion, but I knew. If a body can give a message to a brain then every sinew and signal was saying the same thing. However ill I felt, the sickness was now being rapidly shoved to the back of my mind in the face of what felt like a miracle.

The confirmation came quickly after that. Morning sickness made way for an ecstatic and euphoric feeling of pure joy. I was more thrilled than I'd ever been in my life — I just could not believe it. Everyone around us suddenly seemed in celebratory mood. There were things to do, of course; not least a scan as soon as possible.

But even a case like mine, with all the treatment I'd had, I couldn't go for a scan without an appointment. We made one for the afternoon. There was another reason for delay too: this body of mine, not long since shipwrecked in Malta, now had to take on board plenty of water for the scan to work.

Once I was booked in for the afternoon, there

was nothing for Graham and me to do except go for a walk with a litre of Evian. And for the next couple of hours, we walked on air.

★ ★ ★

Of course, it was at that scan that we discovered I was pregnant with six babies.

It was genuine shock, and probably even a state of fright, that hovered over everyone in the hospital room as the bombshell was dropped. No one in the room had ever experienced a multiple birth of this size.

The ultrasound equipment that had been used to discover how many eggs had been produced had not revealed the multiple birth. It wasn't until now, after the fertilisation part of the treatment had taken place, that the doctors realised that there were six.

No one knew if the babies would survive.

But it was then that I was overcome with that great sense of calm. I made a promise to myself. For, us, and for our future children, I was going to do everything I was told and everything would work out fine.

I was going to make sure I had these babies.

Dr Adrian Murray was responsible for my welfare in Sam Abdulla's absence. He weighed up the situation. Unsurprisingly, he said almost immediately, 'Mrs Walton, I think you have no choice but to come into hospital.'

Thinking it might be good to lighten the atmosphere a bit, I thought I would make a joke and suggest instant admission into hospital. 'Do you mean now?' I said, with half a smile and a nervous laugh.

'Truthfully, yes.' He looked serious. 'But I don't suppose that is practical. No, you must go home, sort out a few bits and pieces and come back tomorrow.'

He gave the impression that it wasn't going to be a short stay — by any stretch of the imagination.

16

Telling the Parents

We walked through the busy corridors of the hospital on our way home, both of us still reeling from the news the doctors had broken just moments ago. Elevator doors opened and closed and people poured in and out of the passageways. Our route was momentarily blocked as a clear chime rang out and a light above one of the service lift doors changed from red to green. A trolley carrying a patient was pushed in our path. I remember avoiding one or two wheelchairs and thinking, *I could do with one of those . . .* I hung on to Graham's arm as he guided me through the tunnels of faceless people.

I saw no expression nor caught anyone's eye. Any thought I had was blurred by the unfolding drama of the past couple of hours. I felt relief that I had been allowed to go home, even if it was only for the night, but I was also, I think, in some sort of shock. The final corridor led directly to the reception area, an open block brightly lit by a mix of neon and natural light. The high ceilings created a crescendo of noise — enough to stir me to focus on a new concern.

Suddenly, as if the huge glass of the atrium had shattered and splintered and shards were stabbing me, I felt the pain and heartache this was going to cause both Graham's parents and

119

my mum and dad, and all the other close members of our family. It dawned upon me that there was very little time and the most important people in our lives needed to know immediately. Yet it was hardly credible. The fact was that nobody would believe what had been confirmed as my medical condition. It was simply — ironically enough — inconceivable that I might be carrying six babies.

If we had been in today's world when Dr Murray had dropped his bombshell on us, the whole family would have been aware of the news by the time we had reached the car park, with the help of modern-day mobiles and text messaging. Back in 1983, it would be a full hour before anyone but Graham and me knew about it.

We travelled almost silently through the Mersey Tunnel from Liverpool to Wallasey to Graham's parents' house. No sooner were we in the lounge breaking the news than the tears began to flow.

Somehow, though, my eyes were dry. My thoughts had already begun to arrange themselves in practical order. I knew this was the first of a number of actions that Graham and I would need to take in the short time we had left before I went into hospital the next day. It was me this was happening to and yet I couldn't cry; it was strange but I felt I had to show signs of confidence to the others. The less I was worried, the more confident they might be.

It wasn't long before we were back at our home in Browning Road, making the stop on the way to Neston. The main reason to stop off was to make a call to the bank. I was due back to work there the next morning, after our holiday in Malta, and that was something that wasn't going to happen.

Even though our time at the house was short, as I wanted to get to my mum as quickly as possible, mindful of my impending absence, I instinctively began to tidy the house as Graham prepared to make the call. He had recovered from the tears he'd shed with his mum and dad and his voice was strong and confident. One of my colleagues, Peter Challinor, answered the phone.

'Hello, this is Graham Walton, Janet's husband.'

'Hello, Graham, Peter Challinor here.'

'Hi. It's really just to let you know that Janet won't be coming into work tomorrow.'

'Oh. OK. Is she alright?'

'Unfortunately, she has to go into hospital tomorrow because she's expecting six babies.'

I don't think Graham meant to be quite so blunt, or even tell him exactly what was going on, but there was no other way of putting it: those were the facts and that was the way it came out.

The answer was even more surprising.

'Oh, that's fine, Graham. Thanks for letting us know. Bye.'

Peter hung up. Graham was left holding the phone, looking at the receiver, completely stunned by what he had just used as an excuse for his wife not being able to go in to work

121

— but even more so by the matter-of-fact way in which Peter had accepted the most implausible, unlikely medical excuse in history!

There was no time to dwell on it or to wait for a call back in case Peter later sought confirmation he had heard correctly.

It was straight out of the house, back into the car and we made haste to my mum and dad's house.

Mum knew how I'd been in Malta, how I'd been feeling and even my suspicion of possibly being pregnant. She had been waiting all day for news and was in on her own.

She was a little surprised that, as soon as she answered the door, before anything else, I told her not to cry. She agreed — and kept her word. Immediately she reacted to what we told her by putting on an amazing act of acceptance and confidence, in so doing showing me exactly where I was getting my own strength from to begin this journey into the unknown.

But, later on, she confided to me that as soon as we had left that evening, she had also burst into tears.

I went to bed early that night. My last night in my own bed for goodness knew how long. Before going to sleep, I turned to Graham. I pulled the sheets a little tighter around me and I told him the secret promise I had made to myself earlier that afternoon.

I looked him in the eye and said firmly to my husband, 'I am going to have these babies. I'll go into hospital tomorrow and I'll be the best patient they *ever* had.'

17

The Royal Liverpool

After all the heightened emotions of the previous day, I woke up the next morning surprised that I had managed to get any sleep at all. I could hear Graham downstairs; knives and forks were clinking together and plates were being moved. Breakfast was being prepared, though I wasn't sure I could even look at food. I thought about the washing that still needed doing from the holiday. Half the things needing attention were still in the cases.

'Breakfast's almost ready, Janet!' The call was clear and confident. Graham was doing his best to act as normally as possible.

'I'll be down in a minute!'

I tidied everything away from the holiday — it would need sorting later, but for now I just wanted it all tidy before I went into hospital. After throwing a few essentials into a weekend bag, I took a quick shower and dressed.

I took a few seconds to look in the mirror and check my appearance. Like so many times before in my life, I looked and all I saw was the familiar but tanned Janet staring back. I couldn't help but stare intently at my belly. Inside me, even now, six little heartbeats were pounding away. I turned to my side to inspect my profile but there was no telltale bump: I looked just the same as I had always done. Here I was with my whole world in total turmoil, trying to face something so difficult to imagine, so incomprehensible it was impossible to take in, and yet my eyes looked back at me calmly, as if to say, it's good, it's for the good.

Something gripped me at that moment. It was an over-powering feeling of confidence. The reactions of all the nurses and doctors at the hospital, and those of our parents and family, were alight in my mind, rushing in and out, fragmented thoughts — but above them all, growing steadily stronger, was the solitary thought that I would listen and do everything the doctors told me. If anything was to go wrong, it wouldn't be my fault.

Yet the thought that was loudest of all was this: *nothing was going to go wrong*.

I was going to have these babies.

'It's on the table, Jan!'

I grabbed the bag and went downstairs, following the scent of marmalade, toast and coffee.

'Not all that hungry, really,' I confessed, coming into the kitchen. After my two weeks of morning sickness in Malta, food wasn't at the forefront of my mind.

'I know, luv, but think how many you're eating for now!' Graham grinned at me across the toast rack.

The humour helped. I was hungrier than I realised and I did feel better for the light breakfast.

After we'd finished, for a moment between us

there was silence, as if we were both overawed by the events of the last twenty-four hours.

'It's going to be OK, luv,' Graham said, into the stillness. 'I know it is. This is the right thing, this going into hospital. It's a big thing for them. They want to protect you from day one and they are going to look after you brilliantly. This way they can keep an eye on you every second.'

He was right. Agreeing with the doctors to go in immediately wasn't difficult. It wasn't really a choice; it was for the benefit of everybody.

For the hospital, who were looking at it from the point of view of doing everything they could to manage a highly unusual medical case.

For me. After all, this wasn't a pregnancy in the normal sense; I was a case that required constant monitoring to ensure a safe outcome for me, the patient. Though the expectation of success at this stage was ranging from nil to even less, what the doctors could do, at the very least, was ensure that I was given proper bed rest, whether I needed it or not.

And, most of all, it was for the benefit of my babies.

★   ★   ★

I couldn't have looked less like I should be in hospital on the sunny June morning when Graham drove me over to the Royal Liverpool Teaching Hospital to be admitted as a full-time patient and part-time unusual case for student medics to examine. There were times in the first couple of days when I felt a complete fraud. I was in a gynaecological ward, surrounded by patients who were there for a variety of serious ailments and illnesses, each being tended daily by the nurses through their individual problems. I, meanwhile, looked like the picture of health, enhanced and highlighted by a bronze Maltese-sunshine sheen.

I was 'allowed' out once or twice during the first couple of weeks in hospital. Graham and I went for a brief walk on the promenade by the river one day, but not surprisingly it was difficult to relax. Everything had changed and now our nerves were on edge, worried in case anything might go wrong while I was away from the safe confines of my hospital bed.

The second time I was given permission to leave was one weekend. But Saturday was market day and, with us both not wanting to lose our place at the market, Graham was going to be out of town, manning the stall. He asked Dad to help out for the afternoon and so responsibility for me was temporarily handed back from husband to father.

It was a beautiful sunny day and I sat with Dad in the courtyard of the nearby Lighthouse pub in Wallasey Village. I was still showing a suntan that was enhanced by my favourite blue-and-white striped summer dress. It had an elastic middle but, with no bump yet showing, there was no need for it to stretch to accommodate my early stages of pregnancy.

For all his joking and humour, age and experience of life, what was happening to his daughter was as overwhelming for Dad as it was for all the close members of the family. All of a sudden he wasn't just Dad, he was a bodyguard. He was nervous and so was I — we just didn't want anything to go wrong.

We left the pub and went for a walk along the front at New Brighton. The view was, as always on clear sunny days, magnificent, with a hazy horizon that separated the two shades of blue given by sea and sky. I was an ordinary young woman, looking no different from any other, enjoying a cool, soft summer ice cream and a walk, surrounded by other ordinary people enjoying the gentle summer breeze of the seaside resort. And yet, somehow, secretly growing inside me were six babies, baffling even the most experienced doctors, at the start of their journey to life. Six babies whose only protection came from that ordinary young woman and her father. No wonder there was demonstrable relief from Dad when Graham got back from the market later that day.

After that weekend, I was too scared to go out of the hospital again. It was just too much responsibility to try to cope without the doctors' reassuring nearby presence.

So as the days and weeks went by I got used to the routine of being a long-term patient in a hospital. The ward had eight beds and there were constant comings and goings, different faces with different stories. Most people were only in for a couple of days. I wasn't quite scratching four lines and a diagonal on the wall but I found other ways of keeping track of time. Other patients became an unlikely source for my calculations, as I added the number of days a case would be in for; the average hysterectomy in those days would be in for a couple of weeks.

I kept myself as busy as I could, keeping in mind all the time from the first day that I wanted to be the best patient they had ever had. Everything I could do I did to the best of my ability. I switched off from everything in the outside world and took a day at a time, although there wasn't a lot to do outside flower arranging, reading and choosing my meals.

The visitors I had were fantastic. In the time I was at the Royal, the quieter moments were always countered by friends. There must have been some sort of allowance made for the special circumstances, and maybe it was partly a sympathetic thing because of the expectation of a negative outcome, but people seemed to be visiting all day. Friends of Graham and mine who worked in Liverpool would pop in once or twice a week. That meant more than the occasional visit from different men. One friend, John Pritchard, worked so close to the hospital that he was able to pop in regularly. Occasionally I could feel a brow being pushed up as the beds opposite moralised on the propriety of the number of 'single' male visitors one pregnant woman should receive at her bedside!

Sometimes you don't realise what good friends you've got until events happen unexpectedly. Time and again I was surprised by simple acts of kindness from people.

I was in for so long that even women who had been in and out of the ward having procedures of their own became friends, and there was one, Rose, with whom I got on so well and who was so supportive that she even came to visit me after she had recovered from her operation and had left the hospital.

Graham even created a time sheet to ensure that I was never going to be without company. It is never nice to have to sit up or lie in a hospital bed at visiting time with or without the curtains drawn and be the only patient without a visitor. Equally, it was no good having ten people around the bed. So we had to have it organised and Graham would tell me who was visiting that night and who would be there the next day or later in the week. He worked it so that there would be at least one person with me at all visiting times, rather than have a big crowd around the bed.

It may have been my body that was changing and me whose life had been turned upside down by fate and fertility, but the months in hospital affected so many more people, especially those closest to me. Their lives were also in turmoil. Normal routines of work life and village life were now completely disrupted, not least because of the distance each had to travel to be with me. The journey from Wallasey that Graham was making twice every day meant changes in working hours and sometimes battling with rush-hour traffic.

Eventually, the sisters on the ward sympathetically bestowed an unwritten honorary status upon Graham and when the bell at the end of visiting went at eight o'clock, everybody else would shuffle out but my husband, under slightly adjusted rules, was allowed to sit there until much later. There were times he would be sitting on his own by my side, but they would never throw him out. He could have been there all night, but in the end he used to go at about half past ten — just in time for a quick pint at the pub around the corner.

The small village of Neston was as good as on another planet in terms of distance from the big city hospital in Liverpool. Dad's daily work commitments meant he wasn't available as often as Mum and Alison. Nearly every single day Mum gathered different things she felt I needed, packed everything for the journey and battled through all weathers on buses, trains and sometimes taxis to be at my side.

I was as good as resident and was on first-name terms with the cleaners. They were a breath of fresh air in more ways than one. One would come in early each morning and once she'd finished her work, she'd pull up a chair to take the weight off her feet and tell me all that was going on in her neck of the woods. When you're just lying there, day after day in the same ward, familiarity sets in. You realise how important each person's job is and how important they are as individuals, all with their own lives and their own set of problems.

* * *

The longer the pregnancy went on, the more a terrible balancing act was unwittingly being performed. For the more time the babies stayed inside me, protected as every baby is in the natural confinement of a womb, the greater their chance of life — but also the greater the danger to my own life.

As is often the case when you are the subject of events, you simply don't see things in the same way as others around you. The dangers that Graham and my family, friends and the staff at the hospital were concerned about, the danger to my life, never occurred to me. Nobody liked to talk about these worries to my face, so I didn't realise what they were saying to each other.

When I look back at some of the quotes from the doctors about my time in hospital before the birth, I wonder whether my attitude and behaviour as a patient really did make a difference. Whether positive thoughts — trying to do everything right according to medical advice, doing as I was told and never losing hold of a constant belief that everything was going to be alright — added to the likelihood of the successful outcome so many seemed to be praying for on my behalf. Our paediatric consultant Professor Cooke said later, ' . . . it was so much better because Janet was the ideal patient . . . she was calm and she never panicked . . . had it been a different patient it might never have happened . . . '

Sam Abdulla agreed with him, saying the same, about how all the way through I had been calm and cool. The truth was I was just trying to be as I had always been at school and at the bank; I was scared of doing anything wrong. It was probably just another form of being conscientious, of not wanting to make mistakes in the eyes of others, of listening to what I believed was good advice grounded in experience and wisdom.

The one thing I was aware of was the significance of the next stage. Care of premature babies had progressed to a point where even the tiniest of babies had a chance of survival. If I could just get through the second trimester — to twenty-three weeks — and give my babies the slightest chance of life, I was convinced they would survive.

If that slight chance existed, I would be moved from the Royal Liverpool Hospital to the Liverpool Maternity Hospital in Oxford Street.

For now, the only option I had was to concentrate on the future, day by day. Nobody, not even the doctors, knew what the outcome was going to be.

18

Liverpool Maternity Hospital

It was early October. I had now arrived at a critical landmark. We were at twenty-four weeks.

The previous week, as I'd hoped might happen through all of my months at the Royal, I had been moved to the Liverpool Maternity Hospital. I was put in a private room. I was now growing at an alarming rate, getting bigger and bigger each day. And I was no longer just a medical case that needed treating. Expectation and belief had begun to spring up in everyone around me, not just the nurses, who of course continued to act in the same ever-professional way, but also the family.

While we were now at a time where it was possible the babies might survive if born, we were still many weeks away from what might clinically be described, under the circumstances, as the most desirable minimum gestation period. I needed to hang on for at least another six or seven weeks to reach that milestone. The medical staff, and especially Sam Abdulla, had to know as accurately as possible what was going on inside the womb. But they had to find a balance of following the babies throughout the progress of the pregnancy without relying on over-frequent scans.

It was still dark when early one morning I was

taken on a trolley and wheeled down to the Ultrasound department. Illa, the radiographer in charge of my scans, was waiting for me.

'Not just me today, Janet,' she said, with an air of importance in her voice. 'Mr Abdulla is coming down. He said he wanted to see for himself the babies' progress.'

'That's good,' I said, trying not to let her think I thought her any less important just because the boss was going to oversee this particular scan. Knowing how many weeks I had now passed, I had been hoping he would be there. 'I have a couple of questions.'

'How have you been feeling?' Illa said with a smile. She had become a familiar face over the last few months and, like all the nurses, she was having to dampen down her enthusiasm and excitement as each week passed. They didn't want to get my hopes up.

'Fine, thanks.'

I couldn't believe I'd said that; why do people do that? But we do — maybe it's a British or English thing that you can be feeling at a ridiculously low point, the world could be caving in, everything going wrong . . . but if somebody asks you how you are, you immediately say, 'Oh, OK, thanks' or 'Great!' or 'Couldn't be better'. I had been in hospital now for four months, and besides bedsores and boredom, my body had turned into Mount Everest. I could no longer see my feet. To top it all, my perm had grown out!

While my determination hadn't faltered, my discomfort and disfiguration had, not surprisingly, taken a bit of the shine off 'fine'. But I

134

couldn't stop myself adding, 'Just fine. Although I think I'm redefining the Battle of the Bulge!'

'That's the way. Got to keep a sense of humour,' she laughed. As she began preparing me for the scan, I noticed even she was surprised as she exposed my tummy and immediately saw so much movement. It seemed the babies were excited about having their photograph taken!

Almost unnoticed, Sam quietly stepped into the room. He was on his own, no entourage or fanfare, no assistants, nurses or student doctors. Just Sam on his own, wanting on this occasion to make me feel I had his full attention and that this wasn't a medical lesson or demonstration for the good of future practice. It was just a doctor and his patient.

'Hello, Janet.' The formality of using surnames and titles had long since gone. While visiting Sam's clinic during the years of my fertility treatment, I had appreciated the manner in which he had always dealt with my case. He was fully aware of the emotional strains and the stresses his patients were under, and was able to encourage and give them confidence, always at the time they needed it most. I always felt lucky for my case to be under his watchful eye. He was careful never to build false hopes, but his enthusiasm for his work was always positive and full of infectious confidence, joy and expectation.

He now had the same question for me as Illa. 'How have you been feeling?'

Same question; different answer. 'Not really been feeling that well, Sam.'

135

A raised eyebrow from Illa, but I needed him to know exactly what I felt was going on inside my body. 'I know it's good that the babies are moving around, but I don't know how much more I can grow. I feel so big.' I was actually, under the circumstances, not doing too badly; more than anything I was being naturally anxious for the babies now they were being so active.

'Well, let's see what we can with the ultrasound and see what positions the babies are in.'

Sam held the scanning pad in his hand and slowly glided it over a river of gel. His face lit up as he began studying the screen. I'd noticed that each time he had been present at the scan and conducted the diagnosis himself, he behaved as though it wasn't just a task that had to be done proficiently and properly, but something more; his interest in what he was doing was clearly more than just a job.

I usually waited to speak until spoken to when Sam was scanning me, respecting his position among the staff around us and the fact that he was basically the boss of the department. However, our relationship had changed from straightforward doctor-patient to one of friendship between two people involved in an extraordinary situation. I now felt at ease with him and able to say what I was thinking.

It seems to me that everyone experiences, at one time or another, people who come into their lives for a reason, but for a reason that they will never understand. For me, Sam was one of those

136

people. There are many consultant gynaecologists and obstetricians working all over the world, and invariably borders are crossed in professional circles and a specialist working in any one particular area could easily find him- or herself working in a city in one country and then in a different city and country as their career moves forward. I have often thought how lucky I was for Sam in particular to be my consultant.

Of all the specialists in this field in the world, there were at the time perhaps a handful who were world authorities on ultrasound. Sam had been born in Iraq in 1937 and after being conscripted into national service he went on to work at a place called Medical City in Baghdad. There he became friendly with Ian Donald, a visiting Scottish doctor who was one of the pioneers of ultrasound. If it hadn't been for his invitation for Sam to join him in Glasgow, we may never have met and I wouldn't have been his patient.

Sam became one of the first to publish medical papers on ultrasound and made new discoveries in diagnosis that helped improve obstetrics. For me that was critically important — because ultimately it was he who introduced obstetric ultrasound to Liverpool. I have no doubt that his exceptional experience made a huge difference in my case.

And it was going to take all his skill and understanding for all my babies to survive. As the leader of the team, it was Sam who would make the tough decision of when to operate. That balancing act again: at which point was it most likely that both the babies and me would live?

I felt more movement across my stomach as the scanner moved forwards and backwards, creating thin furrows in the gel. The gel glistened with the reflected light of the room and flowed across me, creating streams on either side of the great bulk. I kept turning my head to glance at the circular screen on the monitor, but all I could make out were blacks and whites and cloudy areas in between.

'You see!' His voice was a happy one. It was strong, full of the delight of life and wanting me to join in the experience. 'There is one baby. Here is another. And another. And here another and here one more. We can see five babies.'

We can't, I thought. I looked and looked, just as I had done the last time and the time before, but I couldn't, no matter how hard I tried, make out clear distinct shapes of babies or even any parts of them. 'I . . . eh . . . '

'You can't see them? At this stage, it's too cramped to tell whether they are boys or girls. Look, here I will outline.' He carefully marked on the screen where each was, circling them. As he did so, all of a sudden my eyes began to focus on shapes I hadn't seen before. I held on to the sight, trying not to blink even for a moment. Yet my vision blurred as, slowly, tears began to flow. Those were my babies. My babies.

He continued to move the scanner from side to side again and again, backwards and forwards across my abnormally large abdomen, pushing through the waves of gel. I don't think he wanted me to be too emotional so in an effort to distract me he said matter-of-factly, 'It's a very repetitive process but the best way to get the clearest picture.'

He had my attention, and for a moment he reminisced. 'You know, I leapt at the idea when I was asked to come to the United Kingdom to learn about ultrasound. When I first used to do this, we used to use lots of olive oil and the movements we had to make were so repetitive I don't know how we have our wrists intact!' As he turned the scanner pads once again, a trail of gel left a pattern. 'I could even recognise who had done the scan just from the shape of the movement over the tummy and the pattern left in the oil.' He smiled and Illa and I both laughed, feeling privileged that this eminent consultant would share such stories.

★   ★   ★

Although I didn't know it at the time, plans and strategies for my Caesarean operation were now being discussed regularly in meetings between consultant gynaecologists and paediatricians at the Liverpool Maternity Hospital, along with the anaesthesia experts. Yet it wasn't only the medical staff at Oxford Street who had to be involved in these discussions. Whatever the outcome of the operation, the story of this extraordinary event was to become public knowledge and the hospital knew they would have to deal with it, whether or not there was a successful outcome. Consequently, the whole of the hospital's administration department, led by John Lyons, was also preparing meticulously to handle every possible public-relations eventuality they could imagine.

Whenever the operation took place, it was going to be totally unchartered territory for all the staff, including Sam. As it got nearer the time, those who were going to be involved in the operation never went home without a special bleeper so they could be contacted and told to get back to the hospital immediately, should a problem or anything unexpected occur.

Indifferent to anything else going on, my tummy really did seem to be growing at a much faster rate. The lengths to which my mum went to make me feel comfortable never failed to surprise me. She was continually doing things that only a mother would think of to make me feel a little better under the absurd circumstances.

For example, one thing I didn't have to worry about at all was fancy maternity clothes or shopping for my favourite colour smock or trousers with expanding waistlines. Each morning when I woke, I had only one choice when it came to my wardrobe. The question was, which nightie should I wear? But there was another issue. When you're going up a dress size each week, it has the potential to get a bit depressing. So, Mum, in her clever and considerate motherly way, simply cut the sizes out of the nighties. All the labels were gone and I didn't notice at first; I was just pleased to have one that fitted.

The more delicate I got, the more I relied on my mum for things to eat. The variety of favourite foods she brought fuelled both my energy and imagination as the pregnancy progressed and my taste buds changed. I found myself wanting food foreign to Mum's culinary skills, so she did the next best thing and satisfied my cravings by buying things like potted shrimps and smoked salmon. She used to watch over me carefully, observing my changing habits and always finding a way forward.

Eventually, I think I got so big that it was as though my body was saying, 'If you eat any more, you're going to burst.' As ever, Mum's hawk eyes spotted my dwindling appetite and she immediately launched into action.

'Right,' she said one afternoon, as she sat down beside my bed, her voice strong and full of positive energy, even though she'd been travelling for nearly two hours since she had closed the front door at Rose Gardens. 'I can see you're eating less. I've got something that might help.'

She said it as if I was nine years old and sitting at the kitchen table at teatime, having beans on toast.

'I've brought you one of your favourites from when you were little,' she continued, as she opened one of the bulging bags she had only just rested on the end of the bed. Her hand dived into the bag and, like a travelling magician or ancient alchemist with magic potions, she produced pot after pot of jelly. Reds, greens and yellows: each a bright glistening colour. And emblazoned and unmistakeable on each jar was my name in large black block capitals on a white background.

'Have what you want for now and the rest can go in the fridge.'

At that stage, the jellies were just about all I felt like eating. I tucked in with relish, thankful to have such an astute and caring mother, and Mum popped the rest of them in the fridge for me to have later, whenever I felt like it.

A few days later, I found myself stuck between the sidebars of the bed and closed my eyes, imagining the jellies sitting in the fridge. The temptation was too much and, feeling defiant, I flagrantly disgraced my better judgement and somehow managed to find the strength to struggle across the room. I was so big I had to lean right back so that I didn't overbalance! As eagerly as I could, given the enormous extra weight pouched in front of me, I hobbled to the fridge in the corner.

By the time I got there, my eyes were glazed and I was almost licking my lips as I opened the fridge door and . . . nothing! Nothing . . . absolutely no jelly! No colours . . . no labels . . . no jars. NO JELLY! The jelly had gone. How annoying was that?

By the time Graham arrived for visiting that day, I had gone to pieces. The moment he walked through the door, I burst into tears. Goodness knows what went through his mind. I must have frightened the life out of him.

'Somebody's pinched my jelly!' I said it as if the world had fallen apart.

'It's only a jelly, luv.' Graham tried to console me.

'It's not only a jelly. It's my jelly. It's *my* jelly!'

★　★　★

The 'jelly episode' simply underlined some of the frustrations of the extreme confinement I experienced as part of my pregnancy. The hospital staff did everything they could to make me feel at home — the hospital chef even sent me a personal note on my tray, saying that if there was anything at all that I fancied that wasn't on the menu I was just to let him know and he would make sure the kitchen staff would make it for me — but at the end of the day I was essentially locked in the hospital from morning till night, day after day, growing less and less mobile and more and more frustrated and tired.

Each day, I was so relieved to see Graham come through the door. His visits had become proportional to the length of time I was in hospital. He was there for me no matter what and had been brilliant all the way through; and now, each day that passed, it felt like he was there for me more. Love is expressed in the simplest of things that we do for each other. As those days moved on, we would sometimes simply sit together holding hands, watching as the babies entertained us with their movements inside my tummy.

A small hill would appear to grow on the great mound that was my stomach, as a hand or foot pushed with all its strength against the inner wall. It was just as if there was a fight going on or a cartoon. First one, then two, then three or even four limbs at the same time, as the babies struggled to find space within me. But it was always a good sign: because as long as they were moving, they were growing.

And day by day, we came ever closer to the original target date for a satisfactory gestation period that Sam Abdulla had set. The moment I longed for — holding those lively babies in my arms, all safely in the outside world — was creeping closer and closer.

Or so I hoped.

19

Too Soon

It was Halloween and the late autumnal air was filled with the scents of burning embers and gunpowder. For some, Bonfire Night had begun five days early. In a courtyard below the window of my room, between the hospital and the Everyman Theatre, a big firework party was in full swing.

I was at twenty-eight weeks, and the freedom just to be able to go to a party was far away. Nonetheless, I had a front-row seat as the spectacular showers of multicoloured shapes and lights hung momentarily in the air outside my sash window. Every type of firework was lit. As the evening progressed, it seemed they were setting off industrial-sized bombs and canons, creating noises that each seemed louder than the last.

I had been as prepared as possible for my imminent labour, though we were hoping that moment was several weeks away yet. Sam and the other doctors and nurses had talked to me about what they thought would happen in my case when my labour started. Their objective from the outset was to make every effort to control the contractions. I was already being given medicines to keep me in as stable a condition as possible. As for me, I still believed that confidence and a positive attitude was always going to be the way forward.

Suddenly, as the bangs and whooshes from the fireworks flew outside, on the inside I felt a flush through my whole body, unlike anything I'd felt before. In an instant, everything seemed to change. I knew exactly what the discomfort was; every symptom and detail Sam had suggested could happen was happening. Every part of me inside and out ticked each and every box.

Whether I liked it or not, as Catherine wheels, Roman candles and rockets erupted outside, I was having my own Vesuvius to deal with — and I could barely move enough to catch the cord with the emergency call button to bring in the nurse.

Within seconds, the room was full of activity, as if to fulfil a prearranged plan, should that particular button be pressed.

'Sorry,' I said to the nurse, 'but something seems to be happening and I'm feeling really, really uncomfortable.' I tried to express my distress without sounding too distraught, but that was all I could manage to say. Even so, I felt a bit embarrassed for having to bother her.

The sister, who had arrived first, was already preparing a drip. She removed a drug from its packaging, reversed it and hung it upside down on a metal pole attached to the intravenous tubing. Before I had time to blink, she had swabbed my arm, found a vein and planted the needle.

'Right, Janet,' she said, satisfied with her work so far. 'That should do the trick. You're having

146

contractions but the drug should have the effect of slowing things down and hopefully they should stop.'

The drug administered was Ritodrine. I had been given it from about the fourteenth week in tablet form in order to prolong the length of gestation, and clearly it had been doing its job until now. But now tablets alone were not enough. The drip would put up a more intense fight against the contractions.

I kept saying to myself, 'Not yet. Not yet.' Over and over again I was working that positive mental attitude that I had always believed would help. It might just make the tiny, necessary difference.

As uncomfortable as I was, I was alert and acutely aware of the timing. I found the courage to articulate my fears.

'It's too early, sister, isn't it? Mr Abdulla always said thirty weeks would be better.'

She patted me on the shoulder and silently adjusted the drugs. She knew as well as I did that these contractions were coming too soon, but she didn't want to panic me further.

As it was, everyone was amazed that the pregnancy had gone on this long. I was so close to where the best chances lay — just two weeks away from that magic thirty-week mark — so throughout that night, as the contractions squeezed my babies, I made myself stay positive. I counted my blessings. How fortunate I was that I didn't have any other problems; they may have stopped the use of the Ritodrine. None of the tiny souls inside me had shown any significant signs of distress, at least not enough to worry the doctors or for them to consider not using preventative drugs. It was all going to be OK.

The next day, when Sam came in to check on me, Graham had just arrived. They greeted each other and seemed to talk together a bit longer than usual. I heard Sam mention the drugs to Graham and heard Graham talking about milk.

As they talked, they approached the bed.

'Things have settled down now, Janet?' Sam's question was really a statement. His caring bedside manner demonstrated that he understood the trauma I'd gone through the night before. He wanted to give me the chance to tell him my point of view, but the statement also told me more. All the tests I'd had after the contractions told him that, at least for now, the pregnancy was back on track to his target of thirty weeks. As ever, his calm and positive manner reassured me.

'I'm feeling much better, thanks. Not much sleep but I'm used to it by now. Besides, it was a bit noisy last night,' I said, referring to the Halloween party.

'You see what is done for you,' he joked, 'you have contractions and the city celebrates with a firework display right outside! Well, maybe they will again when the babies arrive.'

His confidence was the one infectious thing in the hospital I was happy to catch.

He hadn't quite finished. 'I've told Graham that you must drink milk.'

'But . . . ' I stopped myself saying that I didn't

148

like that particular delicacy. The fact was I just wasn't a milk drinker and never had been. But he was ahead of me, as usual.

'I know it's not your favourite, but I have told the nurses to continue with the drugs to stop the contractions every two hours, and you need to eat and drink something with them.'

I sighed, but I knew my doctor was right. As I had done so many times over the past twenty-eight weeks, I resigned myself to being the perfect patient. Milk drinking it was. Eurgh!

Unknown to me, Graham took in the distaste on my face and concocted a plan of his own.

★   ★   ★

Later that day, after hours of driving around on his mystery mission, Graham came back into the room, carrying a brown cardboard box full of flavoured milks. He presented them to me like a sommelier at the poshest restaurant in Liverpool.

'Well, how about milk with a mint flavour, madam? And if you don't like that, we have a very nice apricot. If that doesn't please *Madame*, we have the chef's special — hazelnut flavour.'

As always, Graham had played the knight in shining armour. My bonus was the smile he brought to my face.

And he hadn't finished yet. With a flourish, he declared, 'And to help the horrible milk go down, we have a selection of the *very* best biscuits.'

He turned to his cardboard box again and, after making a drama of opening it, his hand

149

dived in and out came a Christmas tin. He lifted the lid to reveal a selection of Danish shortbread biscuits sprinkled with crystals of sugar nestling in paper baskets.

Every two hours for the rest of my pregnancy, I ate the biscuits and drank a glass of flavoured milk. It never changed my mind about milk, and to this day I haven't been able to look at one of those biscuits!

Once the contractions had settled down, the idea of taking each day as it came became redundant and was replaced by being grateful for each passing hour. I was like a ship in uncharted waters drifting slowly, without wind in my sails, set in a deep fog, with Sam at the helm giving instruction, ordering his nursing crew to look out for signs of unexpected movement.

You become lost in your own thoughts at a time like that and it is easy to underestimate the feelings of others around you. It wasn't just Graham and our parents and Alison who were going through this with me; other members of the family were feeling the tension too. It was as if a silence and stillness hovered over the final fourteen days, as if everybody's breath was held. It was a kind of twilight zone, a time that was neither night nor day.

Our family were all asking themselves the same questions. Are they going to survive? Will they all survive? Will Janet make it? They wondered whether I was going to be OK and this was what they lived through with me. Their awareness was sharpened; it honed in on the knowledge that, the longer into the maternity I went, the better for the babies — but potentially the worse for me.

Unbeknown to me, a great debate was going on between our family members about when the birth might take place, a discussion that was laced with keen awareness of the dangers. Would I get to thirty weeks? Might I reach thirty-one weeks? Should we even dare to think about thirty-two weeks?

Nobody knew what was going to happen next and an immense weight of responsibility rested on the shoulders of one man.

Sam Abdulla was watching over me, focused purely on balancing a delicate set of scales, with the lives of six tiny babies on the one side and my life on the other.

There was so much to consider, so much to calculate. None of the medical staff had ever experienced anything like my case. I was a huge, fragile unknown; especially delicate during the period of labour, as contractions were monitored and kept under control. All drugs have elements of side effects and those being used in my case had the potential to cause complications, so Sam's eyes were always close to those scales, watching for the slightest tip on either side.

Everything in a gestation period depends on the ability of a foetus to grow, in every birth and for every single baby born. The time comes when the protective environment of a mother's womb is no longer necessary and life outside the womb is ready to begin. In my case, my body was now straining to nourish the babies. As the growing slowed, my uterus was heading

151

to its absolute limit.

A week went by, with nights blending into days, unnoticed as my body clock ticked away in a world of its own, demanding neither sleep nor movement . . .

★ ★ ★

One afternoon during the 'twilight zone', Graham and his brother David were with me when one of the duty doctors began going through what had become a routine of monitoring the babies, in order to pass on the information to Sam. To make sure there was always at least one doctor on duty at all times, Sam had appointed one of the university team, Dr Philip Tromans, as well as a young registrar, Dr Helen Tebbutt, to keep their watchful eyes on me.

Dr Tromans now took a metal flute-shaped instrument from the pocket of his white coat.

The first time this had been used, I had winced at the short sharp shock of the cold metal against my tummy. Now, I couldn't feel it at all. He listened through the other end intently. The doctor then became aware of the two men in the room and looked up.

'Would you like to have a listen?' he offered.

This was nothing new to Graham; in fact, having used this particular medical instrument a number of times before, he now always referred to it affectionately as the 'trumpet'.

Sometimes, it is the simplest of inventions that prove the most enduring and useful. Even at that time, thirty years ago from today, in the hands of a modern doctor, the simple tool seemed rather antiquated, and with good reason; this 'trumpet', as Graham called it, hailed from the nineteenth century. Its proper name was the Pinard Horn: it was named after the nineteenth-century French obstetrician who invented it, doing much in the process to advance prenatal care. Much to the amazement of many modern-day American medics, this simple and most basic listening device is still to this day the most popular of foetal stethoscopes throughout Europe.

'Go on, Dave,' Graham said now, eager to share the benefits of the 'trumpet'. 'You have a listen.'

'Me?' My brother-in-law didn't think it was his place to be so involved. He was a little reticent.

The doctor held the 'trumpet' towards David.

'Go on! It's amazing.' Graham encouraged him.

David glanced at me as if to receive permission. 'If it's alright with Janet . . . '

'Everything has its price,' I said, wily as only a bed-bound patient can be. 'If you want to listen, make yourself useful and help Graham to get me to sit up a little.'

By now, lying down was probably the most difficult thing I was doing. Yet sitting up a bit was about all I could physically manage, even with help. The babies had gone almost as far as they could. The huge mound that housed them, which was once my slim, Maltese-tanned flat stomach, was now a great unmovable mass.

153

Unless at least two people assisted me, it was now impossible for me to move at all.

Gently, standing on either side of me, the two brothers held my tummy and slowly moved it slightly to my left. Once that was done, the rest of me followed and I moved into a more comfortable position.

David then took the 'trumpet' from the doctor, who helped him to find a suitable position to rest the instrument, from where he might best listen to what lay below the surface. While I knew that, especially in the last few days, there was less movement in my womb — things were quite different from the cartoon capers of a couple of weeks ago, when arms, feet and hands had been poking at random and pushing at the surface in their search for freedom — there was still enough going on to amaze and astonish.

David's head turned to one side and he put his ear to the trumpet. There was a pause. After just a brief second, he froze. David looked shocked. His face had completely changed. The expression of amazement he made at the doctor made Graham and I stop talking.

I had always known the differences between the brothers well, ever since Graham and I first started dating; David was always a touch more expressive in his emotions. His eyes now seemed moist as he listened to his brother's babies and pondered about the struggle for life that was going on inside my stomach. After all, the delicate balance Nature presents of the fittest surviving, and the blind role that fate plays, is massively emotive, sometimes overwhelming, even for the toughest people.

'I could hear them all!' He finally found the words. 'One heartbeat on top of another and then another and another. It's like one overriding the other. It's incredible!'

Like Graham, David loves sports and exercise. A runner, cyclist and swimmer, he has entered numerous triathlons over the years. And yet, at the sound of the babies in my tummy, the 'Iron Man' melted with a tear in his eye. More than ever, we all hoped that they would survive the massive challenge ahead.

20

The Day Arrives

I had made it: thirty-one-and-a-half weeks pregnant! But I really wasn't in the mood to celebrate.

During the past forty-eight hours in hospital, 'uncomfortable' for me had moved sharply on the scale to 'extremely uncomfortable'. Back when I had arrived at Oxford Street at twenty-three weeks, I really wasn't very comfortable. Since then, I had barely been able to get out of bed, and in the past week I couldn't even lie down. There were security bars on the side of the bed to make sure I didn't fall out and I was propped up all around with pillows. Now, however, I reached a new low.

Each time I had gone into labour up to this moment — for I had had several more 'false starts' prior to today, each held back by the administration of more Ritodrine — I was aware of a tightening pain inside. However, the 'tightening' was now becoming more and more intense, with every hour that passed. I asked the nurses, who were by now checking on me very regularly, whether this feeling was right. Unbeknown to me, they felt it appropriate to call in the boss.

Graham timed his visit early that day, and his nervous agitation began when Sam, summoned

156

by the nurses, knocked on the door and entered with a smile and a cheery, 'Good morning.' Usually I knew in advance when he was due to see me, but because of the special circumstances he sometimes checked up on me without notice. This was one of those occasions.

He didn't stay long. And yet there was something, perhaps in the glance of his eye or the sound of his voice, just for a second, that made me realise what was about to happen.

'What time did you last eat?' he asked, almost nonchalantly.

Graham and I looked at each other. We knew what that meant. I told Sam and he then dropped his bombshell: they were planning to operate at seven o'clock that evening. It was time and I was ready.

He didn't stay long after that — after all, he was about to have the busiest day of his life.

The previous journeys I had taken into labour had turned out to be the dress rehearsals.

This was the real thing.

★   ★   ★

After Mr Abdulla confirmed the operation would go ahead at seven that evening, members of our family began making their way to the hospital. My dad was already at the hospital visiting and Graham's brother and sister, David and Susan, were to be there throughout the evening — as well as Graham himself, of course. There was no way he was leaving my side today. My mum, who was at work, and

157

Alison were to hold vigil at Rose Gardens.

When the familiar faces of Graham's siblings were shown into my room by one of the nurses, I noticed David was almost in a trance.

'What's up with you, David?' I asked, as if the roles were reversed and I was doing the visiting. Dad and Graham looked up, expecting news from home.

'I was just parking up in the car park round the back and a big posh car pulled up alongside me.' There was a sense of awe in his voice. 'It just pulled up like any ordinary car.'

'Well, that's what cars do in car parks!' My dad quipped, expressing in his own way what we were all thinking. We were wondering, what had been the point of that statement?

'But it was Mr Abdulla,' David continued, almost breathless, 'and I just didn't expect to see him, you know, so close up before the operation.'

For a moment, no one said anything. David made it sound as if he had just seen the Queen, such was the awe in his voice.

'It's just that he's the one, isn't he?' David went on. 'He's the one making all the decisions. I mean, I know he's just normal like everyone, but it was a strange feeling being alongside him, knowing what he was going to do. He's got their lives in his hands.'

He was right. And his reaction showed just what an impact this whole experience was having on each and every member of our family. Though I was the patient, our immediate family were feeling the pressure acutely. The hospital staff had been incredibly sensitive to this and in a

158

low-key manner had cared for all our feelings. There was tension each day around my room, and a nervous camaraderie had built up between the nurses and the family as the time for the birth had got closer and closer. But it was Sam on whom the babies' lives depended. We had all been waiting all these weeks for him to make the decision of when to operate.

And yet, even with all the power that radiated from him, and the respect in which others held him, Sam Abdulla was never aloof. He just got on with his job as any conscientious expert would, enthusiastic and passionate for his work. He went about his everyday life completely normally, because for him saving lives and bringing babies into the world was normal.

Today, however, was a little exceptional even for Sam.

★   ★   ★

As the time for the operation approached, my room seemed to become peaceful. The nervous anticipation previously expressed by both Graham and my dad had settled into a kind of serene acceptance of what lay ahead. They had realised that, as much as they may have wanted to help, this was something out of their control.

As for me, I was uncomfortable but encouraged by the knowledge that all the waiting was about to end. More than anything, I was determined to keep calm.

I decided to take charge. I wanted to speak to Graham, so I asked my dad if he fancied a cup of

159

tea. He looked at me strangely, then immediately realised I needed to be alone with my husband for a moment.

'Good idea,' he said, 'I'll be back in a minute.'

'Gray,' I said, once we were alone. 'It's gone six. Not long now.'

'Not long, luv.' Graham was doing his best to be strong and hide his nerves, but we were too close and knew each other too well. He had been through this with me, every step of the way, and whatever discomfort I was feeling, in his own way he was feeling it too. 'Is there anything I can get you, anything you need?'

'Only an hour or so till the operation,' I said.

The words 'hour' and 'operation' did the trick. We had gone through the plan many times.

An hour before the operation, Graham was to begin making the important phone calls. We had together, over the last couple of weeks, decided on a list of calls that should be made. The idea was that the people on the list were to pass on the information to others, and then they would in a ripple effect make all the other calls to close family and friends. That way those who needed to know would not have to hear anything second-hand.

Graham began searching his pockets. First, both hands disappeared at the same time into his trouser pockets. No list. A rapid search of his jacket brought a similar result. The beads of perspiration that had gently rested on his forehead during most of the day but had recently subsided reappeared, as he realised it was probably still on the kitchen table at home.

He was already having a hard enough time without this little problem, so I smiled reassuringly and said, 'Top drawer of the bedside table — I think I made a duplicate. If not, don't worry. Best just to phone your mum and mine. They'll call everyone else.'

★ ★ ★

I wasn't the only one with a plan that night. It was Friday, the end of the working week, and across the Western world things were winding down for the weekend. But that Friday, 18 November 1983, those people working on reception and at the staff entrance of the Liverpool Maternity Hospital saw a sudden stream of 'off-duty' doctors and nurses hurrying through the doors. Eighteen individuals, at the instant their bleeper had sounded, dropped whatever they were doing, phoned into the department and, if they were not already in the building, speedily made their way to Oxford Street.

I had spent the last six months purely focusing on taking each day as it came, never allowing myself to dwell on the negatives or to look too far into the future. No one knew what might happen, so in a way I had conditioned myself into a state of complete confidence.

Little did I know it, but that confidence wasn't shared by the people who had found themselves at the front line of the operation itself. Having spent weeks on alert, the moment for the team had arrived. Professor Richard Cooke, our paediatric consultant, later admitted that he was scared to death and that all the people in the operating theatre were frightened too.

But I didn't know anything about that for a minute. For over thirty years since that day, Graham and I believed simply that I had gone as far as I could in the term of the pregnancy, carried my babies for the longest time possible, and that it was a relatively straightforward medical decision made by the team that morning that the time had come to operate. When writing this book, however, I discovered that the increasing discomfort I was experiencing by then was causing the consultants great concern, far more than I had ever imagined. That, coupled with signs of maternal oedema, a swelling condition that can rapidly become life-threatening, meant the whole situation had become urgent in the minds of the doctors. There was absolutely nothing routine about what was about to happen. No wonder they were scared.

But frightened or not, the doctors, nurses and all involved in the operation were prepared. The team had been put together many weeks previously, and everyone knew exactly what they would be doing. The operation was planned with military precision. Professor Cooke, aware of its significance, and to give confidence to his team, told them that they should concentrate and enjoy the moment — because they would never in their lives ever do anything like this again.

As the clock moved towards seven, the activity in my room became busier and busier. Graham and my dad stood to one side as the nurses and junior doctors prepared their patient for surgery. Despite the hustle and bustle around me, calmness once again took over. Notwithstanding the discomfort I was in, I felt peaceful, secure in my rock-solid self-belief that things would run smoothly and that everything was going to be just fine.

The door to my room opened again. One of the nurses, Sister Trev, came in, gave a confident smile and invited Graham to accompany the procession along the corridors to the operating theatre. It was time.

21

The Operation

Graham took hold of the rail at the end of my bed and slowly began to reverse it out of the room. Sister Trev oversaw proceedings with her usual meticulous manner.

'Now, take care to look out for the drip alongside the bed. We will wheel it with you. Off we go, they are waiting for us in theatre.'

My dad gave me a quick hug and wished me luck before Graham took control of the bed.

We'd not moved very far when I sensed the responsibility of taking control of the bed was getting more and more difficult for Graham. I was a huge, fragile cargo that weighed a ton, and understandably he was scared for me. With his nerves on edge, he was shaking like a leaf in a storm, and although fit and strong, he was struggling to move the bed along the corridor.

Lying serene in the middle of the bed, I felt the complete opposite. I was calm and relaxed. No doubt some drugs were playing their part in keeping me as passive as possible, but I could sense in Graham his surprise. I was so seemingly together, even this close to the operation, but I simply felt that same feeling that had enveloped me from my very first day in hospital. My confidence in Sam and my belief that everything was going to be OK overrode everything else.

Now I could hear the sharp edge of a voice of caution, warning others ahead to clear the way. There was also an intermittent squeak that seemed out of place as we weaved along the corridors; the bed was letting out a little screech as the rubber of its wheels dug into the linoleum of the corridor floor. We went past the room to where Graham would return to wait with my dad, David and Susan, a relatives' room reserved just for them, where they could wait while the operation took place. As if to underline the serious situation, more and more staff joined the procession as we headed for the operating theatre.

Words of encouragement clouded into the almost incomprehensible murmurings as I closed my eyes and tried to block out as much as possible. I wondered whether I would see Sam before the operation but I had to get to the theatre first. Seemingly reluctant to carry me into the operating room, the bed became more and more difficult to manoeuvre. Graham was even having to stop now and again, unaware of the people behind.

Suddenly, one of the nurses gave a little cough, then, in a quiet voice, tried to catch the attention of the novice hospital porter.

'Er, Mr Walton? I think perhaps the brake might still be on . . . '

But Graham didn't hear the nurse. He leant towards me to let me know he was there for me. His whispering voice shook as he spoke.

'You're in the best hands, luv,' he said, doing his utmost to be strong for both of us.

165

'Thanks, luv,' I replied, ' . . . but I'm not sure the bed is!' I smiled at him, realising he hadn't heard what the nurse had said. 'Take the brake off!'

Graham's tension was, for a moment at least, released. He adjusted the lever and smiled back at me, our eyes locking in that crowded procession, and for a moment it was just the two of us, lost in the moment. Then the bed rolled off again, this time without the squeak, and we were on our way once more.

Finally, I approached the theatre feet first. I looked up to see the double swing doors of the operating theatre before me. Our journey came to a temporary rest just outside the room as the final preparations were made inside. There seemed to be an endless line of people dressed in blue or green moving in and out. The doors seemed to flap open and shut a dozen times. Each time, I hoped it would be Sam, until finally he was there alongside the bed. This was it.

A kiss from Graham and at the same time we both said, 'I love you.' Then, mustering up the last bit of confidence I could find, after storing up so much over the past six months, as Graham's hand slipped out of mine I said as casually as possible, 'Don't worry, luv. See you later.'

When I reflect on those last hours, and read some of the reports and quotes of others who were involved in the operation, in which even the most senior of the professionals expressed fear of the unknown and uncertainty of the outcome, for some reason it seems I was the calmest and coolest person on the day, the only one who truly believed that everything was going to be alright.

My guardian angel was already prepared for surgery, with hat on and surgical mask hanging below his chin, wearing his blue tunic and trousers, which were partially covered with a green apron. The last thing I remember before the Caesarean began was my arm being prepared and a needle being injected and Sam's eyes looking down at me from above. The palms of his hands were on either side of my face, gently holding my head, and I remember hearing his familiar voice quietly and calmly giving me reassurance. Just as I had comforted Graham, Sam comforted me.

'Don't worry, Janet,' he said, 'everything is going to be just fine.'

And that was all I needed to hear. My faith in Sam Abdulla was absolute. If he said it would be alright, then it would be.

As I drifted into a heavy state of sedation, I knew that — because of that trust — there was nothing but nothing to worry about.

★ ★ ★

I was later told by Mr Abdulla that the operating theatre was crowded. The whole team was now in place as I was wheeled into position. Everyone had responded instantly to the call of their personal bleepers, and as they'd arrived they'd quickly prepared for their individual roles.

Usually a Caesarean-section operation would have the normal theatre staff present and then a

167

nurse or midwife ready to care for the baby. In my case, things were slightly different. Besides Sam, in attendance was another leading consultant obstetrician and gynaecologist, Professor John Beazley, who was head of the Liverpool University department in which Sam was a lecturer. He was to help oversee my operation, together with the anaesthetists and necessary theatre staff.

Several hospital registrars and house officers were also on hand to help. There was a team of six paediatricians, led by Professor Richard Cooke, together with nurses and midwives ready to take immediate control of each baby, including Lorna Muirhead, who went on to become the President of the Royal College of Midwives, a Dame of the British Empire and the Lord Lieutenant of Merseyside. It had been decided that there would be a team of three people allocated to each baby. That meant there were almost thirty professionals involved in the birth.

It was reported the next day that so many nurses were put on 'sextuplet duty' that an entire ward at the hospital had to be temporarily closed. As well as six incubators, because of the danger involved, six life-support ventilators were also made available in case they were needed. Because of the special circumstances, with my permission video cameras had been set to record everything and Polaroid cameras were prepared to record the birth.

Though I was not aware of it, the atmosphere in the room became more and more tense as each second passed. While I had been concerned only with the welfare of the babies, the doctors' main concern was for me. I was only later to learn that I was at much greater risk once the babies were actually born.

Another concern the senior doctors expressed was the worry that people in the operating room might panic as the Caesarean was being carried out, because of all the excitement. It was an operating theatre, after all, that was used to a third of the amount of people present.

Professionalism was all. Instructions were calmly given from behind masks and waiting doctors, nurses and midwives, both excited and nervous, ensured everything necessary was prepared for the immediate care of each baby. Their quiet voices mingled with the sound of the surgical staff's aprons rustling as they moved and the gentle clinking of the surgical instruments.

Each member of the team was not only well trained in their respective areas of expertise, they were also equally well prepared to follow the blueprint laid down for that night and the instructions of their leader. With such a high number of staff in the room, Sam Abdulla said later that he felt like the conductor of a symphony orchestra.

Once Sam had been assured by anaesthetist John Beddard that I was ready, he began the operation. As everyone in the room focused, they each felt the incredible atmosphere. The time was recorded as 7.56 p.m.

All the voices, the rustling and the clinking, then suddenly stopped. Richard Cooke told me later that, as the delivery of my babies began, an extraordinary hush came over the room. It was exactly as he had said to his colleagues in his briefing. Everybody knew that they were seeing something that they would never see again. It was, he said, 'An incredibly beautiful moment.'

Then, out of the silence, Sam's voice rang out, announcing the first arrival and proclaiming baby number one a girl. The second swiftly followed, again with his confirmation of another girl. Baby number three: the same!

None of the first three babies had made a sound as they were born, so Sam's voice was still the only one in the room. Then out came baby number four, crying away as if it were the most natural thing in this new world to do. Now the first three began to cry too, already wrapped in green plastic sheets and safely in their own personal incubators. The noise levels cautiously rose, both to compete with the babies' crying, but also with the confidence that came with the successful completion of four seemingly healthy births — and with the literal talking point that all the babies thus far were girls.

Then the excitement in the room rose to another level as the fifth birth brought yet another girl. By the time Sam lifted the last child into the air, there was an almost euphoric feeling as he introduced baby number six to the room, certainly the largest and most definitely another girl!

The time was now eight o'clock. The delivery had taken just four short minutes. Immediately, each of my babies had a team of one paediatrician and two nurses caring for her and monitoring every movement. One of the first things they did was to weigh each of the babies. Their weight had been one of the critical measures in the decision of when to operate, and the target figure was just over 2 lb. Well, the lightest of my girls was a whopping 2 lb 1 oz! That was Hannah Jane. Her name, along with the names Lucy Anne, Ruth Michelle, Sarah Louise, Kate Elizabeth and Jennifer Rose, was nestling, scribbled in a list on a piece of paper, in Sam's pocket.

We had spent many a visiting hour over the past few months talking about names. Not knowing whether the babies were going to be girls or boys we eventually settled on a list of six first and second names for each, as they would be in order of birth. Sam had also asked us to prepare names, as it was clear that there would likely be emergency baptisms carried out, no matter what the outcome.

One by one, the babies were taken to the special care unit, each accompanied by her dedicated team. I was now the main concern of the much smaller team left in the room. The final, delicate stage of the operation began, as Sam and his assistants sewed and sutured me together again, and watched over me as the anaesthetists brought me out of my unconscious state.

★　★　★

First sounds of voices, then nothing, then more voices. From behind my eyelids, a confused kaleidoscope of colour floated. I had a sudden awareness of life as I came groggily round from the anaesthetic, similar to the simple act of waking each morning, but I was instantly overcome by weakness.

Then I became aware of a single voice; a familiar voice.

'Janet . . . Janet . . . Janet . . . '

I could feel a palm on my cheek and my hand being gently squeezed. Senses were rapidly returning, each acting as a trigger to my memory. The same voice delivered the same sound.

'Janet . . . Wake up, Janet. Janet . . . '

My eyes flickered open and I glanced across a sea of green and blue. I looked up and focused on the face in front of me. It was Sam. A little further down the side of the bed was Richard Cooke.

Everything was still groggy. I was very tired and wanted desperately to go back to sleep. I was able to manage just three words.

'Are they alive?'

22

After the Birth

I was really drowsy and as I moved in and out of consciousness I was hearing the same thing repeated in my head, 'They are all alright, they are all alive.' As rare and incredible as it was that all the babies were the same sex, at that moment it wasn't important. Each time the clouds of anaesthesia cleared, the significant thing was that all my babies were still alive.

While I was under the watchful eye of Sam and the recovery team immediately after the operation, and once the babies were settled into the special care unit, Dr Helen Tebbutt went to the relatives' room where Graham was waiting. She knocked on the door and then entered.

Graham told me later that he looked up as the door opened and took a deep breath. He had gone over and over this moment in his head. This was it. After all that had gone before, after all the months of stress and tension, this was the moment of truth. There was nowhere else to go; nowhere left to hide. This was the end of the line.

'Mr Walton?' Dr Tebbutt was a bright, blonde girl who looked far too young to be giving such important information. She was confident and smiling.

Graham tried to respond, his mouth opened

to answer, but his voice wasn't up to the job. As much as he wanted news of the babies, all he could think about was how dangerous the operation had been for me. He didn't have to wait.

'Mrs Walton is doing very well, Mr Walton,' Dr Tebbutt reassured him. 'She's resting now and will be asleep for a little while and you can see her soon. In the meantime ... ' There was a second of hesitation as the young medic took a moment to appreciate the odd reality of what she was saying. ' . . . all six babies are doing well. Would you like to come and meet your family?'

Graham made a number of visits to the special care unit that night. He was dazed and bewildered, but most of all relieved, and these were precious moments with his girls. He was also astonished by the numbers of medical staff tending to the tiny life in each incubator.

As soon as Graham had seen the babies for the first time, he made the important calls according to the list we had agreed before the operation.

Before he went to see our daughters for a second time, he came into my room. I was awake, but only just. I nodded to him in response to his question. I wanted to ask him how he was too, but the words weren't coming out so easily.

'Girls . . . all girls . . . six girls,' was all I could say.

'They're alright. I've been to see our new family and they're fabulous, luv,' Graham assured me.

Most of the brief communication we shared

was through reassuring looks and smiles. Then, totally exhausted, I drifted off into a deeper sleep that took me through the night.

* * *

Back with the girls, as I slept on, the special care unit seemed even more crowded. Sue Williams, the sister in charge, saw Graham come in again and passed him a can of beer.

'Sorry, Mr Walton. No champagne, but this will have to do for now — it's the only one we have in the fridge so enjoy!'

Richard Cooke was there, keeping a watchful eye over all the paediatricians, nurses and midwives; all professional, yet ordinary human beings marvelling at the miracle before them.

But we weren't out of the woods yet. My babies were by now only an hour or so old, and the immediate road ahead was full of pitfalls. The incubation and monitoring process had begun the second they were each born. Everyone gathered there in the special care unit, watching over the babies, knew that the first few hours were critical.

The door behind Graham opened just as he was taking a sip from the can and Father Tony Reynolds walked in. *Perfect timing*, Graham thought with a slightly guilty start. But it was in fact rather apt, as Tony was there literally to wet the babies' heads — though he wasn't celebrating. The emergency baptism had to be done; the danger to each girl's life at that moment was too high to wait.

And so, after a quick sip of Graham's beer, father and Father went from incubator to incubator, the priest on one side with his portable pouch of holy water and Graham on the other, for the first time experiencing the touch of each of his daughters as, one by one, our six tiny girls gripped his finger with their hand.

They held on as tightly as they could. We could only hope now that their grip on life itself would be just as fierce.

23

Making the News

Within minutes the news was out. An hour after the birth, Sam Abdulla emerged in front of the hospital to tell the press about the operation. Still in full battle dress, with his surgical mask now hanging below his chin, he paid tribute to every member of his team and confirmed how pleased he was with the way things had gone.

'The first, second, third and fifth were born bottoms up!' he said, with a huge smile on his face. 'The fourth and sixth were delivered head first. It was one of the most exciting moments I've ever witnessed.'

Then Richard Cooke spoke of how delighted he was with the girls' progress.

Together with the official press release given by the hospital, the news was beamed around the world. News organisations everywhere began distributing a story of a woman in Liverpool who had given birth to sextuplets. And as each minute passed, the scoop was getting more and more sensational.

Inside the heart of the hospital, however, at the special care unit that had become a kind of protective cocoon for my babies, the world outside seemed a million miles away. Graham had just come away from his third visit, this time with David and Susan. It was late. The last time

177

he had looked at a clock it was after half past eleven. Having seen the babies, Dad had gone home, marching manfully through the mountain of media and denying all knowledge of recent events, but Graham, of course, just wanted to be near his new family.

Neither he nor David had a clue that both the BBC and ITV had already headlined the story that night on their television news broadcasts. The two brothers now sat together, tired and weary, but very, very happy, on the simple wooden bench in the hospital corridor that was outside the room where our six babies were struggling through their first hours of life. It had been a long day for everyone and they were ready to go home.

David said at last, 'I suppose I ought to be making tracks. Do you want a lift?'

'Thanks, but I'll take the van. I don't want to leave it in the car park overnight.'

The practicalities sorted, the new father allowed himself a moment to reflect on the amazing events of the night. 'What do you think of it all, Dave?'

'The babies are great. You and Janet have done so well.'

'They're fabulous,' Graham said with pride. 'I can't believe the whole thing.' Then he asked his brother, offhand, 'Do you think it'll make the *Echo*?'

'No idea.'

At that moment, one of the porters was passing. 'If I were you,' he confided, as though passing on a special tip, 'when you leave I'd use

178

the back entrance to the hospital.' He gave them a knowing wink.

'Why's that?' The brothers couldn't understand what the porter was on about.

'You're having a laugh, aren't you? It's all over the news, Mr Walton. Everybody knows about the babies and there are loads of press outside the front door!'

★   ★   ★

He was, of course, quite right. After the two brothers had taken the porter's tip and used the secluded back entrance, David drove away first. He was shocked when he shot past the front entrance. The numbers of press had swelled and a crowd of journalists and photographers had set up camp outside the doors.

What the gathering paparazzi were unaware of was that, only yards away in the car park behind the hospital, the man they all wanted to interview was preparing to leave the scene too. Or, at least, trying to. For while I was sleeping off the operation and at peace with the world, Graham had his head under the bonnet, desperately trying to clean the spark plugs after the van had stubbornly refused to start.

It was clear that the media attention wasn't dying down any time soon. Graham could only hope that this particular anecdote wasn't going to be a part of the huge news coverage the next day.

24

The Morning After

Light streamed through a gap between the cream cotton curtains, where they had not quite crossed at the centre when drawn the night before. I felt a beam of sunshine as it warmed my eyelids. I had been drifting in and out of sleep throughout the night, a million thoughts sparkling like dazzling headlamps, intent on keeping me awake as I fought the lull of the anaesthetic. The hours after the operation had been a battle between excitement and sedation and in a surreal way the number 'six' kept coming into my head, and the word 'girls', again and again.

Girls. Girls. Six girls.

I was feeling tired, groggy and had sore lips from the tubing in my mouth during the operation but I was exhilarated. As I opened my eyes into this new morning, for just a few seconds I had to adjust to reality, blinking hard as though to pinch my mind, to make myself believe the whole thing hadn't been a dream.

Differences. All of a sudden huge differences began to filter through. They made me realise my memory was sound and that it wasn't playing games. I turned slowly to move to a more comfortable position — first gingerly turning my head, as if that was all I should have been able to do, and then surprised when my body could

180

follow. Then I was stopped from moving at all by a sharp twinge from my stomach.

A sister came in at that moment. 'Good morning, Supermum!'

I was still fighting to collect both belief and my thoughts. Things were, though, becoming clearer. Me? A mum? That was the title I'd been striving for for so long; what the last four years had been all about. I was checking reality by the ticking of the clock.

'Isn't every first-time new mum a supermum?' I asked her.

'Not according to the big world outside.'

Suddenly, my heart stopped as my brain cleared to a single, dark thought. I knew what I must do next: a question had to be asked. Time and again before the operation I had been given so many warnings about the multiple dangers and risks to the babies' lives in the first few hours. Whatever confidence I'd had throughout the last six months momentarily disappeared, and I feared for my babies struggling to deal with their first moments.

Just calling them my babies made me feel different to the person I was yesterday. The difference was the feeling of responsibility. I wanted to be with them more than anything, but were they all still alive to be with?

'Are they — ' I didn't need to get the whole question out.

'They are fine. They're all doing just fine.' The sister had anticipated both my question and my thoughts. 'They're beautiful and all crying out for their mum.'

'When can I see them?' Like any new mother, I wanted to see my babies as soon as possible.

'Graham is due in soon and the moment he arrives, we'll make arrangements to get you wheeled down to the special care unit.'

While the joy of the birth had touched all the staff, as one of the sisters on the ward, she needed to contain as much emotion as she professionally could, but nonetheless there was music in her voice, and a soft gentle tone as she hummed while going about her business of helping me to sit up and be prepared for the day ahead.

Then a second nurse came in. She was younger and quite unable to restrain the thrill and excitement she was feeling.

'Have you seen the papers, Sister?' She was in full flight as she swept into the room. 'I've never seen anything like it! I went into the newsagents and there it was on every front page!'

I didn't pay much attention to their conversation — I had bigger fish to fry. As the two nurses carried on tending to me, I drew in a sharp breath, making a loud sound of surprise.

'What is it, Janet?' asked the sister, worried.

I was looking straight down towards the end of the bed, and I couldn't believe my eyes. Then I tried to smile through chapped and cut lips.

'So that's what the rail at the end of the bed looks like!' My chuckle was tempered by the discomfort I was feeling only a few hours after the Caesarean. I looked towards the two butterfly clips that held the boards at the end of my bed, on which the daily vital medical information was recorded, and briefly thought of the tale they could tell. Then I had another thought. 'It's good to see my feet as well after such a long time.'

For the great mound had vanished! It is strange and incredible how the body can change so much; ordinary pregnancy for just one baby reveals the amazing adaptability of the body to deal with nature and childbirth. Even now, when I look back at the pictures of me in those last few weeks, I still cannot believe how my body was able to cope.

'Mr Abdulla and Professor Cooke have already both been in to check up on you and they'll be in again later,' said the sister. And then, as if she was reading my mind again, she added, 'And in case you're worrying, both the doctors have said it's OK for you to go down with Graham to see the babies as soon as you feel up to it.'

I couldn't wait.

★ ★ ★

My night of intermittent sleep was relatively calm compared to the one Graham had had at his sister Susan's house. He'd found himself uncontrollably shaking throughout the night, and he'd barely noticed he was lying in damp, sweaty sheets.

Noises kept him awake. Strange voices. There was knocking on the doors and windows. The clock on the bedside table kept confirming the time his wristwatch told, even if he didn't want to believe it. One o'clock in the morning.

183

One-thirty. Two o'clock. It felt like he was awake the whole night through. And yet, he didn't know whether or not the whole thing he was caught up in was a dream, so strange was the reality in which he now found himself.

Graham could hear his brother-in-law's Irish accent sharply used, almost in anger, as Martin shooed away the marauding pack. 'There's nobody here. Go away! Be off with you!'

But the voice from the street was persistent. 'We know Mr Walton is in there. We just want a word, just a quick word.'

Far from being left alone to reflect on the fantastic joy of experiencing the birth of his first child, Graham found himself caught up in a cauldron of fire that the spreading 'news story' had oiled, bringing with it a chasing pack of people demanding information. It's one thing having a spotlight on you if you are an actor on stage, a performer, a star of the silver screen or the football pitch, but this felt more like he was an escaped prisoner on the run, caught between blinding searchlights.

Eventually, though, even the press found beds to go to that night. By the morning, as the nurses were pampering me, a knackered Graham made his way from Wallasey through the Mersey Tunnel to the hospital.

And despite his tiredness, he felt as bright as a button at the thought of seeing his new family again. He pressed his foot a little bit harder on the accelerator.

★ ★ ★

184

So many heads and faces had appeared around the door to my hospital room that morning. As well as the routine medical things that had to be done, flowers and cards had begun to arrive. Each time the door opened, I felt a twinge of disappointment when it wasn't Graham.

Then, as one particularly large bouquet came into the room, hiding the head and body of the man behind, I recognised the legs underneath. Dodging all the other flower deliveries to the room Graham appeared, looking a little worse for wear after his night of terror. As he turned around to present me with a gift, I felt a flush of emotion and smiled at the romantic sight of a single lonely red rose.

He had arrived at the front door of the hospital with a dozen roses, he said. With a slightly apologetic look on his face, he shrugged his shoulders and explained.

'I couldn't help it,' he confessed, 'I've given all the others away to the nurses along the corridor — they've just been so fantastic.

'But a single rose says it all, doesn't it, luv?'

And it did.

Then he told me everything that had gone on overnight. I immediately thought about Mum, Dad and Alison and imagined that they must have been going through the same thing. I couldn't believe our story had captured the media's attention in the way it had. I only hoped that my family were OK.

Even if Graham hadn't filled me in, I'd have guessed something was up sooner rather than later. The floral deliveries to the room were never-ending. More and more arrived throughout that morning. It was as if the first solitary pink plant that had sat innocently on my bedside table had flourished into a field of flowers. My room could have been mistaken for a florist shop that specialised in pink. Not only were all the flowers pink, but every card as well invariably had pictures of sweet little cherubs in pink.

Suddenly, it seemed circumstance had unwittingly widened my social circle — basically to the rest of the planet! News travels fast; clearly big news even faster. The speed with which the procession of bouquets kept coming was ridiculous. The staff were by now struggling to move around in my room, so Graham made arrangements for the flowers to be moved into the corridors outside, with the thought that the staff could then enjoy the celebrations too.

In the end, only those who acted quickly on the Saturday morning got their flowers to my floor at all. The rest simply helped to decorate the public areas of the hospital.

As well as receiving greetings and best wishes from close family and friends, I was also the recipient of the kindest of words and notes on cards from complete strangers; both names I'd never heard of and names that were familiar to everyone at the time.

There was a personal telegram for me from the current Queen of Comedy, Faith Brown, saying, 'Only a Liverpool lass could do it!' I also received a beautiful bouquet in a large pink ceramic football boot from Liverpool FC legend Kenny Dalglish and his wife Marina. That especially thrilled Graham, who was, like a true football fanatic, still wondering whether there was any chance of him getting to Liverpool's home game that afternoon.

In the end, he concluded quietly, to his credit, that the odds of that happening were larger than the 104-billion-to-one chance the papers were quoting of me giving birth to sextuplets all of the same sex. Some things are just more important than football!

After all, Bill Shankly might have said football was more important than life and death . . . but he never mentioned anything about birth.

25

Meeting the Girls

So there we were on that November morning: Graham and me, just another ordinary set of proud new parents about to see our baby . . . and her sister, and *her* sister, and *her* sister, and *her* sister, and *her* sister!

Not long after Graham arrived bearing his single red rose, I was gently transferred from my bed to a wheelchair. This was the journey I'd been longing to take for almost four years.

The journey to meet my children.

It was difficult to hold back the excitement I felt when Graham took control of the chair and guided me out of the room. As we moved into the corridor, we had to weave our way past yet more flowers. I was amazed as some members of staff lined the corridor, some cheering, others saying well done, all smiling broadly at me.

As well as Graham and me, our little entourage included the medical staff and nurses who were watching over me. We must have made an odd procession. At the time, though, I was blissfully unaware of the extra fuss.

I was focused only on welcoming my babies to the world.

And then, all of a sudden, there they were, all lined up in front of me, in their own private area within the special care unit. Instinctively, I counted the number of incubators. All six sat snugly together in the one room.

I'd thought I was prepared for this meeting — but I could not have been more wrong.

It was an unbelievable moment. All the time I had been in hospital, from the very first day through to the moment I had gone into the operating theatre, I had always believed the babies would be alright. I had always felt that faith and determination were to play such important roles, and that feeling never wavered. So it was a strange sensation I felt — knowing how amazing it was that at that moment all six babies had survived, but also remembering how I'd thought to myself time and again that I just knew they were going to be alright and there was no way that wasn't going to be the case.

It was the loveliest feeling in the world to have been proved right.

My eyes drank in thirstily the vision of my six daughters spread out before me. It was the most beautiful view I had ever, ever seen. I wanted to savour every second. I wanted the girls to know their mother was here with them. I wanted, with Graham, to remember the moment forever.

My eyes focused on the incubator nearest to me, to see which of my babies it was holding. I reached out and took her nametag in my hand and turned it, expecting to see one of the girls' names, possibly Hannah. I was just being my logical self, thinking, well, Hannah's name was the first on the list and they are bound to have positioned the incubators in the order of the names on the list. The tag, though, simply identified the occupant of the incubator as 'Baby Number One', and sure enough down the line they were numbered one to six.

The numbers to me felt clinical, but it was purely medical procedure, providing a simplified method of dealing with such uncharted territory for the hospital. Records were being kept from the instant the babies were delivered. Measurements and more measurements: weight and size, length and movement, together with the more vital statistics of breathing rates and heartbeat, were being monitored constantly. So the babies were identified in the most practical way.

In the special care unit it was compulsory to put on a mask and gown, together with polyurethane bags to cover shoes. Possibly because we were only going to be in a room with our own babies, and not be exposed to any of the other babies in the unit, I didn't have to — but Graham did and looked very impressive in his new outfit.

'You look very medical, Mr Walton,' one of the nurses quipped.

The room was not very big, barely able to fit the six incubators comfortably — let alone me in the wheelchair, Graham alongside and half a dozen nurses and midwives. Nevertheless, we all squeezed in and Sue Williams began talking me through the girls' conditions. Sue was going to be a very important person in the coming weeks. She was the manager in charge of the unit and, therefore, she was the one looking after my babies. There was a warmth about her and she had a manner that made even the parents feel mothered. Care came oozing out of her and that was injected with a shot of obvious expertise in her field of nursing. I immediately felt like my girls were in safe hands.

'Don't worry about all the tubes and wires. All the babies are doing very well. We're just doing a little to help them with breathing and feeding in these first hours,' she said reassuringly.

Her voice was full of both confidence and experience. There were also two elements to her tone that appealed to me greatly — professionalism and practicality. That had always been my way, too, so even in the tired state I was in, I understood. Yet in Sue's voice I also detected, as I had with all the other staff, the sound of sheer delight. To be frank, given the near-miraculous outcome we appeared to be witnessing, to show no joy at all would have been a bit worrying.

Encouraged by my reaction as I nodded at her words, or at least thinking that I needed to know the latest information on the girls' progress, Sue went on. 'Of course, they all had to be intubated and ventilated immediately after the birth. Well, that's standard for prems [premature babies]. One of the girls is already breathing on her own; with two of the girls we were able to take away the tubes after only four hours.'

The nurses monitoring the babies had to keep a constant vigil. We all knew — all too well, for Sam had told us a number of times — that the first forty-eight hours were going to be critical for the survival of the babies.

Confined to the wheelchair, combating my weakness with every ounce of adrenalin I could

191

find, I could still only manage to lean slightly forward and look into each incubator.

'Well, this must be Hannah then,' I said to Graham, as I looked at the 'Baby Number One' tag. 'And this is Lucy,' I pointed at baby number two, 'and Ruth is number three. Sarah is four, Kate five and Jenny is baby number six.'

It was important for me to give them all their proper names. I didn't want to be talking about my babies by number and I immediately felt better on hearing their names.

And as soon as I'd named them, everyone else in the room followed my lead.

My brain was racing at a hundred miles an hour. I was thinking a million things at once. As much as I tried to take everything in, ultimately the only thing I could do in those circumstances was hope. Hope that things would be as I had always believed they would be: that all the doctors, nurses and the other medical staff in the hospital were doing and would continue to do their absolute best to ensure the babies' survival. My confidence and faith in them was enhanced by the fact that every single one of them seemed thrilled to be there and involved in the care of the girls.

It was this that gave me extra confidence and an underlying comfort. The knowledge that the medical team were doing everything they could to ensure the safe passage of my babies, as they made their way on their premature journey from now until the point when they would each be well enough to go home, gave me untold strength.

Yet although I knew the medical team were working as hard as they could, it's not easy for any mother to watch her baby struggle for life in an incubator, let alone all six of her children. I felt so thankful to those little machines: one of the wonders of the twentieth century. How many lives would not have been lived had it not been for the development of premature baby care? The work of the womb carries on after birth, as conditions are recreated to sustain life and help growth. That is a miracle all its own.

As I continued to drink in the sight of my girls, I noticed one or two of the units had a little more equipment in them than others, as each girl was reacting to her new surroundings in different ways. There hadn't been a split of a single egg to create the sextuplets, so there would be no identical features, only similarities.

And in fact, from the moment Sam Abdulla had delivered the girls, their individual characteristics were on display. Despite the wires and tubes, it was important for me on that first visit to be able to see each of their faces. To identify each daughter as a unique and precious person.

Sometimes a tiny hand would reach up to an eye or rub across a cheek as I looked on. Sometimes a foot would kick upwards. With my chair parked at the side of incubator number six, I looked on in amazement at the energy exhibited by such delicate limbs.

'I can't believe all that energy was going on inside you!' Graham's voice was almost a whisper as we watched, in awe of such delicate but vibrant life. 'And that's only *one* of the babies.'

'Jenny,' I said firmly, starting as I meant to go on. 'This is our Jenny. That is the name that goes with baby number six.'

Suddenly, Jenny moved both her arms together upwards, as if to wave to me. Imagination or not, it was as if she recognised me. This caused not only a lump in my sore throat, which was still recovering from being intubated, but also an odd ghostly feeling in my stomach, as I felt a shove that wasn't there anymore.

Each baby had on a tiny pink crocheted hat and cardigan, and above each head sat their first possession, in the form of an identical cuddly bear to keep them company — as if they needed company!

'Plenty of time to get to know them over the next few days, Janet,' Sue said gently but firmly. She was as excited as everyone else about what was going on, but under no circumstances was she going to move one inch outside the boundaries laid down by the consultants. Both Sam Abdulla and Professor Cooke had recommended no more than fifteen minutes for the first visit, in order for me not to overdo it and cause myself some sort of complication.

'I think it's time to go back to your room now, Janet,' Sue continued. 'You'll be able to come down again later, but for now the doctors said fifteen minutes only for the first visit.'

I took a lingering last look at my babies, but I

didn't quibble. These girls were going to need me fit and healthy — and I wasn't going to do anything at all to jeopardise that.

Now, I lived for them.

26

Headline News

I didn't know till much later that two guards had been assigned by the hospital for my protection. As Graham and I made our way back to my room from the special care unit, we were followed — so discreetly that I didn't notice a thing — by our new bodyguards.

When I reached my room, there was a phone call waiting for me.

'Mrs Walton, this is security on the front desk. Please can you describe your mother and sister for me?'

Little did I know it, but the hospital had become Fort Knox. Mum and Alison had arrived to see me a while ago, but they couldn't get through the front door. Not only was the area in front of the building buzzing with activity, as reporters mingled with television news crews, but the huge oak double front door of the hospital had been locked.

The iron ring of security that had descended on the building now affected all the innocent visitors who just wanted to see their loved ones. There was now a 'lock-out' and you had to prove who you were if you were to be allowed into the building. All Mum and Alison wanted to do was visit me, but they had had to wait downstairs until I could confirm who they were and describe them for the benefit of the security guards.

Eventually, they were escorted into my room by yet more security men. All the fuss and attention had added a tension — a fear, even — that they hadn't expected, and it wasn't until they got to my room in the hospital that they felt safe. Like Graham, they'd had a sleepless night, as the phone rang off the hook with calls from newspapers and journalists. Neither Mum nor Dad nor Alison had been to bed, they told me much later, having been kept up all night by the constant ringing of the phone. It was ringing and ringing and ringing but they knew they couldn't take the phone off the hook to get some peace in case the hospital called with news. Invariably, though, it was always just another newspaper on the line.

So Mum and Alison had had quite a job coming in to see me. Finally, here they were. My mum had spent the journey looking out of the train window at the familiar green fields of the Wirral as she quietly contemplated the new and unfamiliar world of being a grandmother. Though she could feel her lips struggling to control a smile, this was tempered by the natural concern she had for my health and the wellbeing of the babies. As for Alison, she'd chattered nervously away throughout the journey, watching everyone at the station and on the train like a hawk. In light of their new exposure to the media, suddenly everyone looked like a reporter or a potential photographer.

As Alison walked into my private hospital

room, leading the way as usual, she stopped dead in her tracks. She came to such an abrupt halt that my mum almost walked right into her. There is nothing like your closest blood relatives giving you a reality check.

'Oh my . . . You look — ' Mid-sentence, she got a sharp shove in the back from Mum, who tactfully realised there were times when you just don't say what you think.

Even though my mouth was still very dry and I was sore all over, considering what I had been through the night before, I was beginning to feel a little stronger, especially having been down to see the babies. To my little sister, though, I looked horrendous. She was shocked by the cuts I had on my mouth and how pale I was. The person she was looking at just didn't look like her sister.

Having come closer to the bed and accustomed herself to my poor physical appearance, Alison's morbid curiosity grew and she wanted more.

'Can I see your scar?' she asked, confidently expecting that it would look something like a normal set of stitches after an operation.

'Alright, but it was a big operation, you know,' I said, trying to warn her that it might not be quite what she had imagined.

'Oh my . . . ' Alison received a second push in the back from Mum, making her walk forward to take a closer look. For a moment she took a short intake of breath as she stared at the huge cut across my stomach, held together by the largest possible surgical suture. To Alison, it

198

looked like a big fat telephone wire, very similar to the wire on the phone in the hall in Rose Gardens, which she had been nervously twiddling in her fingers the previous night as the phone rang off the hook.

I could feel my mum's sense of relief as she took my hand and gently gave me a hug. She had always been there for me, made this journey with me and somehow the world felt a safer place with her next to me.

★ ★ ★

The core of the media interest was focused quite naturally on the hospital itself. The press knew who I was but not what I looked like, and this was a big problem for the picture editors of the national newspapers — indeed, any newspapers, not to mention the TV crews. Bribes were being offered, drainpipes scaled and ladders drawn against walls. Anything for the chance of a picture. Graham and I were both aware of the unique nature of the multiple birth but nothing could have prepared us for the frenzy that followed in the immediate hours and days once the news broke. I had always been a private person, and Graham wasn't looking to be front-page news either, but that didn't come into it. It was out of our hands. It was a story, a big story.

The hospital, of course, had anticipated what a scoop this would be, and had activated a well-rehearsed plan, the blueprint of which had been masterminded by John Lyons, the hospital administrator. They did a remarkable job under siege.

As soon as Sam Abdulla had made the decision to go ahead with the operation, in a kind of domino effect all the other plans to deal with all eventualities moved into gear, and my room became the place they needed to protect the most. Liverpool Maternity Hospital had become a target and they wanted to make sure no harm came to any of the patients or staff in the building.

As the day drew on, the feverish appetite for more and more details gathered a drive all of its own. The media were now making demands on behalf of their readers or viewers for all the 'five Ws' that pad out a news story. It was vital that as soon as possible they knew the who, the what, the why, the where and the when. Vital because, as each second, minute and hour passed, competitor news journals and television broadcasters might just be scooping the story first; and that, from their point of view, would mean the piece was a disaster, no matter how happy the content.

The sooner a second press conference was convened to satiate this mad appetite, the better. It would take the pressure off, at least for the benefit of the hospital and the staff. The demand was so huge that this would be one of the biggest press conferences ever held in Liverpool.

There was excitement everywhere, but it was far away from my hospital room. While I rested in bed, the stars of the conference lined up on the front row of what eventually became a large group of people standing before the assembled press, all of whom in one way or another were involved in caring for me and the girls or in the successful delivery of my babies. All the consultants, gynaecologists and paediatricians were there, along with any other significant medical staff involved in the operation itself and in nursing me before and after the operation.

But of course, while the medical professionals were perfectly equipped to describe the ins and outs and ups and downs of the medical happenings, they couldn't deliver on what the press termed the 'human interest' angle. In my absence and the absence of the girls, the one face above all they wanted to see was that of the new dad.

It was teatime in the hospital. And in between all the pink bouquets and arrangements arriving in my room, one of the nurses hailed for some space in the doorway as she wheeled in a television.

'I think I'm going to be a bit busy with visitors to find time to watch any telly today, Nurse,' I said, puzzled that she or the sister hadn't already realised that point.

'Oh, I think there is going to be something on that you'll need to see, Mrs Walton,' she said cryptically.

She manoeuvred the screen into a place convenient for me to have a good view and within reach of the electricity socket. Within a second of her plugging in and switching on the set, the BBC News headlines signature tune rang out.

And there in the middle of the screen, much to my surprise, was Graham, with his arms raised; five fingers of one hand and one finger of his other hand pointing upwards in a kind of victory salute. Doing his best not to show any nerves; trying to look as confident as possible. I felt like I had never loved him more.

27

The Tiniest Patients

The first forty-eight hours were critical to the girls' survival. Although all of the initial signals the babies had given were positive, Lucy — or 'baby number two' as the hospital had called her — was now, to my horror, 'giving cause for concern'.

One of the most difficult problems encountered in premature babies is the development of the lungs. I, like many other mothers who are likely to experience a preterm birth, had been taking the drug Betamethasone, which helps develop the lungs of the baby while they are still in the womb. But after being intubated and incubated on birth, along with her sisters, Lucy was taking a longer time to breathe on her own. The doctors and nurses were monitoring her closely. They were doing all they could, using best medical practice, to encourage her lungs. All we could do was wait and hope and pray that she would make it.

And Lucy wasn't the only patient giving cause for concern. Throughout the whole time in hospital, I had never considered or worried about my own health. Yet I had gone from being as thin as a rake to the size of a hippopotamus and then instantly shrunk, in true cartoon style, back to the shape of a stick. Such a dramatic transformation came with high-risk dangers attached.

In the immediate aftermath of the birth I was recovering slowly, but as the next day progressed I began to feel pain and swelling in my leg. When I asked a nurse to take a look, she immediately wanted a doctor's opinion. Sam Abdulla was understandably keeping a very close eye on me.

Having monitored the condition of my leg overnight, early on the Sunday morning Sam became very concerned. He came in to see me to talk to me about it. As ever, my primary concern was the girls and I quizzed him for news as soon as he stepped through the door. Professor Cooke and his team of paediatricians were now in charge of the welfare of the girls, but even though they had been making sure I was kept informed of how my daughters were progressing, I was especially happy hearing about my babies from Sam.

'Janet, they are all doing very well,' he reassured me. His smile beamed with almost as much pride as a first-time father's. 'After all, one of the girls needed no help at all with breathing, and all except baby number two . . . '

'Lucy!' I reminded him.

'Lucy,' Sam agreed, ' . . . all except Lucy are now breathing on their own, which really is very good.'

He could see I was still worried about Lucy and tried to set my mind at rest. 'I am sure it won't be long before Lucy is also there as well. The doctors looking after the babies are really pleased with her progress. But now we have to concentrate on you and getting you better.'

I knew he was right.

'My leg still doesn't feel right,' I admitted.

'I know. We need to give it our best attention.' Sam's softly spoken voice, which hadn't wavered even on Friday at the most tense of moments leading up to the birth, suddenly seemed to me to be slightly more concerned. 'I am not 100 per cent happy with the swelling. We need to take a closer look to make sure we can control any potential blood clot.'

I felt like a mountaineer who'd worked really hard to climb a peak, only to find another before them, still to be ascended. The potential blood clot now had to be dealt with — and there was worse news to come.

'To attend to the problem in the best possible way we have to move you over to the Women's Hospital around the corner. Unfortunately, we cannot simply take the normal way because there are the newspaper gentlemen and photographers all around the front of the hospital.'

And so, within the hour, I found myself as though in some sort of spy mystery movie, being led through to the rear entrance of the maternity hospital and helped into the back of Sam's car. I had to hide under the cover of a blanket just in case any of the marauding members of the media caught on to what was happening. We drove no more than a quarter of a mile to the Women's Hospital, where Sam was able to administer dye into the vein in my leg and take an X-ray. I hated being away from my girls, in a different building, even for the few hours the treatment took. But it was worth it. Fortunately, the results showed that I did not have a blood clot.

And by the Monday morning we had crossed another hurdle with the girls, too. Looking for a different way in which the mucus on Lucy's lungs might be loosened, Professor Cooke decided to try a slightly unconventional method: using a soft toothbrush to massage her chest. To everyone's delight, it worked a treat. Within just a couple of days, Lucy had caught up with the others and her cries could be heard equal to those of her sisters.

Knowing how critical the first forty-eight hours had been, the news of Lucy's improvement was fantastic.

For the first time since I'd woken after the operation, I dared to dream of taking my beautiful babies home.

28

Registering the Births

For decades one of the most important offices in Liverpool was situated in a building known as Brougham Terrace. Originally the first mosque in England, it had eventually been converted to the principal registry office of the area. It was here that Graham would register the births of our six precious girls.

Every day that passed, the girls were getting stronger; and the danger to me from potential blood clots had been reduced by the anticoagulants I was now receiving under the care of Sam and the nursing staff. With us seemingly out of the woods for the moment, we now wanted to have the births registered without delay.

There was no danger whatsoever of any last-minute changes to the names. Even after only a couple of days Hannah, Lucy, Ruth, Sarah, Kate and Jenny were so familiar in our minds that even the order in which we said their names had almost become second nature. Besides which, there was also the rather obvious fact that by now the names had been transmitted in one form of media or another around the world at least a dozen times.

On his way to register the births, Graham stopped off at the hospital.

'Where is this place again? I'll have to ask one of the nurses.'

'Why don't you take a taxi?' I suggested.

'I'll be alright,' he said, with typical male confidence when it came to not knowing where a place was. 'I've got my A — Z in the van.'

'A taxi will take you straight there, wait for you and bring you back. That way you'll keep your place in the hospital car park . . . ' I said.

The car park place swung it and he nodded.

'Have you got all the details?' I checked.

'Names and all our details, no problem, all sorted.'

'What about the time?'

'There's plenty of time. They don't close till four-thirty.'

'No, I mean the time of birth! You're going to need to have the time of birth as a record on each register entry.'

The girls were officially born in four brief minutes. Whichever way you tried to work it out, there was never going to be a way for all of the girls to have a full minute next to their names. One of the girls' births was always going to fall in the middle of the four minutes. Graham and I pondered the issue.

'Just a minute, let's check with the hospital record,' I said. I took the hospital's certificate of the births from the bedside table and there it was, clearly written next to Ruth Michelle — time of birth: seven fifty-six and thirty seconds!

I waved Graham off with all the documents.

★   ★   ★

Two hours later, he was standing in the doorway of my room.

'You won't believe this.'

'All done?'

'They didn't want to know about half minutes,' he told me. 'They said, 'It's not allowed.' They said, 'You can't do it.''

I gave him a look that said: you're having me on.

'Seriously. They've not seen anything like it. It's never happened before. I had to go through it with them. I said to them, 'No, it's *got* to be this way. Six girls were born in four minutes.'

'I went through it all with them, in detail. It was seven fifty-six, seven fifty-seven, seven fifty-seven *and a half*, seven fifty-eight, seven fifty-nine and eight o'clock. I showed them the hospital certificate and said, 'That is what it says on there.' And they said you couldn't have that; you can't have halves.

'And I said, 'We have got one. And the half is Ruth.''

And there was more.

'Not only that, I think the whole thing is going to be broadcast!'

'What do you mean?'

'You won't believe who went with me to the registry office.'

Graham didn't wait for a reply, but I could have guessed. It was Roger Summerskill, who was at the time one of the most familiar voices on BBC Radio Merseyside. Graham and Roger were already acquainted because, purely by chance, the last pub Graham was taken to by his friends on a celebration tour on the Saturday night after the birth had been Roger's local, near our home in Wallasey.

As Roger was the acting news editor at Radio Merseyside, this was a huge scoop for him. Simply being in the same pub as the father of the moment was a story in itself, and sure enough he had filed the story with the station at half past eleven that night. By Monday, their camaraderie had grown and Graham was doing a tour of the radio station with his dad, John, and my mum, Nancy, doing his first live broadcast. We had decided that, no matter what else was going on or being offered by the national press for exclusive deals, whatever arrangements we made would also have to allow us to talk to the local paper and radio stations. And so as it turned out, the first full-length interview that Graham gave was to Roger at Radio Merseyside.

Consequently, by the time Graham set out on his mission to get the births registered and spotted Roger outside the hospital (he, like many other journalists, was on daily duty outside the front door), they knew each other well.

'You're the one who suggested a taxi,' Graham told me now. 'He asked if he could jump in with me!'

And so, as the taxi doors slammed, all of a sudden Graham had found himself listening to a running commentary from Roger.

'Before the driver had asked where we were going Roger was talking into a microphone wired up to a tape recorder!' Graham exclaimed. 'You should have heard him: 'We're now going to register the births . . . How are you feeling, Mr Walton?' I said, 'Oh, I'm feeling very good, smashing!' He said, 'It will probably take all day, won't it?' And I said, 'It very probably will . . .''

I had to stop myself laughing at the absurdity of it all.

Graham finished relating the story. 'I tried to explain to him about the times of the births and I got all mixed up and he had to re-record it and do it again. If that's what being on the radio is like, I think I'll stick to painting and decorating . . .'

'Well, never mind,' I said, having regained some composure. I was more concerned about whether or not my little girls had had their births recorded accurately. Had Graham managed to persuade the registry office that each girl needed her own unique time of birth?

He passed the finished certificates over to me and I checked each of the girls' names and the times carefully.

And, sure enough, Graham had won the day. There, emblazoned in fine ink alongside Ruth's name, was the totally unique time of seven fifty-seven and thirty seconds.

I smiled up at my husband. 'Six perfectly detailed certificates for our six perfectly precious girls.'

29

We're Going to Need a Bigger House

From the morning of the first press conference, all the major newspaper groups were repeatedly asking the same question: could they buy the exclusive rights to photograph the girls? The pressure wasn't going to go away and although there was advice available, ultimately it was a decision only Graham and I would be responsible for; it would be our girls who would be photographed, no one else's.

It became clear to us that the right path was to agree to an exclusive arrangement with one newspaper; believing that once an agreement was in place, the situation surrounding the hospital would get better. Graham and I agreed to one photograph of ourselves, the happy parents, with the *Daily Star* soon after the births, and that was published on the first Monday morning after the girls were born. We also gave an interview to the *Liverpool Echo*, and there was Graham's interview on Radio Merseyside. But what the press really wanted were pictures of our six little miracles. It seemed everyone wanted to share the joy and to see the babies.

In a way, we were dealing with three things at the same time. We were helping to gain financial security for the future — which was much needed now that we had six little mouths to feed, six little bodies to clothe and six little minds to stimulate and entertain. We were also sharing the brilliant and wonderful blessings we had been given with millions of people. Finally, we were also, or so we hoped, releasing an enormous pressure that had been built up in the media frenzy.

I have no doubt that, had we agreed to it, many newspapers would have been happy to publish pictures of the babies within hours of the birth, struggling for their lives in their incubators. There was no way Graham or I would have agreed to any such image. When we decided to agree to family pictures with the *Sunday Mirror*, it was on the strict condition that they had to wait until all the babies were coping happily, without any tubes aiding their breathing or wires monitoring their every movement.

★　★　★

Eventually, a couple of weeks after the birth, the doctors gave me the all clear to leave hospital for good. With the girls recovering fast — they were putting on weight and, bit by bit, losing their reliance on various medical technologies — our national newspaper shoot was imminent. As a security measure to protect the story, the *Sunday Mirror* put Graham and I up in the luxurious Prince of Wales Hotel in the nearby resort of Southport until the photographs were ready to be published. Yet, as plush and palatial as it was, all we wanted by then was to go home.

Once the *Sunday Mirror* had published the

first pictures of the girls there was no need to prolong our stay. As the rest of the world began a new working week, it was time for us to leave the impressive Victorian architecture, colonial-style restaurant, sculptured surrounds and ornate gardens — and go home.

We stopped off at the hospital first to spend time with the babies, then headed back to the safety of our own little stronghold, returning to the two-and-a-half-up-and-two-down reality of Browning Road.

The feeling was at the same time both triumphant and empty. Triumphant — not because of any heroic feeling, but because whenever I had travelled or been anywhere in life, whether on holiday or while staying away for work, it was always the best feeling to get back home to my own bed. Six months was certainly long enough to be away. But the emptiness . . . Well, that was pretty obvious: all my children, six sweet, tiny miracles, were still in hospital. We were a family now but we hadn't brought our babies home. At least, not yet.

Caution was maintained by those looking after us on behalf of the newspaper, and as we turned the corner onto Browning Road in the chauffeur-driven limousine they had provided, I could sense the relief of pressure Graham felt on seeing that the tidal wave of paparazzi photographers and journalists had withdrawn from our doorstep. Little did we know this lull in the chase was not going to last, but nonetheless it was an oasis of time that gave us a chance to catch our breath. We had now experienced life as

Me as a baby, in 1953. I'm in a Silver Cross pram – very posh!

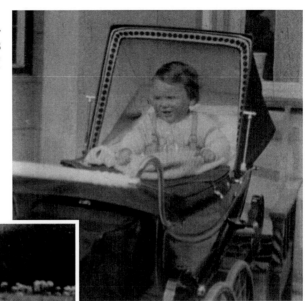

With my little sister Alison.

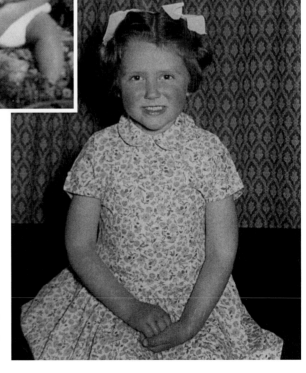

Me, aged 7.

Shortly after meeting Graham, in 1970.

On holiday with Graham.

Graham and I on our wedding day, 25 November 1976.

The trip to Malta in 1982. I may have sat on that fertility stone a little too long!

At twenty-eight weeks pregnant, just three-and-a-half short weeks before giving birth!

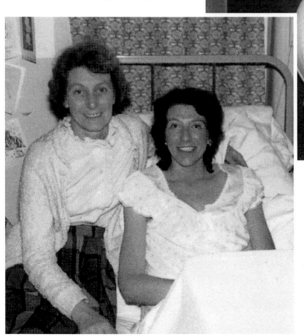

With Mum, the morning after the birth.

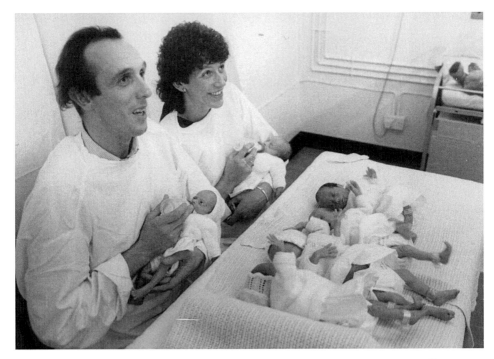

Graham and I with our six little miracles. Graham is holding Hannah, Ruth is in my arms, and on the table we have Kate, Jenny, Lucy and Sarah (*left to right*).

At the christening. Jenny with Sam and Linda Abdulla; Kate with Reg and Kay Feeley; Ruth with Martin and Sue Moroney; Graham and me with Canon Kehoe; Hannah with Dave and Chris Walton; Lucy with John and Lynn Pritchard; and Sarah with my sister Alison and Kenny Phillips.

Me holding Ruth, with Grandad Bill and Nanny Fox. How proud are the great grandparents?

Me with Jenny.

With Lucy in the garden.

Hannah and me.

Teaching Sarah how to walk.

With Kate in 1987.

I love this photo – the only one we have of all the girls with the grandparents. My parents Peter and Nancy are on the left, with Graham's parents Betty and John on the right.

Growing up – the girls' last day at St. George's Primary School. (*Left to right*) Lucy, Jenny, Sarah, Kate, Hannah and Ruth.

The girls aged thirteen.

Meeting Phillip Schofield aged fifteen at the stage door of the Empire Theatre in Liverpool.

The girls celebrating their thirtieth birthday in New York! (*Left to right*) Lucy, Jenny, Kate, Sarah, Hannah and Ruth.

With my granddaughter, Jorgie Louise, born 7 October 2014. Another little miracle!

media prey for nearly two weeks. If we were to remain sane, it was something we would have to come to terms with — and quickly.

We thanked the driver and the people from the paper, said our goodbyes and finally turned the key in the lock to come home.

Opening the front door, though, was not so straightforward. We had to wade through an avalanche of envelopes. It had been a few days since Graham had last been at the house and in those days alone the quantity of mail that had arrived at the house was incredible.

Graham gathered them all up and put them in the lounge, ready for opening later. He was a few minutes, as he glanced at the writing on the front of some of them, fascinated by the foreign stamps, before joining me in the kitchen. I was staring intently at the surfaces, musing over how we were going to cope with a production line of bottles in such a small area.

'You want to see some of the addresses on the envelopes, luv. I can't believe they ever got here!'

'What do you mean?' It had never occurred to me that complete strangers would want to write to me, let alone people from abroad.

'One of them has just got 'Sextuplets, somewhere in England' written on it!'

The mail we were receiving was coming from all four corners of the world. Well-wishers touched by our story — who may have only caught part of it on the news or heard about it from a relative or friend — felt moved to make contact in any way they could. What still amazes me is how people went to so much trouble to get in touch: taking the time to buy cards, investing in the thought process of writing and then getting to a mailbox or post office to make sure it was sent. Today, sending a message is so different and easy. Using Facebook or Twitter, or one of the other social networks, people can now express their feelings instantly, moving the minimum of muscle. Back then, they genuinely put time, money and heartfelt effort into reaching out to us.

As I continued my look around the kitchen, I glanced at the copies of the *Sunday Mirror* that we had brought back with us from the hotel, which were now resting on the kitchen table.

'Aren't they fabulous?' I said, so easily distracted by the picture of my girls, all huddled together in a line. I sat down to rest my legs. I still had a long way to go to recover full fitness, something I was reminded of every time I saw photos of myself in those first few weeks after the operation. But despite my exhaustion, looking at the girls now, for a moment the emptiness I'd felt when we'd crossed the threshold of the house without them turned into confidence, which seemed to give me more strength. We knew the girls had come through the critical period; they were all doing really well. Surely it was only a matter of time now before they would be coming home.

'They all look smashing, luv.' Graham, reading my mind, had already put the kettle on. With our drink to fortify us, we both sat at the table, which we had always felt was just the right size for our little kitchen. It was set against the wall, opposite the sink, and although perfectly cosy for the two of us, there wasn't a lot of space for much else.

'I think Jenny is going to be the first to come home.' The world had definitely changed. The babies were constantly on my mind. It had been less than an hour since I'd been with them at the hospital, but in the same way that I was desperate to see my children as soon as possible on the morning after the operation, now I wanted them all home as quickly as possible. Jenny, although 'officially' the youngest, was much bigger than the others and was making such good progress. I knew it wasn't going to be long before she was home.

'Well, if they come out two at a time like the hospital have said, then Kate will probably join her. She's putting on weight just as fast as Jenny.'

'You'd better hurry up and start making the cots then,' I joked, enjoying just hearing the girls' names in my own home.

Making up a cot is something I think most couples look forward to as first-time parents. It's part of the natural excitement of having your first child and no matter how good or otherwise you are at building and putting things together, even if you have to have a bit of help, it's still a special moment. But with the best will in the world, making up *six* cots was going to be a big task. At this stage, the babies would only be in large carrycots on frames, but still, six of them was going to take a bit of time to sort out, and they would need more space than most of the rooms we had could accommodate.

'All organised.' Graham was now sitting

217

reading the paper, scanning page after page inside. Each time his hands spread the paper out to a new page, another picture of our girls confronted me. 'According to this report,' he continued, 'there is a construction team of carpenters on their way! Although I think we may need planning permission . . . '

Later that evening, we went into the lounge and settled down on the same settee we had last shared over six months ago, but my mind was restless. I was still thinking about where everything was going to go and how we were all going to cope in such a small house.

'Seriously, though,' I said to my husband. 'Somehow we are just going to have to think about more space.'

As much as Browning Road meant to us, as our first home together as a couple, it had served its purpose. We had already made the decision to move house to accommodate a family, back when we had been accepted for adoption and were interested in giving a home to twins. When I fell pregnant with the sextuplets, it had been apparent that we would need more space — assuming everything went well. But with me in hospital and the future so uncertain, moving had not been a priority.

Throughout the pregnancy, we had never made plans about how we would do this or what we would do about that when the babies were born. But now the babies were here, we were going to have to address the problem of space — and soon.

It was a worry. Even living in the house with

six babies for just an interim period of a few months wasn't going to be easy.

'Hopefully,' Graham said encouragingly, 'we'll move house before the summer. Somewhere where there's a bit of garden for the girls to play.'

'That sounds good.'

As I spoke, I yawned and leaned back into the cushions of the settee, letting my head fall on Graham's shoulder. I was suddenly feeling the effects of yet another hectic day. I was tired but happy that, for the first time in a long while, we could at last begin to make plans for the future.

'Everyone says that babies and toddlers should get as much fresh air and sunshine as possible in their first few years,' I told Graham.

'And a couple of extra rooms,' he carried on, enthusing, 'a playroom and one we'll keep for best, for visitors and that kind of thing.'

'Well, I have a feeling you and I at least will be moving a lot sooner than you think,' I said.

'What do you mean?'

'Well, you saw the size of the carrycots we were looking at in the shops. We can't possibly keep the babies downstairs; it just wouldn't be practical or safe. The only way all the babies are going to be together in one bedroom is if we evict ourselves from the main bedroom and turn it into the nursery.'

And, as if we needed another incentive to make the move a priority, it would only be a few weeks before the girls were going to need full-size cots.

We tried to relax in front of the television after that, but it wasn't so easy. No sooner had we switched the set on than the clarion-call music of *The Nine O'clock News* was being played, the newsreader crying out, 'Here comes some more history!' We sat in jaw-dropped, open-mouthed silence, astonished as our story featured once again as one of its headlines.

It seemed that five minutes ago we were just an ordinary couple, happily married and living in a small semi-detached house, and privately doing what we could to realise our dream of becoming a mum and a dad. Now, it felt like we were public property — whether we liked it or not.

30

Coming Home

We were right in our prediction that Jenny and Kate would be the first two babies to be given the all clear by Richard Cooke and his team. As a new year began, so too did a new stage in our lives. Jenny had already passed 6 lb in weight by 3 oz and Kate was not too far behind at 5 lb 9 oz; both having almost doubled their original birth weight. With the two of them now clearly healthy bonny babies, it was time for them to come home.

Wrapping the two girls in layers of crocheted bonnets and blankets, we said our goodbyes and thanks on behalf of our daughters to the staff, made sure Kate and Jenny also said 'see you soon' to their sisters, and then the four of us set off on our journey back to Wallasey.

Leaving the others behind was difficult, but even if they had all been at a weight acceptable to be allowed home, the advice would still have been for the girls to go back to the family house in sets of two rather than all at once. We knew it was only a matter of time, a few weeks at the most, before Hannah, Lucy, Ruth and Sarah would be at a weight that would be satisfactory to the hospital to allow them to join their sisters. And I had a feeling my hands were going to be rather full in the intervening weeks before we had all six of them under our roof. The time was going to go quickly.

In fact, it felt that the time since the birth had moved at lightning speed. With so much excitement and so many things happening at once, it wasn't surprising that each day seemed to pass by so fast.

We had enough common sense to know that support was going to be a big issue. Anyone who has experienced having twins knows the massive difference that doubling up everything makes. And we had to cope with doing everything six times over. As much as I wanted to care for my babies one-to-one, I was realistic enough to accept that this was just going to be impossible at first.

So I was more than a little happy, when we arrived back at the house later that day with Jennifer Rose and Kate Elizabeth in our arms, to find a welcoming party of relatives at the ready. Both Betty, Graham's mum, and my mum were waiting, well prepared and confident, with sleeves rolled up and more than enough years' experience between them to help. By the time the news was being broadcast — Bernard Falk had been filming the homecoming exclusively for the BBC — the girls were fast asleep in our specially prepared 'care unit', where my husband, the hero, had completed phase one of the construction of the carrycots.

Only four more to go!

★ ★ ★

The plan was for Hannah, Lucy, Sarah and Ruth to follow as soon as they had gained enough weight to satisfy any concerns of the hospital. The expectation was that this should take another fourteen days.

During those two weeks, while Graham and I got used to our new way of life and to having babies of our own at home for the first time, each and every day one or both of us, if my mum or Graham's mum were available for babysitting, made sure we spent as much time as possible at the special care unit with the others. The first pangs of guilt were felt as I was torn between two places, desperately wanting to be with all my girls at once. Often, I would get a sudden sharp feeling of painful emotion, which I tried to combat with thoughts of being sensible and telling myself not to be so silly. But even though I had dealt with the fact they were so small and was totally used to it, they were still tiny babies reaching out for their mum as any baby does, and if you're not there for them when they cry, the short, sharp stabs of self-reproach are real.

★ ★ ★

A few days later, I was in the kitchen cleaning bottles and preparing for the next feed when I heard Graham calling from upstairs. I went up and into our bedroom. Or, should I say, into our former bedroom. The room had been transformed. Our double bed had been dispatched to the much smaller rear bedroom and in its place all six carrycots were now lined up, all with matching mattresses, blankets, covers and teddy bears. Opposite the cots there was one table for changing and one for bathing. On a side wall there was even a chest with six drawers. Perfect! Our own unique nursery was ready for action. All we needed now was to bring home the rest of our family.

There was, however, one first I enjoyed before all the girls were home. Determined with Graham not to be held back by the cold and grey skies of the winter morning, and using a borrowed pram with enough room for both Jenny and Kate, our little group of four set off on foot to visit Graham's parents, Betty and John. We were over halfway to their house, too far gone to turn back, when the weather suddenly turned very nasty. In an instant we were fighting driving snow. Fearing worse to come, we covered up the pram as much as possible and battled our way to their home in the very appropriately named Folly Lane. We felt a little foolish, a lot colder but very happy. We'd achieved one of the things we'd dreamt of ever since we began trying for a baby: the simple act of going for a family walk.

★   ★   ★

Our original plan to bring Hannah, Lucy, Ruth and Sarah back to the house from the hospital in two's was abandoned due to the strain of the daily journey, now that we were looking after Jenny and Kate at home. On the day they were finally discharged from Oxford Street, Lucy had grown to an impressive 6 lb 9 oz, Sarah was weighing in at 5 lb 7 oz and even Hannah, who was the smallest at birth, was deemed by the doctors at 4 lb 14 oz to be big enough and well enough to go home.

But as always in life, things don't necessarily go smoothly or as planned. The joy of taking the girls home to join their sisters was dampened by the fact that the doctors decided to keep Ruth in for a little longer. The hospital told us that they didn't discharge babies from the special care unit until they were fully fit. Ruth, unfortunately, had a slight cold. They said she should be allowed home in a few days' time.

Graham had had a bit of a shock when he'd gone to visit the girls the day before, in fact. He'd walked into the room where the girls were and one of the cots was empty. He immediately went to the nurse on duty and asked where Ruth was, only to be told that they'd had to isolate her because she was suffering from a little cold and they didn't want to take any risks of infection spreading.

It wasn't until recently, over thirty years later, that I discovered that there was actually more to the reason as to why Ruth couldn't join her sisters. In a medical paper published many years afterwards, authored by a number of eminent professors and doctors including Richard Cooke, focusing on the outcome of preterm sextuplets, it indicated that one of our babies, 'case number four' as she was referred to, had 'a serious apnoeic attack at fifty-six days'. That would have been three days before Hannah, Lucy and Sarah left hospital. It meant Ruth had stopped breathing.

I would have been totally devastated if I'd lost one of the girls. After all the doubt during the months in hospital, all the determination they were all going to be alright and all the days that had passed since the birth, as the girls came safely through all the critical moments, each one progressing from being incubates and incubated to becoming healthy enough to come home, it would have been soul-destroying.

Happily, the consultants and nurses, who had done such a brilliant job all the way through, once again must have worked wonders to save 'case number four'. And we knew that as soon as Ruth's 'sniffle', as Graham called it, cleared up, we would finally have a full house. But the relative calm of just Jenny and Kate at home was gone already. Now Hannah, Sarah and Lucy had joined them, the house already felt more like a special care unit!

★　★　★

For now, it was enough to cope with having five beautiful babies at home. But just as we were carrying our little hat-trick back to Browning Road, a second situation dashed a shake of salt on our vulnerable family.

In the whole of the thirty years since my girls were born, there has only been one time when the story became one of controversy. This was it.

Following the original press conference, there were suddenly a host of questions about how

Graham and I would possibly be able to cope. Both the Wirral area health authority and the local social services were caught up in the biggest story that had ever crossed their desks, and both were under pressure to react to media demands of what they were going to do to help. On the day we went to Oxford Street hoping to bring the remaining babies home, both authorities had decided on holding a joint press conference, with everyone being consulted — except us!

In that evening's *Liverpool Echo*, huge block letters on the front page proclaimed 'THE FREE BABY-SIT'. A piece above told how the 'nurses were on rates as sextuplets go home', while under a picture of a trio of smiling nursery nurses who had been assigned to us, another headline in large type asked, 'Is the help too generous?'

The details given at the press conference were personal, giving the world financial information that in any other situation for any other couple was absolutely private. By the next morning, all the national newspapers had latched on to the story and 'The Free Baby-Sit' had spawned new headlines. It was now 'Bumper Back-Up for Supermum', 'Thirteen Helpers for Sextuplets', 'The £8,000 Baby-Sit', and the classic 'movie' style heading, 'Storm Over Baby-Minders'!

I was so upset at the betrayal of confidentiality.

It seemed that while the vast majority of stories written and reports given had been totally supportive and joyous in the celebration of what was, after all, the most incredible blessing — even, as some said, a miracle — there were some who simply couldn't see it that way; and

227

others who felt too much attention was being given to one family by the authorities. People began debating publicly all the things a normal couple would take for granted to be something that was a very private matter.

Following the incredibly intrusive press conference held by the authorities, there was a backlash of support expressed over 'leaks' of information and some wonderful letters of support printed from members of the public. They meant such a lot to me. Within a week, the authority, acknowledging our right to privacy, issued a further press release. They confirmed that the conference had originally been called as a result of enquiries and admitted we had not been consulted. They also released a statement saying there would be no further press conferences.

In a way, although I was disappointed at the time, I was fortunate to be sheltered from much of what went on purely because my focus was entirely on the day-to-day welfare and care of the girls. We hadn't asked for anything, we were grateful for whatever we were given and entitled to, in whatever form the help came. When I look back now, however, at the way in which the privacy to which we were entitled, just like any other couple, was taken away, I still find it upsetting.

Thankfully, on that day and on the days that followed, we didn't have the time to dwell on it. Caring for our family of five daughters at home, while we continued our daily visits to see Ruth in hospital, left no room at all for thinking about the thoughtlessness of others.

31

The New Routine

There were no brass bands playing in the street, no bunting, flags or indeed any outward signs of celebration on the day Graham and I carried 6 lb 2 oz Ruth Michelle across the threshold. Inside our hearts, though, was a carnival of joy. We looked at each other across her little bonnet-clad head and knew the significance of her homecoming.

We had said our goodbyes to the hospital staff and to all the wonderful nurses in the special care unit for the last time, with promises of one day bringing the girls back to visit. Now, we were home for good.

But in the end, 'home' was only Browning Road for a short time. In all we were only in that house with all the babies for about ten weeks. Somehow, between juggling baby bottles and changing nappies, Graham and I were able to hunt out a house with a bit more space, which was something we clearly and desperately needed before anything else.

During that ten-week period, though, it was as if our home had become converted into a clinic — a very busy clinic. It was our own very special care unit; without the expensive equipment, but with six of everything required to give the girls the best and make them as comfortable as possible.

The kitchen in Browning Road was so small, anyone going in or out had to squeeze past another person if they happened to be going from one room to another. There was no place to cross over. Any spare space there might have been was taken up by the table for two we had once used for quiet meals and which was now an essential work area in a room that cried out for more and more surfaces on which to place bottles — which had to be made up in advance of the busy feeding times — and all the other essential equipment.

The work always began the night before, when it was easier and quicker to do more things at once. We carried spare stocks of everything, but the bottles we had used still needed to be cleaned out and washed and sterilised. By the end of an evening, we had usually accumulated thirty-six bottles, which then had to be made up and prepared for the next day. The kitchen felt at times like a factory, as we would always try to anticipate the needs of the next day.

The mountain of tinned milk powder that sat on top of the cupboard would shrink each day as the plastic scoop shovelled the contents into a waiting jug. The scoop conveniently gave a precise recommended measure; useful to most but totally meaningless to us. We were learning the best way as we went along; there was no manual on rearing sextuplets.

In no time at all, instincts and common sense once again ruled my day. Rather than make up each bottle with its own formula individually, which would have taken all night, we always made one large jug full to the brim, and then divided it into as many bottles as we could at a time. Anyone helping was given the simple instruction to make, whisk and pour!

* * *

Our small semi-detached house in Browning Road was at times as busy as a department store on the first day of a sale. It seemed a never-ending stream of people every day were ringing at the bell or rapping away at the door-knocker, all with good reasons and intentions.

The phone was a major thing at Browning Road. Invariably, Graham or I would have the receiver in one hand and a baby in the other. The same phone that had played such a significant part in my life when I was going through the years of fertility treatment was not to be left out of the excitement of the arrival of the babies, the new residents at the house.

It was constantly ringing, determined to make its presence felt as everything else was going on, with people moving about all the time between the rooms of the small house. I would sit on the bottom stair and people would be going up and down passing me while I was talking to one well-wisher or another. If ever there was a moment of quiet, it was sure to be disturbed by the shrill bells of an incoming call. If people weren't coming to the house personally, they were ringing to see how I was coping and to ask

231

if we needed anything. The answer was always 'more hours in the day' or 'an extra pair of hands would be good'. I didn't think it was likely that I was about to sprout the arms of an octopus, but more than one person had joked that that might have been useful to me.

We had accepted the fact that our home was not going to be our own, at least at first, from almost the moment we had arrived home with Kate and Jenny. We soon realised that privacy and intimacy, already a thing of the past due to my extended stay in hospital, would continue to be scarce for many months. I became conscious of having to lower my voice at times when talking to Graham, or having to strain to hear what he was saying to me if he felt he had to whisper. Familiarity is a friend when trusting your baby to the care of a stranger, but over-familiarity was never far away. On one occasion, when a boyfriend of one of the nurses called early for her, she felt it acceptable to walk in on me having a bath!

We had points of reference that helped give some focus and establish a routine to the day. Firstly, there was the preciseness of the 'changing of the guard' — the times during the day when the night-nurse shift came to an end and the day nurses arrived to take over duty. However many 'helpers' had been publicly talked about, once the girls arrived home, there were only ever two nurses at any one time who actually gave day-to-day care to the babies: two nurses came to the house during the day, and two were on night duty.

After our parents, our most amazing help came from the wonderful Sue Thomas.

Sue joined us as a home help, to do the mundane jobs like cleaning and ironing. 'Help' couldn't have been a better description, and like the nursery nurses she wanted to do the best she could to fulfil her role. But, unlike the nurses, she had no certificates or qualifications in baby care — except, of course, that most valuable of all qualifications: experience.

Sue was on the same wavelength as us. The most important attribute she had was initiative, and she had a personality to match Graham's and mine. She immediately became a good friend and she also had a close relationship with my mum and with Graham's mum Betty, getting on really well and working alongside both in the 'factory' and the 'clinic'. She simply wasn't the kind of person who could just dust a table in the lounge when there was so much going on, so before long she was asking to help more. With two young daughters of her own, she turned out to be more of a mother's help than a home help.

★ ★ ★

It was no fault of the nurses who were at Browning Road to help us, who did an impeccable job, but when the time of day arrived that left just Graham and me to look after the girls — the hours between five and ten when we had the house entirely to ourselves — we felt immediate relief at finally being 'home alone'.

For the first few months, these were the hours

233

I looked forward to the most, and it was the time I felt the least tense. There was an obvious irony, in that this was the time when I would be the busiest. There was no one else to turn to and just the two of us to deal with whatever new experience parenthood could throw at us without a safety net.

On the first evening we had on our own, we stood together just inside our old bedroom, the new one for our daughters. The girls were all soundly asleep in their cots: fed, changed and content. There would be no difference in our affection for the girls. They were equal to us and they were equal to each other. Although we may jokingly refer to Hannah as the eldest or Jenny as the youngest, the four minutes that separated them was the same moment in time. Our little girls would always be different to us, each her own person, but we would always love them just the same.

Already, the girls were highly skilled at capturing my heart and making me feel like a million dollars, six times over. As each gentle breath came and went in the nursery that night, softly punctuating the stillness in the evening air, we still couldn't quite believe our luck.

32

The Christening

When the papers were finally signed and the contracts exchanged on our new four-bedroom home in Bidston Village, situated fairly close to Wallasey, both Graham and I felt a huge sense of relief.

The new house we had chosen was absolutely brilliant. In return for a PR photograph the house builder had given a small discount which had helped seal the deal. Without doubt, the increased size and extra bedrooms were going to be of huge benefit for all the family. We knew that the garden especially was going to be a wonderful place; in the first instance just to rest the babies safely in their pushchairs, then to let them crawl about on the grass, discovering in the garden some of what nature has to offer with all its curiosities. Eventually, Graham and I could already see the girls running about playing during future summers.

But as somebody once said, time and space are relative, and I realised from the first moment of the first morning in our new home that nothing had changed in respect of the essential things that had to be done for the caring of a new baby in your life. They were a given whether it was one baby or six.

Inevitably, in our home, the waking cries of

one baby woke another and another, until all six babies were alert to the start of a new day. The routines and schedules, as had been listed on the wall of our old bedroom in Browning Road, fully occupied Graham and me and the day nurse, and we were all immediately back into the same system of feeding and nappy changing, simply in a new, slightly bigger, setting.

We were getting through each day on pure instinct at times — but then, that's what it's like for most couples experiencing a newborn baby in their lives for the first time. No matter how many baby classes you go to in advance of giving birth, and I had not been to any, nothing you can learn there can substitute for the learning curve of each real-life experience.

There is an element of mystery and the unknown, and in a way those experiences are the first beautiful adventures that mother and baby share together. Advice and help from parents, if you are lucky enough to have them and they are close enough to be there, is great. But I think that the things I enjoyed most were the first tentative moments of caring for the babies when they were at their most delicate on my own, and learning day by day what their own individual needs were and doing my best to give them what they needed.

One of the last phone calls we had received in Browning Road before we moved was from Canon Kehoe. As priest of the English Martyrs Roman Catholic Church in Wallasey, he was going to preside over the ceremony for the christening of the girls. I'd promised to call him back as soon as we had got the move out of the way and were settled in the new house.

I needed a couple of days, in any event, to talk the arrangements through with Graham. Yet finding the time to do a simple thing like have a quiet chat about anything that wasn't related to the immediate needs of the babies wasn't straightforward; and for the christening there was another balancing act to perform.

As part of the initial arrangement we had agreed with the *Sunday Mirror*, they were to be given exclusive access to the celebrations and service relating to the christening, alongside a television crew, who were going to be sending film to the BBC. It would be the first time the girls would be outside the protective bastion of their own home. So I was worried about juggling the christening itself, the media attention, and — my primary concern — the safety and welfare of the girls.

We were becoming more and more conscious of the fact that people actually wanted to see the babies. Even with all that had happened over the past three months since the news broke, it was still difficult to understand the extent of the interest that had been created by the birth.

'It's going to be difficult for the church,' Graham said thoughtfully, concerned about the details, as he slowly peeled back a nappy that needed changing. I was doing the same and glanced across. His face drew back an inch or two and his nose seemed to contort to one side as he attempted to block his nostrils with the area above his lips.

The smells were something I had got used to a little quicker than Graham. 'You should see your face,' I laughed.

'You should see this!' I could only just understand him through his distorted lips. 'It's disgusting!'

'What do you expect?' I said, mine wasn't anywhere near as bad.

By now, Graham was well-practised in nappy changing and deftly removed the offending one, binned it and in an instant had wiped and cleaned everywhere necessary. 'Can you pass me a fresh nappy, luv . . . and the powder?' (Talc was everywhere.) He put on the replacement and was rewarded with a smile from me. His mind went back to the point.

'We need to ask the Canon about the media people. He might not be happy about them being there.'

'He's obviously seen everything that's gone on up to now. When I spoke to him a few days ago, he seemed to be expecting photographers and television people. At least, he said, 'I presume they'll be there.' I think he was looking forward to it.'

'I'm more concerned about having it on a Sunday. It's going to be overcrowded. It'll have to be a Saturday.'

Graham was right; there were going to be so many people in attendance that it was only fair that the weekly Sunday congregation should be left in peace to pray.

'But, what about your football?' I suddenly exclaimed. 'What if it clashes with a home game?

The season won't have finished by the beginning of May, and I've no doubt Liverpool will have at least one more game at Anfield before the end of the season.'

With the round-the-clock dedication he was giving to domestic life, the one thing Graham had to release pressure and give him a chance to be in a completely different atmosphere was when he went to watch the team he loved and supported. As much as he now had a team of his own at home to love and support, I felt it was important to try and make sure he didn't miss a game.

'Don't be silly, luv.' I detected a tiny artificial edge to the tone, but he was resolute. 'How can a football match be compared to the christening? You just give the Canon a ring tomorrow and sort the date out.'

The next morning, receiver in one hand and fixture list in the other, I called Canon Kehoe to make the arrangements, not only avoiding Liverpool's home game, but also a couple of the Canon's tee-off times; his enthusiasm for golf had not waned since he had first told me about his second passion.

We agreed that it would be sensible not to hold the service on a Sunday and so, with all sporting considerations sorted, the date was finally decided for Saturday 12 May 1984. Just six days short of six months since my six girls had made their entrance on the world's stage, they were to take their first bow in public.

★　★　★

239

I appreciated that, although in one sense the christening was a private family celebration, Canon Kehoe and all those who had functions to perform in connection with the church were more than likely to come under a lot of pressure from the media. I told the Canon that we had decided to limit the amount of media people involved by making arrangements with one newspaper and one television crew.

The truth was, though, that due to the very public circumstances, we were never going to make it easy for the church. I was hoping for too much, but in as diplomatic a way as possible, I hinted that it might be best for there to be as little public notice as possible about the event.

In the meantime, I got on with the rest of the arrangements. One morning, not long after we'd set the date, I received sample invitations to the christening from a lady, out of the blue. She wasn't connected to us at all, but her timing couldn't have been more perfect. The cards she had sent were rough sketches of what she imagined I might like as a design; it was a purely speculative approach and she didn't really expect to win the business. Six babies in bonnets and Moses' baskets with blankets, each bearing one of my girls' names, were beautifully illustrated on the invitations, three babies on either side, leaving space in between for the guest's name.

I immediately thought they were just right. I couldn't help but be enthusiastic about her designs and to her delighted surprise placed an order for 200 cards, for sending to our close friends and family, and all the assorted doctors and helpers who had assisted us thus far.

A week or so before the big event the church notice went out . . . and all hopes of the 'private' event went out with it, as it clearly informed all members of the church of the date and time of the christening. Within hours of the notice going out, the phone began to ring; the press had picked up the scent and they were on our trail.

Three days before the christening, the only sound in our house was Graham turning the pages of the *Liverpool Echo*. The girls were all soundly asleep upstairs in their cots. The day nurse had gone home. We were having some precious peaceful time to ourselves, relaxing in the lounge with a glass of wine.

Graham suddenly closed the paper, making me look up. The gesture wasn't unusual and I waited, expecting his comment or opinion on some local or world news, or more likely on a decision Liverpool Football Club had made, or on a frustrating injury to one of the players that would keep him out of the lineup for the next match.

'Well, that's it!' He said it in a resigned tone that I instantly recognised.

'What's it?'

'It's going to be mayhem on Saturday. It's all here in black and white. Everything except the time the service begins. It says, 'Canon Kehoe said seats will be reserved for the Walton family and their friends and the remaining places will be open to the public. It's a church and everyone is welcome.''

Graham passed me the newspaper. The article

241

even had a picture of the girls in hats similar to the ones I had prepared for the christening; that photograph had been taken from the house builder's public relations department. As I scanned the story, my eyes focused on one particular paragraph.

'Canon Martin Kehoe will officiate at a service where Graham and Janet Walton's world-beating six baby girls will acquire twelve godparents.'

Well, I suppose 'world-beating' was one way of putting it, but it wasn't a competition.

It 'revealed' — another great newspaper word — as if showcasing a piece of sensational information, that for baptisms the Canon's memory aid was to 'write the child's name on the palm of his hand'. It also said, in an act of astonishingly astute clairvoyance, that the christening service was likely to attract a huge crowd of well-wishers and pressmen. Well, it would now.

'It's not Canon Kehoe's fault,' I said, in the end. 'He can't say anything else — the church is for everyone. We'll just have to go with it and hope everything's OK.'

I was trying to be positive but I was beginning to feel a little apprehensive and took a slightly larger gulp of wine.

★ ★ ★

On the morning of the christening, the phone by the bedside table rang out. Brittle and shrill, it woke me instantly. It was a different tone to the alarm clock and as I checked the time, I realised it was half an hour earlier than I'd set it to wake up. So much for my plan to give myself an extra fifteen minutes' precious and definitely needed sleep. Graham let out a disagreeable snore and I picked up the receiver.

The familiar voice didn't wait for a 'hello' or 'good morning'.

'I know you are busy and I know you've got a thousand things to do and I know this isn't very important, but it *is* important because if it's not right it might spoil everything and I don't want to spoil everything!'

'How did you know it would be me who answered, Alison?'

'You always answer if I ring early in the morning.'

One of the girls had reacted to the ringing and was now looking for some attention. It was Kate. I wondered if the other girls would wake up.

'Who's calling at this unearthly hour?' Graham had stirred; after the last six months he was fully accustomed to unorthodox sleeping hours. 'If that's Canon Kehoe, tell him we'll be there on time!'

The small transom window at the top of the window frame in our bedroom had been left open through the night. Outside, I could hear voices instead of the usual tweeting of birds. Who on earth was it at this hour?

I got up, still talking to Alison, and held the phone in one hand as I moved towards the window. Slowly I pulled the edge of the curtain slightly back.

There were half a dozen men outside the

243

house, armed with cameras, tripods, pads and pencils.

I suppose I should have expected it. Our deal with the *Sunday Mirror* meant they were going to continue to have more intimate access to the exclusion of the other papers. Arrangements had already been made to allow the *Sunday Mirror*'s photographer, Howard Walker, into both our home and Graham's parents' house, where we had decided the girls would be dressed before going to church. However, even though the rest of the national press were aware of the deal that had been done, any editor of a national newspaper worth his or her salt was not going to let the occasion pass without insisting that their most intrepid reporters and photographers were on the scene, expecting them to get the pictures and a story at all costs, deal or no deal. The fruits of those Fleet Street briefings were now camped outside our house.

I let the curtain fall and tuned back into my sister's conversation.

'Cream, Ali, wear the cream. It will be perfect! Your goddaughter Sarah will love it and it will look nice on the telly. I have got to go — the troops are rousing. See you later.' I turned to Graham. 'I'll shower first.' I then pointed towards the front of the house and added, 'And we have got company!'

Hannah was awake next and within minutes all the girls except Jenny were awake, creating more decibels than all the phones and all the alarm clocks on the estate.

Usually it was Sarah who woke first, and

sharing a room with Ruth, Hannah and Lucy she would trigger a chain reaction. In the other bedroom, Kate at her loudest couldn't stir Jenny. As sure as sunrise, one by one their morning vocals created a choral harmony of baby cries fit for the cloisters of a church. And church was where we were heading that day.

As Graham and I busied ourselves with our usual hectic morning routine, the press, draining the last drops of coffee from their flasks, realised they weren't going to get any quotes or 'line-up' photos at the house, and went off in search of Canon Kehoe to ask for permission to take pictures on his patch.

We then put our plan into action. Instead of dressing the girls at home, we went to Graham's parents' house, where we had arranged to meet Howard. It was situated just around the corner from the church — the last thing we wanted was for one of the girls to be carsick on the way to the christening, so the shorter the distance we had to travel with the babies in their very first 'best' outfits, the better.

I laid the special clothes I had bought for the girls on the double bed in John and Betty's room upstairs. Within minutes — with help from the ladies of the Walton clan — all the girls were lying on their backs fully dressed: three near the pillows at the top of the bed and three below, as always in the now-familiar birth order of Hannah, Lucy, Ruth, then on the next row Sarah, Kate and Jenny, each bright white outfit now complemented by a pretty mobcap. They were ready for their big moment.

Before the days of instant communication and mobile phones, other methods were found to get information from one place to another rapidly. Part of our entourage today was the same *Sunday Mirror* team as had worked with us for the first exclusive pictures, and messages were being relayed between them over their walkie-talkies as to what was happening up at the church.

The information being dispatched was of huge crowds gathering and more and more people arriving and hanging around the car park, driveways and entrances to the building.

Even though it was close by, walking to the church was completely out of the question.

In our plans for the day we had been expecting that we would have to take the car. But what we hadn't bargained for — at all — was the size of the crowds we were being told were massing around the building. However organised we had tried to be with the christening — arranging the exclusive pictures to try to limit press intrusion, creating formal invitations in an attempt to have a private function for family and friends — nothing could have prepared us for this. It was as if the Beatles were playing in the sixties.

I could hear the noise of the crowds when, a few moments later, Graham pulled the car into the driveway of the church. People were actually cheering. But even if we had wanted to try to let everyone see the girls, or had tried to prearrange some kind of event for them to do so, it simply would have been impossible, and more to the point not safe.

We had been expecting that the large crowds were going to be made up, for the most part, of all the people who had received the specially printed invitations . . . but they were apparently already in the church. The people outside were members of the public, local people from Wallasey and the surrounding areas who were curious and wanted to see the babies. None of them wanted anything other than to catch a glimpse of the girls and wish them well on their special occasion. It was all with good intentions.

We drove past the gates and I looked up to the church tower, but my eye was diverted to an iron fire escape at the side of the building where, high up, a group of teenagers had gathered and were peering through one of the windows. The front doors of the church had been, by necessity, shut, simply because there were already too many people inside.

We had to slow down to a crawling pace and even through the protective metal of the vehicle, I could feel the pressure of a human wall as thuds of hands, knees and bodies hit the car. Suddenly, another large group of journalists and photographers seemed to take over the momentum of the vehicle and we finally came to a halt with the front fender buried in a brick wall close to the entrance of the church.

The police had arrived to help with the control of the crowd, but notwithstanding their presence, worse was to come. As a small amount of space was cleared for us to open the back of the car, so that those family and friends who were carrying the babies into the church could move, the mass of people trying to get a closer look at the girls suddenly lunged forward.

That was the breaking point for me. Just for a second, my composure was replaced by an instinctive defence mechanism. I was a mum who felt her children were in danger, and I shouted at the journalists to 'stop pushing and get back!'

And that was it. They had got what they wanted. The newspapers that didn't have access inside the church had a story outside.

As bad as the moment was, luckily that was all it turned out to be, just a moment — a bit of a scary one, but just one bad moment among a million brilliant ones inside the church.

While, later, there was the odd attempt to spoil the story by some papers using headlines like 'Storm Over Sextuplets', they were drowned out by the majority saying 'Six Babes Bright and Beautiful' or 'Six Tiny Reasons for Big Smiles' or 'Bless the Babes'.

And blessing the babes was, of course, what this day was really all about. The struggle to get to the church on time meant we arrived in the nave nearly a quarter of an hour late, just in time to hear an inspired canon, who had climbed to the pulpit early to ask everyone in the church to be patient. Smiling broadly, he gazed across the people in the pews and aisles below him and made an announcement.

'You will all know the babies are girls, and girls will be girls. They do have to spend some time getting ready!'

The *Ode to Joy* of Beethoven's Ninth

Symphony, resounding from a team of ten schoolgirl handbell-ringers, welcomed in the babies to their special ceremony. One by one, Graham and I made sure the right baby was given to the right set of godparents. The girls settled into the laps of each of the godmothers. The television cameras quietly focused on each baby's face while a crescendo of clicks echoed off the stone walls as members of the congregation took their own photos.

Alison's nerves were shot, being in front of such a big crowd of people. She was, along with Graham's friend Kenny Phillips, to be a godparent to Sarah. She would have happily been godmother to any of the girls but it was Sarah we had paired with her, and Sarah who was to sit upon her lap for the service.

The other godparents were a mixture of friends and family. They were: for Kate, Graham's friend and workmate Reg Feeley and his wife Kay; for Lucy, our friends John and Lynn Pritchard; for Hannah, Graham's brother David and his wife Chris; his sister Susan and her husband Martin, who had sheltered Graham from the media storm on the night of the birth, were there for Ruth; and finally, for Jenny, because she was the last of the girls to be delivered and therefore the youngest, we asked Sam Abdulla and his wife Linda to be godparents.

There was an enthusiastic crescendo of sound as the organist pumped a little extra pressure on the foot peddle and the opening hymn 'All Things Bright and Beautiful' began. It concluded with music and voices resounding throughout the church. As the final notes echoed off the bare stone walls and floor, the soles of Canon Kehoe's shoes could be heard clicking their way to the pulpit. A thousand ears waited for his opening line. There was silence for a moment.

And then Jenny beat him to it, crying out sweetly as if to make the point that the girls were the stars of this particular event and were going to have their say and she was the official representative of the sisters. A brief murmur of joy came from everyone, then a pause with a beat of time, and then there was silence again.

I looked up at Canon Kehoe, standing there in his white smock emblazoned with a cross to the left of his chest, and reflected on our journey together. One of the first people I had told of the pregnancy was Canon Kehoe. It was a few days after I'd taken up residence at the hospital. It had been made clear that the chances of survival were remote and Graham and I had decided it was right for the church to know as soon as possible.

When I'd told him how I felt strong and confident and truly believed everything was going to be alright, he'd seemed moved by the positive outlook I had taken. I'd told him that I looked forward to having them all and was prepared to do everything I was told to give my girls the best chance of life.

Canon Kehoe had been there for me then, and he was there for me today, too. He had absorbed a huge amount of pressure in the hours before the ceremony. In a calm and collected manner he had held back wave upon wave of press enquiry and, like Moses at the Sea of Reeds, had cleared a passage for the 500 congregants to take their seats safely in the church. Now, he was about to give the address to celebrate and bless the lives of my little girls.

The Canon's finger pulled gingerly at the black collar that crowned his smock, as if to release some of the pressure of the occasion. His hand continued upward until his palm swept across his bald head, removing the delicate sheen the occasion had settled on him. He was as nervous as the rest of us sitting on the dais in full view of the congregation, which included Lynda Chalker, the local MP, the Lord Mayor . . . and the 10 or 12 million who would be watching the BBC News that night.

Canon Kehoe coughed to clear his throat and in a confident, experienced manner spoke out.

'In June last year, Janet told me a specialist had confirmed she was going to have sextuplets.'

Glancing at his notes, he straightened his glasses and continued, 'I asked her, 'What on earth are you going to do?'

'And she replied, 'I have faith and I am determined to have them all.''

Another pause, then he smiled. 'On 18 November, I was at home watching the TV when the announcer said that a Liverpool mother had given birth to sextuplets. My reaction was automatic. I stood up and waved my hands in the air.' There was laughter from the pews.

Jenny let out another little cry as if to say, 'That was me!' In fact, the cry was because she

251

was teething and the problem had been bothering her all morning. My hand gently slipped into my handbag and I extracted a tube of Bonjela teething gel and passed it along the line to Linda, hoping not too many people would notice.

'The babies,' the Canon continued, 'have already been given an emergency baptism immediately after their birth by a priest from the cathedral, but today's celebration will bring together all of the ceremonies used for christening and admitting the children into the Family of Christ.'

Once he had finished addressing the congregation, Canon Kehoe signalled for Graham to join him in performing the ritual acts of the celebration.

Beside the momentary frets Jenny expressed, the girls were on their absolute best behaviour as far as crying was concerned. In fact, the only other tears that were shed that day were purely those of joy from the adults. I even noticed a tear in Graham's eye once Canon Kehoe had passed over each of the girls in turn and claimed each on behalf of the Lord Saviour, as his finger moved in the shape of a cross on the babies' foreheads.

If anyone had looked closely enough, they would have caught a glimpse of some blue lines scrawled across the palm of each of the Canon's hands. On his left palm were the names Hannah Jane, Lucy Anne and Ruth Michelle; and on his right Sarah Louise, Kate Elizabeth and Jennifer Rose. It's a wonder he had the room for all that information.

I watched Graham then take a candle to each of the godparents. And as I thought of the future, when the same candles would be used for confirmations and perhaps weddings, I also thought of the past, as I wondered about the first time Graham had helped to baptise the girls, as they struggled for life just hours after the birth.

Bernard Falk and his team, who were filming the BBC News report that would be seen around the world, were literally like flies on the wall. They were unobtrusive and blended in, avoiding spoiling views for congregants. We never regretted allowing the media to cover the event. Even those members of the press who had managed to gain access to the church behaved well and there were no disruptions or problems that affected the service. They all were able to record what they wanted and to cover the story for their readers.

Everyone — press, general public and locals alike — seemed to want to be a part of the ceremony. The only sensible and logical way for strangers to see the christening and to witness the celebration was for professional cameras to cover the event. If it had been an 'open house' and free-for-all for the press, the chances are each would have understandably wanted to get the best point of view and, as often happens when multiple photographers are trying to get the same picture or the attention of the subjects, the whole scene would have lost its dignity. By allowing only exclusive cameras in, we managed to ensure that people who wanted to see the celebration, whoever they were and wherever they were, could. Most importantly, it meant the service went smoothly — without any of its little stars being upset.

It was a fabulous and overwhelming day that was filled with huge swathes of love, joy and happiness. Once we were inside the church, we were oblivious to the frustrated press and disappointed crowds outside. Instead, we were able to take in the service and enjoy every moment of what was such an important early milestone in our daughters' lives.

As for the girls themselves, it was almost as though there was awareness within their tiny souls that this was a special day. They were marvellous throughout the whole ceremony. Graham couldn't stop beaming with pride at his 'smashing' daughters.

The rest of the day was one long celebration as we partied away at the nearby Leasowe Castle Hotel, where the girls were introduced to everyone, and everyone wet the babies' heads with copious amounts of champagne.

33

Six Buggies

After the joy — and upheaval — of the christening, life at Bidston settled into some sort of normality. The crowds outside the church, though, had not only been a surprise but also a reminder that life was never going to be normal whenever we stepped out of the front door.

One of the things I had always looked forward to whenever I used to dream about being a mum was the simple idea of taking my baby for a walk in a pram or a pushchair. Before I had the girls, I would occasionally see someone pushing a double buggy and observe how heads would always turn to give a second glance, perhaps even stop and stare. After establishing twins were the occupants, the next question from the passer-by would be: 'Are they identical?' I could only imagine what the reaction to sextuplets out for a stroll would be.

As it was, before we could even consider going out for a walk with all the girls, we had to work out the logistics and practicalities of just how it was to be done. Like so many other ordinary everyday considerations, this was just another that, for us, had to be thought out and planned with precision timing. The last thing we wanted was to be walking too far from the house when they all needed changing or feeding. And then there was the question of exactly how they would all be taken out and transported in the first place.

I was determined, nonetheless, to make sure that the girls got as much fresh air as possible. While we were working out the best way for walking our new family, we were at least mobile and able to travel *en masse* by road. We had accepted a loan vehicle from a local car dealer in return for some photographs of our family for marketing purposes. It was large enough to accommodate six carrycots in the back. This gave us the freedom to be able to visit Graham's parents or go to Neston.

Both my mum and Graham's mum Betty were always well prepared with any emergency supplies when we were away from home. Now and again I would get that cold rush when we were short of a nappy or some other vital item of baby care that had been left at home, and they would always come to the rescue. Each, in true and reliable grandmother style, would magically produce something that would make do from a secret stock that they would keep 'just in case of emergency'.

When Graham and I began to consider what was available in terms of baby transport, nothing seemed to be a sensible solution. Six single buggies were out of the question. That would have meant always having half a dozen adults on hand every time we wanted to go for a walk. There was little chance of that being the case. It was totally impractical, as nice and normal as it might have been for the intended occupants. The nursing help would be coming to an end soon and even with the extra pair of home-help hands, I could never be sure that all the babies could go out at the same time. Noticeably, there wasn't a pushchair specially manufactured to accommodate six babies on display.

'I don't think any of the pram manufacturers make buggies for sextuplets,' I finally declared, after hours of further research.

I stood at the door of the playroom and watched Graham relaxing there as the first signs of summer spread through the large picture window: a reminder, as if I needed one, of the pressing need to find a solution to our problem.

Graham didn't respond at first — but then again, relaxing wasn't exactly what was going on. The babies, topless in the warmth, were swarming around him, crawling about, having discovered the adventures that movement brings. Graham was dressed casually in a T-shirt and jeans, and was sitting with his back propped against the wall, one leg stretched out before him and the other bent at the knee to form a bridge. As I watched, smiling at this little moment of joy, a bright white nappy disappeared through the gap made by Graham's raised leg. Hannah was hauling herself over the other leg but was hindered by a tug of her toes as Ruth did her best to grab her sister's foot. More nappy-clad bottoms were at each of his sides as Kate and Lucy held precariously on to each of his arms, while Jenny, using her height, had somehow managed to almost squeeze behind him and had hung on to his neck with both arms. Sarah, opting for the easy life with less struggle, had decided to take a rest, taking up a sitting position between his legs. I stood there and simply laughed at the human climbing frame.

'They do make triple ones, you know, luv,' Graham had been looking at some brochures that had been given to us as a suggestion of the ideal answer to our requirements.

'It *sounds* great. Imagine: just you and me and the girls . . . ' And it would have been great — but there were too many problems, ranging from expense to collapsibility to common sense. 'Sounds like trouble to me,' I concluded. 'All I can see is the two of us struggling in the rain to collapse the uncollapsable. What if we had to get on a bus or through a door quickly? And the weight! Doesn't sound too clever to me.'

'We could always go for backpack carriers and slings. What do you think, Jenny?' He playfully pulled her gently over his shoulder down to his knee. She giggled all the way.

'Don't joke, it might be the only way!'

The first walk we had taken with Jenny and Kate, when they were the only two to have arrived home, was in a borrowed pram. By the time the others were home, the idea of a family walk had seemed a long, long way off. And it seemed even now, a couple of months after the girls had first arrived in the world, we were no closer to that dream I'd once held of taking my babies out for a stroll.

The answer came with the help of one of the baby pushchair manufacturers. In the same way the car transport issue had been sorted by one

258

company who saw the benefit to them in the appeal of a publicity photograph, our shining knights in the pushchair world struck a deal with us for some PR shots and in return delivered to the house three double buggies. They were brilliant and perfect for what we needed, being both manageable and practical. It meant even if only two of the girls were going out, we could use just one of the buggies, however, at first it did mean we had to have three adults on hand to take all the girls out at once.

★ ★ ★

The sun seemed to shine for the whole of the girls' first summer in 1984. We were out and about every day as soon as they had been bathed, changed and fed. It felt as if we were walking all the time and I am convinced that the health of the girls benefited tremendously from the long days of endless walking and the fresh air on the hills of Bidston.

The summer gave way to autumn and the walks continued under the orange-and-gold canopies of trees that lined the pathways in the forests and parks near the house. By the time the girls had reached the milestone of their first birthday, I think we must have been breaking the record for quantities of nappies used and bottles of milk drunk. I never had time for calculating anything, but along with changing something like 12,000 nappies we must have prepared at least as many bottles.

The first birthday was always going to be an

emotional and very special day. Graham and I felt it an opportunity to thank all our family and friends for all the kindness and support they had given throughout the year and invited them to celebrate the day with the girls at a party in a local hotel. Also, as a thank you to all the staff at the hospital, we arranged to take the girls back to the special care unit for a visit.

There is no definite moment that is absolutely right for 'next stages' as children grow up. Experts will say babies should be off bottle-feeding by one year to eighteen months, or that nappies should be a thing of the past and potty training complete by a certain age, but those 'rules' are just guidelines. The girls each had their own ways and although at times more than one would move on to the 'next stage' at the same time, for the most part it was one by one and when each was ready. What helped, of course, was a baby seeing a sister do something and wanting to try it for herself, so there were many times, especially at breakfast, lunch or teatime, when as soon as I'd turned my back I'd miss a new moment when one of the girls would mimic another holding a fork, spoon or cup.

Sue, our home help, was the sole survivor of the team of helpers supplied by the local authority and social services. Whether it was helping with the girls first thing in the morning, going for walks or making sure the had a sleep in the afternoon, she had crossed the line from home help to overall 'ACC' — assistant in charge of children.

It was a huge relief for Graham and me to

arrive at a point where there was no one else in the house. We were a proper independent family dealing with daily life and the only thing different was that everything we did was in half-dozen measures. It was six of these or six of those; whatever they were, it was always six. I was constantly relying on the instincts I had nurtured as a child and found to be a reliable resource in life, especially at work and going through the years of treatment. It was so important to keep everything organised at all times.

Any let up and one thing would have got on top of another and before we knew it life would have been much more difficult. More than that, without keeping measure of times and schedules, Graham and I would have lost all possibility of having the quality time that was so important with the girls. A child's expectations are high: their demands don't go away, their needs are basic and their responsibility is zero. So preparation was everything if we were to swim and not sink in our sextuplet world.

The average day began around 6 a.m. when Graham or I would stir to the sound of the ensemble in the adjoining rooms. Whimpers and cries would be some sort of secret code or signal between the girls, one waking another until they all made it clear they were ready for the new day ahead.

There was nowhere to hide and six nappies to change. Tiredness wasn't an option. The only practical way was working together, at least at the start. Then when the majority of the girls were ready to go, one of us, usually Graham, would start the breakfast with plenty of toast while I finished changing the last couple of babies. The girls were never changed or bathed in any particular order. There was never even time to think . . .

The girls were now on solid foods and bottle feeds were already a distant memory. The hundreds of bottles that had been prepared each week had given reasonable expectation that once we had moved on from the mixing of formula, and the washing and sterilising of bottles, things at least from a feeding perspective might get a little easier. In our dreams!

The most important machine in the house sat in the corner of the kitchen, appropriately enough right opposite the six highchairs the girls occupied during mealtimes: the washing machine. There were times I lay in bed late at night, when all the girls were asleep and Graham was gently snoring next to me, and in those rare moments of near-silence I could just hear the washing machine humming away in tune with the drier, which was strategically positioned directly above it, so that I wouldn't waste any time moving clothes out of one porthole and into another. Listening to the machines do their work, it was peaceful but more importantly comforting to know the 'Battle of Bidston Kitchen' was being won.

Basically the battle line was drawn across the middle of the kitchen floor. On the one side there were the clean machines — the washer and the drier — and on the other six children heading for the 'terrible twos' were finding anywhere to put their food except where it was supposed to go!

The number of clothes changes going on in any one day was almost equal to the nappy changes. But one look at the toddlers eating their meal and it wasn't surprising. I never knew where the spaghetti was going to land next!

Speed was an essential element that ensured success at mealtimes. There were still moments amid the chaos, however, when in the middle of a meal my heart would suddenly melt.

On one particular evening, the bibs were secure and the plastic spoons and dishes full of spaghetti letters were already sitting on the highchair trays. I had just finished filling the drier with another never-ending pile of washing. It had twisted and spiralled itself into one long colourful line of cotton and linen and formed an umbilical link between the two portholes of the machines. The sight of me struggling to get it all in was something that always amused the girls.

I turned to tell them not to laugh at my misfortune, contorting my body — only to see Ruth attempting to feed Sarah, caringly but clumsily mimicking what she'd seen her mummy do so many times. Ruth had been showing strong independence of late and had been insisting on taking hold of her own plastic spoon and feeding herself for some weeks. Sarah, on the other hand, was still as relaxed as ever and was happy to be fed by an adult or, in this case, her sister.

In a way, the highchairs were their first classroom. The girls were going through each experience of life at the same moment. There were no elder siblings to learn from or follow, so if one of them picked up something before the others and passed on what they had learned, every meal was a form of education and learning with a full class of six pupils. Ruth was now trying to show Sarah how it was done.

With the red sauce of the spaghetti stuck to her own mouth like smudged lipstick, and her eyes concentrating intently on the plastic spoon, Ruth made attempt after attempt at getting food to scoop into the spoon from the dish. Invariably, even when successful her hand then wobbled, landing the food back in the dish, but mostly her efforts just scooped it over the side of the bowl and onto the white surface of the tray. Sarah watched, fascinated.

Each of the girls' Mr Men bibs was adorned with strings of spaghetti, altering Mr Silly's smile or giving Mr Busy a decidedly stringy pasta wig or an orange moustache for Mr Bump and Mr Chatterbox a mouthful of food. Jenny, not concentrating, made half her food go in her mouth while the other half fell off her plastic fork, cascading down her chin. Her alphabet spaghetti spelt disaster all down another outfit, letter by letter dripping from her bib, to her dress, to the floor depending on her body movement.

I drew my eyes back to watch Ruth and Sarah. Feeding themselves with spoons in an 'across the high chair operation' was an ambitious process. Yet as Ruth at last held the food-laden spoon towards her sister, Sarah leant over to help and opened her mouth and . . . success! All the food was going in the right place and I thought, *OK, this is good. Getting the girls to feed each other could save us so much time . . .*

But just as I was dreaming of the future, the next attempt was made. This time the mission was aborted halfway through and left spaghetti nestling in Hannah's lap on the other side of Ruth.

This time my thoughts ran: *OK, this is bad. The food is not necessarily going in the right place. Second dress of the day and not even twelve o'clock . . . Time to intervene!*

I wanted to encourage them in all their new moments of learning, but that needed serious tempering with common sense.

The routine was similar most mealtimes at this stage. I always had a wet cloth ready and waiting because what doesn't go down can always be washed off. But the clearing up was a challenge in itself. With my left hand firmly on Ruth's head, keeping it in place, I would use my right hand with the wet cloth to wipe her face. With her eyes closed tight as the cloth cleaned her face, she would shake her head from side to side, and pull back in an attempt to stop the action. Then I would have to be quick to slide her dish away before too much mess ended up on the floor. A quick rub of hands and Ruth would be ready for a drink.

But what you don't realise is, as your two large hands are perfectly and successfully controlling the face-cleaning operation, two tiny two-year-old hands are happily swinging a plastic bowl from side to side out of your eyeline, from which more spaghetti than ever is going all over the place.

Cleaning the girls up after a meal was like what they say about the painting of the Forth Bridge — a never-ending process, you finish at one end and have to immediately start again. And so it was: as soon as I'd wiped Sarah's face and highchair surface at one end, it was back to Jenny to perform the same operation at the other. It was a never-ending cycle.

The bottom line was that somehow Graham and I had to stay in charge and gradually, one by one, the girls learnt the 'kitchen rules'. Each had their own moments of discovery and glory, each in a different way. But to keep control, everything had to be done by us with a 'no messing' attitude. We had to use our ingenuity at all times to divert attention with things like talking when giving out drinks and saying their names repeatedly as we went along the line. Hannah, Lucy, Ruth, Sarah, Kate and Jenny would understand, and eventually they became used to the parental voice — wielded with an authoritative tone when it was necessary — and they would hesitate, knowing you were in charge.

Oh, that winning feeling!

34

Mishaps, Accidents and Illnesses

With another move behind us, as our toddler girls settled into life at our new home in Wallasey, Graham would find as much spare time as he could to work on redecorating both the inside and the outside of the house. Outside was a job for the spring or summer and whenever the opportunity for DIY arose, some of the girls liked to help. While the idea of six little assistants might be considered a bonus, when your six apprentices have a combined age of eighteen, it's more of a potential calamity. If any serious work was to be done, the girls needed to be occupied in other directions.

The summer months were always a delight. The trees and bushes around our home were lush in different shades of green and the grass on the huge front lawn — seemingly always in need of a trim — would gently brush against the ankles of the girls as they played in the garden on bright days and learned to amuse themselves with every new discovery.

The garden was rapidly becoming a place of wonder to the girls. Everything nature had to offer at any one time was a source of amazement to each child, whether it was a flower or some horrible soily creature. I would always do my best to express equal joy whether a gift came in the form of a bunch of daisies from Hannah, Sarah or Kate or a wriggling worm squirming between a tiny finger and thumb of Lucy, Ruth or Jenny.

At each stage of the girls growing up, there was much to learn. At times I felt as if I needed all the wits I could muster as my imagination was measured against the creative demands of my daughters.

They were soaking up so much of life at once; every little thing was a source of wonder and intrigue and at times a challenge. The curiosity of children knows no bounds. As any parent could anticipate, our intrepid little explorers were keen to get into everything and everywhere, given half the chance. It meant a mixture of wonder and pride for us at each little milestone multiplied by six — but it also meant a different set of health-and-safety issues that we had to deal with.

One particular morning stands out. The four large bay windows at the front of the house, which overlooked the garden and play area, were looking tired and jaded and had been on the 'to do' list for repair and decorating since we had arrived. I had been hoping that Graham would find some time to tackle the outside of the house now summer had arrived and was pleased when he announced at breakfast that morning, to an attentive audience of six, that painting the bedroom windows at the front of the house was his job for the day.

Whatever Dad was on about, it sounded exciting to the girls . . . but their minds were already on the old suitcase in the hall. They always got excited when I brought this case down to the hall and, mindful of Graham's plans, it seemed the perfect thing with which to distract them from the messy paint and towering ladders that were to be used outside. The suitcase was a playtime signal: it was full to the brim with old clothes, hats and shoes, contributed collectively by my mum, Graham's mum and me.

A great favourite pastime of the girls was to dress up and they would spend hours walking around the house and garden with their little feet lost in my shoes and draped with bead-and-bauble necklaces of all colours. Mum or Betty, when either was at the house, or Sue, would keep the girls amused by helping to set up impromptu market stalls for the glamorous 'ladies' to shop at, using empty cereal boxes and other colourful items of redundant packaging for 'stock', which in the girls' heads made things real. But neither Sue, nor Mum, nor Betty was there that day.

The morning moved on and Graham was making progress, removing the old paint from the wooden window frames and preparing them for undercoat and gloss. I was busy gardening with the girls, half of whom looked like a stage act as their little feet scraped along the tarmac of the path, tottering along in their enormous low-heeled boat-like shoes, which they still wore.

One or two of the girls looked up at their dad on his ladder as the noise level rose. He was trying to force open a window whose hinges hadn't been exercised for years. It was glued together with old paint and stubbornly refused to open.

The only way Graham was going to be able to open the window was to prise it open from the inside. He quickly got down from the ladder and made his way upstairs.

Suddenly, I heard him calling me from inside the house.

The moment he had opened our bedroom door, he had heard Ruth's voice calling, 'Dad . . . Dad!' He thought she must have followed him and instinctively half turned, but stopped himself, certain that, although it was completely illogical, her voice had come from in front of him and not behind.

'Dad . . . Dad!' Once again she called. This time Graham looked straight ahead, to where the sound of his daughter was coming from.

On the outside of the window, a blonde mop of hair blew gently in the breeze and two bright blue eyes innocently blinked as she called out once again. He was face to face with our three-year-old, a storey up in the air. 'Da — ad!' There was a touch of impatience this time, as she proudly showed her dad her grand achievement of climbing to the very top of the ladder.

I had detected the urgency in Graham's voice and was at his side within seconds, just as he was beginning to talk to her.

'Ruth,' he said slowly. He knew how important it was to remain calm. 'Don't move. Stay exactly where you are.'

We swapped positions and I kept talking carefully to her as Graham shot downstairs and within an instant was up the ladder. To my relief, a moment later he had hold of Ruth. Then, as calmly as he could, whispering gentle lessons in Ruth's ear, he slowly brought her back down from her adventure.

While all this was going on, Sarah and Lucy had carried on walking up and down the path, each wearing a pair of my shoes, a hat that covered their eyes, a necklace in a matching colour and a chiffon trail. Having made themselves presentable to go out shopping, they were too busy attending to their grocery needs at Jenny and Kate's stall to notice any fuss going on with Ruth. In the meantime, Hannah, bucket in hand, had in her role as my assistant gardener abandoned her weeding job and been worm hunting. She was also far too occupied with these important matters to be bothered about Ruth's risky ascent.

There are lots of little accidents, illnesses and mishaps that are part and parcel of bringing up children, and with one child you can be no less vigilant than if you have six small spirits exploring every nook and cranny they can of life. But while most parents need eyes in the back of their heads, I needed eyes all over — and more besides.

The ladder episode was a lucky escape. It was a real hairy moment and a stark reminder of the danger that can happen in a split second.

★ ★ ★

Being on our guard for potential accidents was not the only thing constantly on our minds.

271

Right from the moment the girls first came home from hospital, we were always careful to look out for illnesses and symptoms that could turn out to be more than just a cold.

It was during our second winter at the house in Bidston that I experienced one of the biggest frights since the girls were born.

We had been fortunate with the girls' health overall, having until then mainly had to deal only with the mild traumas of coughs and colds. It was late in December and there was snow on the ground; something that was proving quite exciting for the girls, as they had begun to comprehend the changes in the seasons. The breakfast lessons that morning had included stories of snowflakes and snowmen. Other than the fact that the poor weather had postponed the morning walk, all was normal in the Walton household.

Sue had spent the morning dividing her time between her regular chores of cleaning and ironing, and her extra service of keeping the girls amused. Having finished her morning hours by helping to put the girls in their highchairs for lunch, she was now about to go home.

'What do you think we're having for lunch, girls?' I said to them. They were not quite ready for conversation, but words were beginning to come thick and fast, although they mostly each liked to hear the sound of their own names.

''Getti!' Hannah had already spied the cans I was opening and, recognising the colour, knew what was on the menu for lunch.

That met with an approval rating in the

majority and cheers echoed off the walls of the kitchen. A chorus of ''getti . . . 'getti . . . 'getti' led by Kate and Sarah was harmonised by Hannah and Ruth.

'No — o — o — o!' Lucy dissented.

'What's the matter, Lucy?' I gave her a funny quizzical face, close up.

'No — o — o — o!' She repeated herself but was louder. 'Lucy has beans!'

Before the word 'beans' had left her lips I'd already deposited six large ladle-sized portions of edible orange letters into each of the girls' bowls.

'Well, just try some spaghetti first, Lucy, see if you like it, then we'll see. OK?'

'OK!' She smiled, happy with the individual attention.

Alphabet spaghetti was the girls' favourite delicacy and, having served up equal helpings one by one along the row of highchairs, to various cries of approval, I quickly went to the sink to get the plastic spoons.

Graham, having finished giving the playroom a quick tidy after the morning's activities, popped his head around the door of the kitchen.

'I'll just see Sue to the door,' he said.

'OK. Say goodbye to Sue, girls. See you tomorrow, Sue!' I shouted above the girls' chorused farewells.

It had taken no more time than that to collect the cutlery, but as I turned back to my girls to give them their spoons, I felt my whole body go as cold as the weather outside.

'Jenny!'

The manner in which I'd called her name sent

273

immediate alarm through the hall and brought both Graham and Sue back into the kitchen.

Jenny had slumped in her highchair. All you could see was the whites of her eyes. They rolled up into her eye sockets alarmingly. A quick touch of my palm on her forehead indicated a ragingly high temperature. By now we were used to dealing with the usual coughs and colds, temperatures and runny noses, scraped knees and bleeding fingers that come with parenthood. It took a lot to shock us. And I was truly shocked. For the first time, the situation was frightening. Jenny was by now floppy and semiconscious.

'Call an ambulance!' I directed the plea to Graham, who had momentarily stepped back in disbelief, as Sue and I took Jenny from the chair. He ran to the phone as we put her on the draining board and began loosening her clothes.

'We need to cool her down as much as possible.' Common sense between the two of us was instinctively taking charge of the situation. She would probably have benefited from a bowl of the snow that quietly sat on the ground outside, but removing her clothes and applying cool water was the only logical thing we could do until an ambulance arrived; Sue was already soaking flannels under the cold tap. We stripped her off and started dabbing and gently rubbing the cold water all over her.

'More 'getti, peez!' Ruth had deposited much of her lunch into Sarah's bowl. The usual giggling, laughter and mealtime antics continued down the line as the other girls, oblivious to their

274

sister's distress, carried on eating and playing with their personal bowls of letters.

'It's on its way. How is she?' Graham was back in the kitchen, looking ashen and distressed, as we worked on Jenny to try to bring her temperature down.

'She's coming round a bit.' Slowly, Jenny had begun to react to the attention Sue and I were giving her. 'She's awake but only just. Keep an eye on the others.'

The usual pebbledashing was in full swing as the five highchair occupants created illegible words with their lunch on their clothes and on the floor.

Both Sue and I were aware of the symptoms of febrile convulsions, seizures which are often prompted by a high fever, and both thought that might be what was happening to Jenny. As with everything, the chance that something like that could happen in our house was six times greater than average. Although that didn't stop the shock, it did in a way help to avoid panic. We both just got on with doing what we thought we had to do and waited until the ambulance arrived. And waited . . . and waited.

'Do you want to go with the ambulance or should I go?' Graham was thinking ahead. We were so grateful that Sue had not already left and was there to help with the emergency, but she had been about to go home and that meant only one of us could go to the hospital.

It took an absolute age for the ambulance to arrive because of the icy surfaces on the roads. By the time the paramedics were in the house,

Jenny was showing signs of improvement but, confirming our fears, they too thought that it had been a febrile convulsion and they insisted that she had to go to hospital.

'You both go with the ambulance. I'll stay and look after the girls until one of you gets back,' said Sue, as heroic as ever. She insisted that it would be no bother and waited at the house until Graham returned a couple of hours later.

Jenny was in hospital for a couple of days. They ran tests on her while I stayed and slept in a chair beside her bed. It had all happened so quickly that the other girls weren't aware of it, but Graham assured me that they missed her very much while she was away.

The doctors confirmed what the paramedics suspected: it had been a febrile convulsion. It seemed that her temperature had become too high and that can be one of the causes. One of the most difficult things about bringing up the girls was that one of them nearly always had a cold. So it was possible that Jenny had had a cold with a high temperature. That illness, coupled with the fact that, because there were so many people around, it had been quite hot in the kitchen, might just have prompted the seizure.

The doctors told us that febrile convulsions were something that happened to lots of children, and that they weren't a cause for continued concern. Thank heavens for that.

★   ★   ★

Things settled down after that episode. It had been one of the most frightening moments I'd had with the girls and, from then on, the awareness of the possibility of it recurring with any of the six never went away.

We were really quite fortunate that there weren't any other similar episodes, but the colds and coughs did keep coming. The difficulty was that an illness was never in isolation. Either more than one child would catch something at the same time or noses would endlessly stream for days as one would catch something off another and pass it on; it could go on for weeks. We kept cupboards full of Calpol to combat infections and help us cope. It became a necessity, as it was just about the only thing that seemed to bring down temperatures and soothe feelings effectively.

We decided from the start that we would have to judge each medical problem as it came along and generally, as long as it wasn't a clear danger, we gave things a couple of days to settle down, giving whoever was under the weather a little extra personal attention. If we had taken a different approach, we may as well have taken up residence in the doctor's surgery waiting room! It is understandable to want to rush your children to the doctor's each time there is an illness, but for us it was impossible and far better to wait and see if anyone else went down with the same thing or if the symptoms worsened.

We had made sure the girls each had the MMR vaccine to avoid measles . . . but not before the next thing to hit us at Bidston: the mumps. First to contract it was Lucy. I used to wonder in cases like this whether it would be better for all the girls to be ill at the same time, or whether it might be easier to cope if they, as they inevitably would, caught it off each other one at a time. This time it worked out that there was a two-week incubation period for each of them and so the next one got it after the other . . . and the other . . . and the other . . . The house became a temporary clinic in which lethargy ruled and limply clinging to Mummy or Daddy was a never-ending episode lasting a very long time.

Graham and I, like all parents, absolutely hated it whenever any of the girls weren't well and when they held on for comfort, I always felt their suffering, sometimes feeling helpless once the medication was given and all I could then do to ease their pain was hold them close.

Overall, though, the mumps and the colds and coughs aside, we were quite fortunate in that the girls throughout those early years were quite healthy.

But as well as illnesses, as Ruth's ladder adventure had shown, accidents or at least the avoidance of them were also always on my mind. I was very conscious that everything had to be as safe as possible. The more children you've got, the greater chance of accidents, and so the more you guard against it. It was just another thing, as with so many other situations, in which I felt I had to be ahead of the game.

One of the reasons I think there were so few bumps, falls, mishaps and scrapes, especially considering all six were so active, was the fact that, in order to maintain our own sanity, we basically created a nursery school environment in our home.

Once the girls had started crawling and walking, they began to find their own way from the playroom to the kitchen. Along the journey, they had to pass the staircase. We knew that after a while it would prove too tempting to their curiosity. Graham decided to be doubly sure of safety and, because it was an open stairway design and not suitable for a standard baby gate, he set about making the stair gates himself, tailor-made to our needs.

One of the early house safety rules was that no adult was allowed to have a cup of tea or any hot drinks near the girls. Graham bought a pile of plastic covers for the electric plug sockets in case any of the girls put their fingers in the holes too. We were constantly trying to think ahead and combat potential threats.

With so many little curious minds to consider, making sure they couldn't wander when outside was also a necessity. The gates at the house in Bidston were all constantly checked and the garden area itself was enclosed so they couldn't wander off, which meant we knew they were always either in the playroom, kitchen or garden.

Both in Bidston and in Wallasey, we made the gardens into a safe environment and had a section of them paved so that the girls would have a level area on which it would be easy for them to push their dolls' prams. We thought about whether or not to follow what some regarded as sound advice about not letting little ones play outside in the winter. In the end, we didn't agree. With plenty of hats, scarves and warm anoraks on, the girls were just as happy playing outside in the autumn and winter as they were in the spring and summer.

Whatever the weather, the centre of attention in the garden was the large, luminous green-and-yellow multi-swing. The girls loved it and spent hours sitting and swinging in all seasons. It gave them, along with other activities in the garden, a chance to begin to explore their own feelings and find a spirit of adventure and discovery. Whether it was the new-found courage of Ruth and Jenny excitedly shouting, 'More . . . more . . . ' or the exhilaration of Lucy and Hannah demanding, 'Higher . . . no . . . higher!' or Sarah and Kate's pure joy, the brightness of all their eyes spoke volumes as they experienced the speed of the swing and the rush of air against their faces whenever Graham or I cautiously pushed from behind. It became an important well-used addition to activities for all of them.

At the back of each garden was a large shed, brimming with the favourite outdoor toys. It was full of all their prams and became a second playroom of sorts — although before they could get in Graham had to unlock the shed door. He had to be careful each time he did, as there was so much stuff inside that whenever the door was opened, a river of brightly coloured plastic seemed to flow into the garden.

It was all about getting by, being as practical as possible, working together and using our instincts and common sense and always having an eye for safety. All the decisions we made were what we felt were the right ones at the time for the good of the family. Thankfully, the lack of accidents seemed to reassure us that those choices were the right ones, at least for us.

It's much the same advice I give the girls today — never reproach yourself because making a decision is right for the time. Things always change and situations differ. You can only do what you do with the knowledge you have at that moment.

35

Assessments

Throughout the first five years of their lives, the girls remained under the watchful eye of Professor Richard Cooke. As well as the clinical assessments they were given by the local health authority as a matter of course, we revisited Oxford Street annually until the girls' fifth birthday.

There was always going to be special medical interest in their progress, if nothing else due to the fact that, at the time the girls were born, there were only three other sets of sextuplets in the world. The Rosenkowitz sextuplets were born in Cape Town in 1974; in Italy six years later to the day, the Giannis were born; and three months before the girls arrived, a set was born in Belgium.

The girls, though, were the first to be born all of the same sex. So the opportunity to study the different changes in them over the first five years was quite special. The fact that they had identical beginnings made the assessment very interesting to the medical profession. While Graham and I were always careful to have the girls' needs as our priority, we were so grateful for all the doctors had done for us that we felt as if we owed them something. We knew they wanted to assess the girls and so whatever they wanted us to do, we would do.

One of the things that illustrated the differences in the girls was the fact that they are not all of the same blood group, with Jenny differing from all the others. This apparently reflects the natural influence a parent can have on a multiple birth. Jenny, who was the biggest at birth, kept her position and has remained the tallest of the girls all the way through to adulthood. Overall, it seemed that the relatively low birth weight had not resulted in anything to worry about and each year we went to the hospital, Professor Cooke indicated how pleased he was with our girls' progress.

If we had had time to dwell on the assessments, we may well have found ourselves more apprehensive about how the girls would do each time, but the fact was we never had time to prepare ourselves mentally for anything, let alone worry about whether or not they would pass the assessment. Each time we went to Oxford Street, or the one time we went to the local clinic in Seacombe, by the time we'd got the girls dressed and ready, we only had a few minutes to get into the car and go in order not to miss the appointment. Besides, our instincts told us the girls were fine.

In all the five years of visiting Oxford Street, there was only one occasion when one of the assessments didn't quite go to plan. As usual, we arrived en masse at the clinic and took up half the waiting room area. One after the other, the girls were called in to see Professor Cooke for their individual assessment. This illustrated the point that unless there were at least two adults involved in the outing, these basic things like doctor's appointments would have been impossible to fulfil.

When it came to Jenny's turn during the final assessment, she was simply not in the mood for playtime. I knew she had been playing up and thought she might be a little reticent when it came to responding to requests. I couldn't have been more right. When it came to the basic test of catching a ball, the serious-minded and very professional professor attempted to engage Jenny in the 'game' — only to be met with an absolute brick wall of disinterest. Having exhausted his resolve, he eventually gave up and reluctantly but definitively awarded his young patient a big 'R' on her report for 'Refusal'!

One lovely thing about the annual visits to Oxford Street was that we always took the opportunity to visit the neonatal unit. The delight on the faces of all the nurses who had been there when the girls were born was special.

Another special thing was that, whenever we visited there, there was a chance we would see other parents who were living through the pressures and traumas that premature births bring. I remembered that time so well. The girls' visits were a golden opportunity to show that, even against all the odds, there was always the possibility of 'light at the end of the tunnel'. I hoped seeing the girls, who had once lain in those same incubators, struggling for life, might give those families some hope in their darkest hours.

The other, more common, assessments in which the girls would be monitored — as all children are — were regarding general development, weight, height, speech, behaviour and various social skills. Under normal circumstances, those assessments would have taken place at the local clinic close to where we lived. That arrangement was almost a non-starter, as after the first time, we went, we were politely asked not to return. Not for any behavioural reasons relating to the girls, we were simply too large a group in one go for the, then relatively small, clinic to cope with. They suggested home visits instead.

One afternoon, the health authority sent one of the clinic's health visitors on a mission to our house to attempt to go through all the standard measures, tests and general follow-ups required to assess behaviour and things like talking and walking. One of the bedrooms was seconded and became our home-made clinic for the day.

All the girls gathered around to be examined and waited in a line on the landing. Unfortunately, they were in a mischievous mood and their antics were more like a Marx brothers' movie, much to the dismay of the health visitor.

Following her yellow card from Richard Cooke, Jenny's point-blank refusal to talk warranted a second yellow and a sending out of the room. In the end, the health visitor gave up. The moment she left the room, however, Jenny began talking fast and fluently, saying that she absolutely was *not* going to do *all* those silly things!

Luckily, Jenny's excuses had been heard through the door and all was well.

36

Stars of the Show

Sue Thomas was experienced, gentle and sweet, and her easy-going manner made her a hit with the girls — and me. It wasn't long before her duties extended to baby-sitting, and eventually she found herself part of our 'travelling circus' on those occasions when we had agreed to do a photo shoot or make a new documentary.

For we had found that the media interest in our family didn't die down once we took our babies home, had them christened and popped them in their double buggies for their morning walks. No, the girls' unique status as the only all-female sextuplets in the world meant this story was going to run and run. In fact, today, over the thirty years since the girls were first born, there have been over a dozen documentary films made following the girls' progress from their first days in the special care unit all the way through to a special celebration of their thirtieth birthday in New York. There have been many moments throughout the making of the films that have made me both laugh and cry, but for all the sequences and set-ups it has always been the natural things that have created the most enduring and endearing memories.

Graham and I were concerned each time we agreed to allow the film crews and cameras into our lives. We were so very aware about whether we were doing the right thing by having the girls filmed, especially when they were young, when they weren't making the decisions themselves nor had the choice. Sometimes, if they started crying, Graham used to say, 'Are we doing the right thing? Is it right for them?' But while any financial reward that came was undeniably useful in enabling us to give the children things we might not have otherwise been able to afford, we never looked for anything that I might call unnecessary. I think the main reason for that was that Graham and I already had what we had always wanted, and that was a lovely family.

When the girls were born the idea of full-length films documenting every aspect of our lives couldn't have been further from our thoughts and even when we agreed in the first instance to be filmed, we never imagined that so many people would follow the girls' progress.

As it was, the first film was watched by one of the largest television audiences in the UK with almost 15 million viewers. Each year, for the following five years, there was a film broadcast at Christmas time, allowing an insight into how we were coping and the progress of the girls.

Yet although, especially in those first five years, there were huge television audiences of millions of people tuning in annually to watch Christmas 'specials' and we were massively in the public eye, we still somehow managed to stay the very private people we had always been before the world popped in for tea with the sextuplets.

No matter what new experiences came our

way, my upbringing, I hope, kept my feet firmly on the ground. Sometimes life seemed an eternal picnic — mainly because picnics were one of the simplest forms of family enjoyment and possibly because few other days out brought so much pleasure. As if to underline the point, to this day, whenever Graham and I have time to reflect on and watch some of the films we've made, we always stop and rewind to some simple scenes that were shot in the sands, such as when we walked the girls to the beach with their own little picnic basket. It was a simple pleasure, just doing something we naturally loved to do.

We didn't spoil the girls at all: we saved money where we could; we went to quiet places. We never shunned the publicity, but we did it as a separate thing to family life. We never threw ourselves in entirely. We've enjoyed, really, the best of both worlds, because we had a bit of the fame, which is nice in small doses; it enabled us to travel and have new experiences.

One of them came when it was discovered that 18 November, the girls' birthday, is shared with that of the world's most famous mouse, Mickey of Disney fame (who actually does have an official birthday that is celebrated every year at the various resorts). The then President of Disney, Michael Eisner, personally introduced the girls to the world's press when they were asked to be the official openers of the Wonders of Life exhibition hall at the EPCOT centre in Disneyland in Florida.

Another incredible experience was the time we finally decided to accept an offer from Fuji television to take the girls to Japan. We had turned down offer after offer, thinking the very idea was ridiculous in the first few years. But, eventually, we travelled across the world and we could not believe the welcome we received as television cameras recorded our arrival and broadcast it on the main evening news.

And we were fortunate that Sue was available to travel to Japan with us when Graham's mum, Betty, wasn't able to go due to having an operation. The whole journey would have been impossible without an extra pair of hands. Another reason I was grateful to Sue for being there was that on the journey I developed a bout of flu, which then decided to accompany me for virtually the whole six days we were in Japan.

As it was, we had been through a lot of deliberation as to whether to accept the invitation from the TV show in the first place, and not just because it seemed such an extraordinary thing to be asked to do. Knowing we had enough people we could trust with us to give the girls full attention was one part of making the decision to go. The other part rested on something that Graham and I had felt strongly about since the girls were born. The programme producers wanted them to be dressed identically when they were to appear, but Graham and I stood our ground, holding on to the principle of the importance of different identities. We reached agreement to appear only once we found a compromise on the issue. I got the girls multicoloured pastel pinafore dresses, and bought six matching, but differently coloured, T-shirts. Unable to get the last couple of pairs of similarly matching socks anywhere, I ended up borrowing them from a friend. There was also a little bit of last-minute tailoring to do as the dresses were all too long for the girls.

From the moment we arrived at the airport, we were shocked at the welcome we received. Before we had even learned the bowing etiquette when greeted by our hosts, we had to run the gauntlet of 'frenzied shutterbugs', as the Japanese paparazzi are known.

Before appearing on the live show itself, we agreed to do a press conference. 'Wardrobe manager' and 'dresser', Mum and Sue, had been a huge help in getting everyone ready in the hotel bedroom and we were taken by minibus to the studios. We were greeted by one of the producers — the one who spoke the best English. He bowed towards Graham and then to me.

'We would like for photograph, please, all girls in order. Thank you.'

'Order?' Graham was asking what I was wondering. Order of size, birth, hair colour? Photographers were always asking for a different type of line-up. Size order usually meant Jenny first and Sarah at the end of the line. Hair colour brought Jenny, Kate and Sarah on one side and Hannah, Lucy and Ruth on the other.

'Ah, yes!' The producer thought we understood. Big smile as he read from his clipboard. 'Please, as it is saying. Hannah, Rucy, Luth . . . ' (expected hesitation) ' . . . eh and Sara and, eh, Kate and Jenny. Please. We have crayons for colouring and paper.'

Hannah gave him a strange look as if to say 'you are rubbish at our names'.

'Oh, you mean in order of their birth,' said Graham.

'Ah yes. Thank you. Walton-san.' He quickly corrected the honorific. 'Ah sorry, I should be saying Mr Walton.' He bowed again. Graham bowed back.

He led us out into the studio area, where they had set up a line of six small chairs, with others for the adults, behind a long table. In front of each child's place was a full set of coloured pencils and a drawing pad. Ignoring a crowd of three rows of journalists and photographers, and before a camera had had a chance to flash, Ruth ran round and placed herself firmly out of order in seat number four.

Sue ran after her and whispered in her ear that she needed to move to the next seat. She was number three.

This meant nothing to Ruth. The crayons in front of her, the pad and that particular chair were now hers and that was the way it was going to be, no matter what anyone said about order of birth. She was in *her* place.

The curled lower lip of determination had rolled out, casting a shadow over her chin. This was Ruth's sign that her mind had been made up — and anyone wanting to change this little girl's thinking was going to do so at his or her peril!

Ruth was quite remarkable because what she was really doing was covering her doubts and lack of understanding as to why she had found herself suddenly in front of a load of total strangers calling out her and her sisters' names, asking her to do things she didn't really feel like doing at the time. She acted as if she was oblivious to the crowds of people and simply concentrated on the drawing, as if she was doing it on the kitchen table at home. Whether she was braving it out or genuinely cool as a cucumber, no matter what gentle coaxing took place, she didn't budge an inch. In the end, the production team decided they were happy with the girls in a different order after all.

It was the fourth time since the girls were born that we had been asked to appear on one of Japan's most popular programmes of the time, *Naruhodo the World*, which means 'I see' or 'to understand', but the first time we'd said yes. The programme focused on other cultures around the world, looking at amazing events and weaving them into a quiz-show format. That made us basically an answer to a question put to contestants — and a huge surprise for a live television audience.

As we filmed the show, on cue two enormous doors flung open, revealing us to a hugely worked-up excited audience, who were cheering, clapping and whooping. Only moments before, Jenny had been crying with an earache that had been building up during the day at the hotel. She was clinging to Graham as I held hands with Ruth and Sarah. Lucy and Kate, using Graham's legs like the trunks of trees to hide behind, peered out from behind him and then confidently followed his footsteps to resounding applause. Hannah, on the other hand, exhibiting her cautiousness, hesitated and studiously took in her surroundings, momentarily holding us all up.

Feeling the full force of my flu, I broke out into the biggest smile in front of 400 live faces and millions of television viewers. After a quick check that we were all there, with no hands available I instead gave my 'eldest' a gentle nudge of the knee as I guided her on to the stage.

The madness of that trip to Japan represented the insanity of our lives. We were rushed off our feet every day as it was, coping with feeding and washing and entertaining the girls, but every now and again the curveball of an international television appearance or a glamorous photo shoot would be thrown into the mix.

In amidst the chaos, I was more grateful than ever for the help we received from our family and friends, and especially Sue. And in fact Sue was to play another important role for the family when I was to be matron of honour at the wedding of my sister Alison.

The girls, then at an adorable bridesmaid age of nearly four, would have looked absolutely wonderful had they all lined up at the church. I had bought six pretty white dresses with pink sashes for the occasion, but Graham and I felt uncomfortable about the girls being in the church for the ceremony.

As the date of the wedding approached, Graham and I talked about it a number of times. The problem was that most people in the village who would come to see the bride had not seen the girls, and it was important to avoid the possibility of taking the shine off Alison. We decided instead that they would all go to the reception after the church service.

But then, as often happens, the unexpected landed in the form of sickness.

By the day of the wedding, Sarah was not at all well. She was sad and suffering and clearly the idea of six going to the reception had fallen to five. The plan had changed and Sarah was now to be looked after by Graham's mum, while the others were brought over to the wedding reception.

But Sue, in an effort to make Sarah feel as if she wasn't missing out, still made sure she dressed up in her special party dress. When Sarah arrived on Betty's doorstep with Sue, aware of her special party dress, she still managed a brave smile for her nanny, who made a big fuss of how pretty she looked and made her feel very special. It was a rare occurrence that any of them went to Nanny Betty's on her own, so to get one-to-one attention from her nan was probably a real tonic for poorly Sarah.

As a surprise to Alison, we also arranged with Sue, who was looking after the girls while Graham and I attended the ceremony, to bring just two of the sisters to the church to present the new bride with a horseshoe.

We added a little excitement for ourselves by allowing Sue to choose which of the girls would bring the gift. She knew them so well we knew she would choose well — and she did. Sue thoughtfully chose to bring Jenny and Hannah, the youngest and the oldest of the girls while the others were looked after by a family friend.

There had been no advance warning or announcement about the presentation; it had been a well-kept secret and intended as a brilliant surprise for the bride. And the idea worked a treat, bringing tears of joy to Alison's eyes and making the day complete for the blushing bride, as she embraced her little nieces.

37

Going to School

In the days leading up to the girls' very first school day, there was huge pressure from the media to have the 'event' covered for both press and film. At the time it was a difficult decision to make as to whether or not to agree, mainly because, even without all the media attention, we thought that from the girls' perspective making the transition from nursery to 'proper' school was enough of an event in itself.

Graham and I often talked about whether we should agree to the girls being photographed, as the beginning of their first school term loomed over us. The problem was, their arrival had been reported in such a sensational manner throughout the world — and it appeared media types had long memories. Five years on, they were still eager for more. As ever, for us the same issues were there as when the news of the birth was announced. The same issues had been there six months later at the christening, too. And now they were here again.

In the first instance, we were always trying to avoid too many journalists and photographers being in front of the girls. Most of the photographs were taken under controlled circumstances with as few people as possible involved. But because our 'event' had been such a big story, there were always going to be moments when it was impossible to avoid a whole crowd of photographers, and we had to plan accordingly. The first day at school was one such day. Like everyone else, we were going to enter the school through the front gate; but unlike everyone else, there would be twenty, thirty or even forty cameras flashing and snapping away alongside as many journalists, who were under pressure from editors to get the story, did everything they could to nail their shot.

In the second instance, we were conscious that sharing the moment with the public, who had been so kind in so many ways and had expressed so much joy and enthusiasm for us, was something we wanted to do.

Finally, there was the ongoing issue of expense, with six of everything always being on the list of necessary purchases — and school uniforms and accessories weren't cheap.

In the end, we agreed to stop as a family just for a moment at the gates of St Georges Primary School so that all the photographers and journalists could get the shots and the story they wanted; we agreed separately for the Mirror Group once again to have access 'behind the scenes' at the house a couple of weeks before.

One of the outcomes, as it turned out, was one of my favourite pictures of the girls. After trying a few different set-ups in the house and the garden, the photographer asked if it would be OK if the girls could sit on the garden wall. I think he was a bit worried that one of them might do a humpty-dumpty, but in fact they were well past the age of such worrying wobbles. Once in position, they were not just comfortable but thought it a great idea themselves.

Because the photographer wanted the girls to wear their school uniforms in the shots, this was evidently one of the very few occasions that they would be photographed wearing the same clothes. It had been a burning issue for Graham and me throughout the years that we wanted to avoid the appearance of all the girls being dressed identically. So to deal with the problem, and at the same time add an educational touch, each of the girls held a book and each book was different; I also made sure Hannah, Lucy, Ruth, Sarah, Kate and Jenny were each wearing different coloured socks. So I managed to maintain that precious but most important little bit of individuality.

The result was pure joy and one of those rare photographs, when so many faces are in one shot, when all eyes are looking in the right direction and every face is lit up like a beacon.

★　★　★

The primary school offered four classes for the new intake of children each year. The girls had already spent some time at St Georges at the preschool level and the staff knew them well, so I had left it to the teachers to choose the way the girls would be split. We made no suggestion to the school to help them decide which of the classes the girls would be in and who would be with whom. We weren't abandoning the girls to their fate but we decided that we would be just like any other parents and not interfere unless we had to.

As it happened, the way it turned out, with two of the girls together in each of three of the classes, was more than likely the way we would have done it. Jenny and Hannah were in one class; something Jenny made good use of, cleverly employing Hannah's spelling skills to help with her own. Kate and Ruth were in another class together, and Sarah and Lucy were together in a third.

The class structure sorted, all too soon the first day of school dawned. The years had passed so quickly. Yet now the house was about to become a completely different place with the girls being away so long during the day.

On that first day, Graham and I were both clock-watching all day, anticipating the end-of-school bell more than the girls. They just took the whole day in their stride, but as a mum I missed them and felt pangs of loss, as for at least part of the day I devolved some of the responsibility to the teachers.

When they did finally come home that day, a new ritual of telling stories from school began around the kitchen table. The big news of the day came from Kate, who simply could not get over the fact that there was a set of twins in her class. Sarah also had something to report: at lunchtime, all the children were sitting around one large table — and some of them weren't Waltons!

Each day I would wait at the school gate with all the other mums. Each day, one by one, the other mums would say a cheery goodbye as they collected their little one. As they disappeared, the circle of children around me grew until I'd counted in as many as I had counted out in the morning. The smothering of kisses was followed by excited chatter as we waited for everyone to arrive.

Jenny and Lucy, after the novelty of school had died down, couldn't get out quick enough and would run to the gate; others took their time. Ruth and Sarah were often busy chattering away, comparing notes from different classrooms. Kate would be checking her schoolbag, worried she may have forgotten something she wanted me to see, while Hannah would always be last across the playground, with her head in a reading book.

Whatever schedule I had, with plans to get things done, wasn't a concern of the girls. There were important matters to report; always some headline news of something a teacher had done or an astonishing act of naughty behaviour that had resulted in someone standing in the corner.

Artworks of differing degrees of accomplishment would cascade out of the classrooms into my hands and then onto the walls of the kitchen. Some of them involved the girls painting family portraits, which on occasion would have one or two of us missing for lack of space on the paper or lack of time, as there were too many faces, arms and legs to paint. Kate loved the art and creative lessons in school and more than the others would thrust her latest piece of art in my hand for approval when she ran out at the end of the day.

Schooldays for the girls brought about more house rules, some of which worked smoothly, others . . . Well, six personalities meant six sweet little perspectives.

For example, there was no way I was going to give myself extra work by allowing the girls to remain in their uniforms once they had got back from school each day. The washing machine and drier, my two trusty weapons in the war against grime, had enough to keep them on duty every day without unnecessary additional work. The girls didn't take much persuading, as they all wanted to get out of their uniforms as soon as they were home, however — as ever — they all had different attitudes to keeping their clothes clean.

Hannah and Kate cared most about looking after their school uniforms. Hannah because she was the most tidy; and Kate because she didn't want anything to go wrong with it. Lucy was the opposite. She was forever rushing in with coats and bags flying everywhere, usually reversing within a couple of steps to the tune of Graham or I shouting, 'Lucy! Will you pick that up?' Or 'I've just tidied the hall, Lucy!' She just wasn't bothered. Throw it on the floor, that's the type of character she was; and Jenny and Sarah were much the same.

I remember one occasion, a few years later, when Graham and I had been asked to do an interview. The journalist was sitting on our settee, chatting in the lounge by the bay window that overlooked the front garden. The girls, old enough to be making their own way back from school at the time of this interview, were expected home at any moment. The topic quite naturally had moved on to the girls and Graham was taking his turn in answering a few questions, proudly talking about his daughters' different ways of dealing with the end of the school day.

He had just finished singing the praises of Hannah and Kate, telling of how they were so neat and tidy when they got back.

' . . . and then there's Lucy.' He let slip a slight sigh of exasperation. 'Every day it's the same. She'll arrive home 'on a high', chattering with excitement about her day.'

'Sounds lovely!' The journalist remarked, then, as astute as ever, asked, 'Why the sigh?'

I smiled. I knew what was coming.

'Whether it's her mum greeting her home or me here,' Graham continued, 'she'll run over to give us a kiss which — you're right, that's lovely. I love all that. But Lucy is definitely the . . . *untidy* one.'

As we all responded to the description with a short laugh at the idea, the gate at the bottom of the garden clanged as a couple of the girls — the first wave of arrivals — led, coincidentally, by Lucy, took a moment to struggle with the ironmongery. At their age and height the gates loomed large and they took a little extra effort to open and close. Once through the gate, they scampered at speed with their pumps pounding the tarmac path, but paused for a moment as they caught sight of us in the window. Lucy's face lit up with a massive smile. She stopped, dropped everything and almost off-balance gave an exaggerated zany wave. They were then caught up by a second set of sisters who were also coming through the gate.

Graham continued, 'By the time she has made her way from the front door to where we are now, she'll have left a trail of bags and coats and shoes and cardigans, mark my words.'

I detected that our guest, thinking Graham a little creative, was a touch sceptic, but before she could ask another question the noise level in the hall was raised a few decibels. Having picked all her stuff up from the garden, Lucy and her sisters made their way into the house and clattered through the back door. Lucy didn't stop until she was in the lounge, where, in the time it took her to get from one end of the room to the other, schoolbags, books and coat had flown all over the place, landing half on the settee and the other half on the carpet.

Once the kisses, greetings and introductions were made, Graham, clearly amused by the accuracy and timing of his description, simply looked up, gave his throat a little clear, and said, 'As I was saying . . . ' We all roared with laughter.

Never one to be embarrassed, all Lucy wanted to know was what was so funny . . .

As for Ruth, she would always conform to the 'house rule' of no uniform after school, but only in her own way. It had to be something she wanted to do. Luckily, she, like the others, wanted to be out of the uniform. Phew!

I still see today the small differences that they began to express in those early days. If Ruth doesn't want to do something now, she usually has a good reason — and she won't do it. If something makes no sense to her and needs an explanation, she will always want to debate the issue and put her point across. It shows independence and a single-mindedness that gains respect. At first, though, it felt as if it was just a stubborn extension of the terrible twos . . .

The good thing was that all the girls settled at school very well. We had worked hard over the early years, even from a very young age, to make sure they had what my Nanny Fox would have called 'people skills'. From the first day that we had managed to coordinate getting all six babies out of the house, I had been to a mother and toddler group near to where we lived in Bidston. I had made friends with a lot of other mums who had children of that age, therefore Hannah, Lucy, Ruth, Sarah, Kate and Jenny all had friends their own age from outside the family right from the off; it was never just the six of them. All the girls, at differing levels, were outgoing. They were used to playing with other children, either from nursery and playschool or from mixing with their cousins, and as a result none of them was introverted or over-shy.

Once at school, they soon discovered that it was not just an institute of learning and education but the fertile land of newly formed friendships. In those first years at school the girls made some of their most important and enduring friendships. They all had lovely friends.

Yet their new social circles brought with them another unplanned job for me. Their friends were arriving on the doorstep thick and fast. I was now, among other things, a social secretary.

Almost the moment they had started school, invitations began to arrive for the girls to go to parties. This was potentially a minefield. For at first, if it was a party of a friend of just one of the girls, the mother would, perhaps feeling pressurised, ask all the girls to go. It was understandable: some thought that they couldn't ask one without inviting the others — which may be reasonable for twins, but with sextuplets that kindness would, in some cases, almost double the attendance and that wouldn't be right.

The other mums and dads were being kind and thoughtful, not wishing to be the cause of any upset between our girls if any felt left out. I wasn't comfortable with letting it go on, however, so I decided the right thing to do was to make it clear to the other mothers that they didn't have to ask all the girls. Once the message had been given, if, for example, Hannah and Jenny were invited to a party by one of their classmates, then only those two would go.

It could have been a different scenario and gone horribly wrong, resulting in no invitations for any of the girls. That would have been awful, so pre-empting the issue after only a couple of parties once the girls had started school went a long way to solving the sextuplet party-invitation dilemma.

It did help that many of the mothers I knew already; they were mums I'd met long before, in nursery and preschool days. I had thankfully developed some good friendships and even if it was only a passing acknowledgement at the school gate, we all got on well and I felt able to speak frankly to them.

Like the girls, I too was making new friends. Joining other mums on the school's parent teacher association straight away not only gave me an opportunity to give something back to the school, but it was also a natural and sensible way of keeping an eye on the girls, at least in those early years.

One of the ways in which I was able to help the school during the primary years was to go along on the school trips, assisting as a supervising parent. These would take place usually at the end of a term and we would travel to places of interest, not too far away, including the old Roman town of Chester, the bird sanctuary at Martin Mere and Thurstaston Hill, where I had spent many happy days out when I was a similar age to the girls with my mum or dad.

Ironically, everywhere I went in my home life I looked after six children — but on the school trips, the rules dictated that I was only allowed to have five in my personal group to look after at any one time!

At St Georges, the pupils always went on trips from school a class at a time. I would always have a group that included my girls, but of course because they were in three separate classes, it meant that I would go to the same place three times! They were supposed to be 'places of interest' but invariably by the time I had been to the same ruins of a Roman fortress and given the same nod of acknowledgement of thanks to the same Roman soldier three times in a week, they were rather less interesting for me.

38

The Multiplying Masses

'Going to the baskets' was one of the ways in which I managed to maintain the girls' individuality. As the girls went through primary school, I would always have on hand one big basket full of different coloured socks and another one full of ribbons. As they got older, whatever they were wearing, I would always ask them to go to the baskets and choose their socks or their ribbons. Each would select a different shade and in so doing mark herself out as independent from her sisters.

The colour coordination later moved on from ribbons and socks to include underwear. At first, when they were little, they used to wear any old vest and pants from the laundry basket, but as they got to primary school age I decided that the time had come for them each to have their own.

This was not as straightforward as it might seem; sorting one or two or three of similar age or size is one thing, but all six — well, the easy answer was just to let them keep going to the baskets. But I wasn't comfortable about it and knew at some stage the same thinking would eventually go through the girls' minds.

The solution began when I was inspired by a new and exciting recreation the girls now enjoyed. They all equally loved going to disco dancing, and for their lessons each of the girls had a one-piece leotard in her favourite colour. Lucy loved navy blue; Jenny, purple; Ruth's was pink; Kate's yellow; Sarah, turquoise; and Hannah, red. A few years earlier, they had all worn the standard blue ballet outfits, but the disco clothes gave them a chance to express their individuality by wearing the colours they each liked best.

My plan was simple: a few nights of sewing were set aside as I stitched onto countless vests and pants cotton threads in the colours that went with the disco leotard shades. So instead of the girls sharing everything that came out of the washing machine, I watched with a very satisfied smile as six young ladies sorted out their own underwear, all coordinated to their individual taste. They knew they had their own colours, so they simply picked their own things. I think in some ways it was probably something I did for my convenience, as at that stage the girls wouldn't have cared, but I also thought the time was right.

Over and over I heard the phrase 'take one day at a time'. That was all very well but if I hadn't looked ahead or tried to be as organised as possible, things would have fallen apart. It was so important to have as much as possible prepared in advance. Whether it was clothes for the following week or sorting out Christmas presents, it was all about being ahead of the game.

Graham and I didn't want to miss anything of the fun times if we could help it; it is common sense to get things planned ahead so as to be able to enjoy the moment. We knew intuitively that things had to be prepared in order to fulfil the importance of enjoying 'one day at time' — but the only way I could truly do that was to have half an eye on the future. It was instinct born out of the conscientious schoolgirl in me, or the bank cashier who wanted her columns to balance: both striving to fight the fear of not wanting to make a mistake or get things wrong. As it had always done, that fired me up to try to be as prepared as possible. And in truth, thorough preparation probably meant the difference between sinking and swimming. As the girls grew older, that organisation remit grew to include preparing the girls for the academic challenge of school too. For once they had settled into primary school, my six little five-year-olds would come home each day with progressively more homework. Homework was now a part of their lives and each of my girls had her own unique approach of how to deal with this new responsibility in her life.

Right from the start it was clear that Hannah was going to shine in this particular area. She would do her homework simply because she actually wanted to do it. Kate would do it because she was scared not to do it. So Hannah and Kate would both do their homework straight away, but for different reasons. Ruth would eventually get around to doing it, mainly because it seemed to come relatively easy to her, so she just got on with it when she felt the time was right, always managing to balance her timings to

310

avoid Graham and me having to get involved. Sarah wasn't that bothered, but adapted herself to the idea of having to do her homework — and both Jenny and Lucy would try their best not to do it at all!

With all six going through each element of learning at the same time, anyone would be forgiven for thinking that the breakfast room was an extension of their classrooms. Within a few weeks of the new school term beginning, the breakfast room cupboards were festooned with multiplication tables and mealtimes never went by without question-and-answer sessions as the food was served.

A certain amount of diplomacy was required on my part, as each of the girls' skill levels when it came to mental arithmetic progressed at speeds commensurate with both attitude and aptitude, but more than anything I tried to make it as much a fun thing as anything else. It also, in a way, felt like a natural extension for me after all the adding up I'd been involved with throughout my life, whether working at Nanny Fox's shop or the cake shop, adding Dad's scores up on the bowling green or making columns balance at the bank.

I had my little tricks of encouragement. As I brought the girls' tea to the table, I would be spooning mashed potato on their plates and then going, 'Five twos? . . . Three times four? . . . Seven eights?' They all had to answer their question and I used to go around everybody.

If they weren't learning tables at the table, the girls also learned from the multiplication tapes

311

we had, whether everyone was listening to them together in the living room or in the car on every journey.

Most of the girls grasped their multiplication skills quite quickly, and there were plenty of laughs learning, but Lucy's answers for the first few weeks remained firmly based on the two times table. Not even singing along with the tapes helped. Graham would sit down with the girls as well to help them learn the tables, and he began to spend more and more time with Lucy to help her grasp it — but she just didn't get it! She laughs today about it, saying it's still not her favourite subject.

It took a tremendous amount of parental patience before — after weeks and weeks of Graham taking her aside and going over and over how to multiply, and them both practising and practising more — there were cheers and whoops of joy from dad and daughter as Lucy made the mathematical breakthrough and finally mastered the two times table.

With the usual encouragement, I said, 'That is brilliant, Lucy. You'll be ready for your three and four times tables now!'

The smile vanished into a cloud of shock. 'What?! There's more?'

She had worked so hard that she couldn't face anymore. She promptly burst into tears — and Graham wasn't far behind!

I couldn't teach them the 'ologies' they were going to learn at school, but the least I could do was to do my best to help them with the basics. So, even though it was really difficult to find the time to give the girls one-to-one attention, reading was practised day and night and arithmetic, even as they grew older, became a constant game at mealtimes.

But all work and no play is no fun for anyone. Graham and I became accustomed to having even more children in the house as the girls began to have their friends over. Since the girls had begun school they had each made several new pals. There would of course be a crossover in places, where one would be a friend of more than one of the girls; some of those friendships have lasted throughout their thirty years.

At first, coming back to our house for tea was a special occasion. Then it seemed that it was such a special occasion that everyone wanted to do it. The numbers increased until in the end I had to put limits on how many friends each girl could bring back at one time. After all, even with them each having just one friend over, you suddenly had twelve children under your roof.

Without those limits, it would have been party night every night — and chaos no doubt would have ruled the house.

And chaos was what we were always striving to avoid. I had realised early on that only the right mix of order and variety would work to keep the household running smoothly in the long run. Establishing certain patterns to keep some sort of rule came in the form of little things like being strict about the girls all preparing for the day properly each morning. This rule emanated through the house — because unless all the girls understood that, at times, Mum or Dad knew best, the result would have been chaos. It was a case of a modicum of discipline or definite disaster.

There were no von Trapp whistles, far from it, but there were times after breakfast, when the last-minute gathering of coats, bags and homework began, that all six shot from the table like spokes from a hub, all running in different directions to find both necessary and unnecessary 'stuff'. Graham would go out, unlock the car, open the gates and start the engine. I would take up my post at the front door and give the three-minute warning in an even, controlled and clear motherly tone of concern.

By the time the three minutes were up and it was time for the third and final call, my tone had sharpened to ensure it shot through to every corner of the house and planted its message inside every car: 'Get in the car . . . NOW!!' This was a time thing — and it had just run out.

Yet variety was just as important as managing to keep the structure together, otherwise I think we'd have all gone mad. And without at least trying to be versatile, embracing all the girls' different ways, all the order in the world would have failed miserably — because family life would have failed. While things had to run like clockwork, each cog needed its own chance to spin. Time and time again it was apparent that talents like resourcefulness, and all-round adaptability, together with a touch of elasticity, would not just be handy but necessary.

Sadly, none of these attributes were available in offers of three-for-two or half-price on a 'parent' shelf at the supermarket. I tended to find that no matter how often I might have stopped and wished for some or all of these things, the only answer was just to get on and deal with the next thing. Invariably, I surprised myself, adapting and stretching what limits I thought I had to try new things all the time to keep the girls busy and keep up with their interests. That was becoming more important than ever, as school life was broadening their horizons at an ever-faster rate.

39

The Caravan Years

The girls' schooldays were complemented by the long school holidays. Graham and I were acutely aware that when it came to holiday locations, we needed to find somewhere relatively private. The girls were still a big draw for press and public alike. Ever since the girls were small, we wanted our holidays to be an escape, a chance for the girls just to be themselves. When they were two and a half, we'd found the perfect spot. It became over the years of the girls' childhood our little paradise. It was brilliant for Graham and me but, more importantly, brilliant for our six little ones.

Our holiday haven was a caravan site at Dinas Dinlle in North Wales. We'd had no idea of the natural beauty of the surrounding countryside or its historical and archaeological significance when we first booked it, on a friend's recommendation; all that came later. What we'd wanted was a simple bolthole or hideaway where we as a family could experience the natural elements of an ordinary holiday, which wasn't going to cost a fortune, but was going to give plenty of fresh air and days to remember for the girls.

It wasn't long before we began to appreciate how special the place was: the sea air, the beach within yards of the site, and the contrast of the countryside with the farms and open fields to play in. All this, set at the foot of Snowdonia: its mountains gracefully rising with snow-peaked tops to the blue skies in the summer or to the clouds on early spring and autumn days. It formed a dramatic backdrop to the site that became our retreat year after year as the girls grew up.

While our caravan was one of the biggest available, in reality it occupied not much more space than the lounge at Bidston. It was not surprising that once or twice we had conversations concerning sardines! Nonetheless, going to the caravan became a big event for the whole family. As well as the importance this little second home accrued for the girls during the long summer holidays, we used it as often as we could for weekends, too.

Planning once again proved well placed. We cut out much wasted time by preparing everything that the girls would need (including any special cuddly toys) and waiting outside the school gates for them on a Friday afternoon in a fully loaded vehicle. Invariably, they would arrive at the caravan site in full school uniform.

In the spring and summer, Graham and I always got a good feeling as the car climbed the A55 highway through the Halkyn mountain range at the summit, where the rocks on either side of the road form a gateway to a magnificent view. As we headed through, towards the sun, it would set over endless green fields and distant forests.

We were lucky in that a journey that would have taken hours and hours along the Welsh coast had been halved when a tunnel, under the estuary of the River Conwy, completed the North Wales Expressway not long before the girls' first adventure to the caravan. It was designed to speed up travel from the North of England to the tip of Anglesey and it certainly did its job. Most importantly, it meant we received fewer enquiries from those of the girls who were fully-fledged members of the AWTY club. That is, the 'Are we there yet?' club, to which I don't know a child who doesn't belong.

Once we had passed by every town and junction there was to pass by on the highway, and had left both Conwy and Caernarfon Castles still standing, there were two ways to get down to the caravan site. One was down a lane and the other way was down a main road.

'Let's go down the lane — can we go down the lane?' the girls used to shout out, almost in unison. It was clearly their preferred route.

And the reason was that going down the lane was when they started with the animal noises. One of the first times we went down there, one of the children said, 'There's a sheep.' And so they started making sheep noises; somebody else started doing pig noises and that caught on. And so, every time we went down the lane, they all started with these noises.

'I can see a snake!' . . . followed by hissing sounds.

The excitement in the car was infectious. It was great fun and the two adults in the car

318

usually laughed the loudest.

Sometimes, though, the noisiness in the car did get a little out of hand. Not surprisingly, after long journeys tiredness set in and if it didn't lead to sleep, then irritation took over. Children, no different to adults, have their own desires and opinions. A single child can be demanding. Two can argue with each other and sometimes, if you have children of different ages, the older ones can help keep the younger ones under control. But when six siblings the same age decide to fight for the right to be heard, bedlam doesn't begin to tell the story! Now and again, in the closed space in the back of the car, the scene could become horrid.

On one occasion, we had been for a day out to Criccieth and a crescendo of noise was coming from behind. It was hot, we'd had a long day and the girls were all arguing in the back of the car. I was tired from a full day of all the girls running about on the beach. As the pure dulcet tones of one of the family's favourite car entertainers, Doris Day, softly soothed my mind, I began to succumb to slumber.

'You get some sleep, Jan,' Graham said. 'Doris will soon quieten them down and they'll probably be asleep as well soon.'

'*Que sera sera*,' sang Doris, who had the attention of Kate and Lucy at least as they joined in the chorus.

As my head nodded, I could hear the noise levels behind rising. The girls became more animated in their conversation and louder. Each time my head fell, it jolted to wake me, but I couldn't fight the tiredness and eventually the noise became distant and the motion of the car sent me to sleep.

As Graham concentrated on the driving, the heat of the summer's day that had raised the temperature inside the car began to affect the girls' moods. They were hot, sweaty and tired: a recipe for trouble. Even open windows and the breeze that was created as the car wound its way through the country lanes didn't help. Everyone awake was feeling tired and uncomfortable.

And then Ruth objected to Doris.

'I don't want this tape, I want the other one.' She was referring to the tape with the girls' favourite nursery songs.

'Another tape!' Jenny shouted, agreeing a change was necessary.

In an attempt to keep the girls quiet on the way home to the caravan, I had given them each a small pack of sweets. That proved to be a mistake. All of a sudden, the top of Hannah's voice range woke me up.

'Give me that!' she screamed.

'No way, it's mine,' came the swift response from Sarah, 'I had it first!'

'*Hannah!*' Graham's voice had taken on the tone I knew was expressing exasperation with the girls' behaviour.

'No, you didn't!' Hannah yelled, indignantly. Each word got louder as she tried to retrieve the rogue bag of sweets.

'You've got your own!'

'Whatever will be, will be . . . ' Kate and Lucy were still singing at the tops of their voices and were not being diverted from their favourite song.

'Are we there yet?' Jenny was minding her own business, not getting involved in the confectionery dispute, but she knew that phrase usually got a response from her dad.

'Jenny,' Graham ignored the 'Are we there yet?' 'Sarah's sweets are somewhere on one of the seats, will you look for them, please?'

'Mummy, my feet are sore.' Ruth now felt she needed to be heard above the others and her crying only added to the noise.

All the girls were hyped up. The music, sweet and feet problems had fully sharpened my senses.

I turned round, twisting uncomfortably in my seat as the safety belt restricted how far I could twist. We were all tired and I could see that Gray had had enough.

I said to the girls, 'If you don't stop moaning and crying in the next few minutes, I am throwing this music tape through the window!'

Of course, they carried on and nobody took any notice — so I pushed the eject button on the cassette player, pulled the tape out, wound down the window and threw it into a field!

Stunned into silence, the girls were quiet as mice after that.

'Well, I told you,' I said, 'I told you I was going to do that.'

Out of the silence, I heard one single whisper. It was Graham's voice, next to me in the front of the car, coming from the corner of his mouth. 'But that was my favourite tape!'

Later, back at the caravan, I gave each of my girls in turn a silent kiss on the forehead as I tucked them into bed. We had done a lot of walking that day around the castle at Criccieth, and a lot of playing on the sands, so it was easy to sympathise with the exhaustion of my six sweet little souls — especially once they were fast asleep. I left them to their dreams of buckets and spades and ice creams, and probably fields with sheep and horses dancing to Doris Day.

I went into the lounge area of the caravan, looking for Graham, to tell him how peaceful they all looked after such a riotous journey home. It was a warm evening and through the window I saw he was sitting outside in a deckchair. He had a tired but contented look on his face.

I opened the door. As I stood behind him, I said, 'Are we there yet?'

His hand came over his shoulder and looked for mine, and he said, 'We're not doing too badly, are we, luv?'

It certainly didn't feel like it at that moment in time.

★ ★ ★

Fast-forward to another summer, and it was a different story. One day, when dark clouds fulfilled their promise and the heavens opened, we decided to take the girls to a real live circus for the first time.

It was throwing it down, absolutely throwing it down. Not surprisingly, the place was full. We trooped in and found space for eight on one of the wooden benches that circumvented the ring, where the entertainment was about to begin. I noticed that there was a bit of a gap at the back of the seats as each row behind rose to give a better view for the audience. They were also a bit damp and slippy, so I told the girls to keep their coats on and not to jump around.

Each of the animals came on the centre stage in turn — and they were soaking wet! Long-faced horses trooped miserably into the ring. The poor things had been in an open field by the side of the big top — which was beginning to form ominous bulges in its canopy roof above as the rain fell even heavier than before. It was all a bit grim, really. But it was about to get grimmer.

In came the elephants. Very impressive! The girls were getting excited, despite the cold and damp. Children can't help wriggling about a little, especially if there's a ten-foot-high elephant with an eleven-foot trunk pointing right at you.

Graham nudged me. 'Isn't the bloke sitting on the elephant the same guy who sold us the candy floss?'

'I think you're right,' I said, laughing, 'and the assistant who was taking the money at the ticket office.'

The ticket office — it snagged in my brain as a reminder. It was where I'd last done a head count. I instinctively turned to the girls and did a quick tally.

Immediately, my hand grabbed Graham's arm

so hard the blood must have hesitated in his veins. 'Five!' I cried.

'What?' Graham said in disbelief. By now he had Sarah and Kate's heads in his lap; the elephants had proved a little overbearing.

Not believing my eyes, nor wanting to, I needed an instant independent recount.

'I can only see five of the girls!' I hissed to Graham, hiding the small element of panic growing inside me.

'But I've only just counted them!' Graham cried. He did a quick head count. Sure enough, there were only five. Ruth had disappeared!

We tried to collect our thoughts and not panic. It was seconds since Graham had done his own count, when Ruth had been present. Everyone was too tightly packed together to think anything sinister had happened. There must be a simple solution to the mystery.

And there was. It turned out that the approaching elephant had proved too much for Ruth. She tried to make herself smaller and smaller and shrink further and further away from it — so much so that she slipped through the wooden slats of the seats and fell through the gap in the seating. It was quite a drop, but thankfully to lush grass below.

We found her moments later. While she was a little shaken from the shock, I think she was actually more in a state of relief at having escaped the 'giant' elephant's trunk.

★ ★ ★

In between holidays at the caravan, the girls would plan their favourite things to do for the next visit. Sometimes, to distract my six little girls — who were by now seeming not quite so little, as they fast made their way through the years of St Georges — I would ask them to make lists of what they would like to do on the next trip. The one thing that was always common to each of their lists was a visit to the Rabbit Farm. And each girl would write its name with the two letter Bs each growing two enormous rabbit ears, emulating the sign on the gates of the farm itself.

The farm has now been open to the public for over thirty years, making the Walton clan some of its earliest pioneering 'watch where you tread' visitors. Not far from Criccieth Castle, hidden away in the small village of Llanystumdwy, the pet farm was a perfect paradise for the girls. They were absolutely the perfect age for it as youngsters and they used to ask to go there every day. If we went to the caravan for a week, we would always go at least once. They loved it there.

And so did I — because it was the perfect venue to take away concerns about one of the girls slipping out of sight or worrying that head counts were not always going to add up. Here they could run about to their hearts' content while also learning about the responsibility of caring for the smaller animals, by holding the rabbits, the lambs and the little puppies and stroking and feeding them with the help of the staff.

Of course, the farm's status as a collective

favourite also meant it was one of those essential sanity tools to keep the girls' behaviour levels where I needed them. It was always, 'If you are good, we'll go to the Rabbit Farm in a couple of days!' Common sense rule number one with lots of children is to learn how to dangle a carrot; in the case of the Rabbit Farm, it literally was a carrot!

Whenever any of us talk about the caravan it's always a source of joy and happiness reflecting on some of the best years of our lives.

40

Going Places

An essential skill for any child, but especially those going regularly to the seaside on weekend trips to a coastal caravan, is to be able to swim. During the girls' time at St Georges I decided the time had come to make sure all the sisters learned to swim. My mum and dad never took me to swimming lessons and I thought it important that the girls were given the chance I didn't have to learn.

It had been a concern for us for some time for a number of reasons. Firstly, of course, the summers we were spending at the caravan site had highlighted the importance of swimming. With the caravan site's pool being so popular with the children and the sea so close, it was important they were always going to be confident in their own ability in the water.

We had also experienced a fright when Graham had taken all the girls down to the pool one weekend while I stayed a little longer at the caravan to make the sandwiches. The girls were excited about going in the water and didn't want to wait so, although we both had usually watched over them in the pool on previous occasions, Graham, being a proficient swimmer, gave us enough confidence that everything would be alright until I arrived with the picnic.

As Graham watched over the girls, each with their inflatable wings and rubber rings, he suddenly became aware that the constant count to six was one short. Quickly glancing around, continuing counting and mentally naming the girls as he checked the faces bobbing in the water, he was horrified to realise Ruth's ring was empty. She had slipped clean through her ring and was submerged completely under the water. Within seconds, Graham had dived in and scooped her from below the surface, fishing her out and saving her from any serious trauma.

As well as these experiences, Graham was also always reminding me that it was a sensible move for us geographically. Living on the Wirral we lived on a peninsular surrounded by water, so to take the precaution of making sure all the girls were given the opportunity to be good swimmers seemed a no-brainer. It was something that had historically been such an important consideration in the generations of the Walton family that Graham and his siblings were even given swimming contracts for the local baths as Christmas presents each year.

Dealing with the logistics of teaching six girls to swim, though, would prove to be another challenge. All six at the same time was not going to be easy. The local baths situated by the Town Hall in Wallasey were in an aged and architecturally antiquated building known as Guinea Gap. It was always packed out so giving the girls one-to-one attention or at least the full attention of an instructor was not going to be easy.

Like most things, however, the answer to our problem came unexpectedly. A much-needed refurbishment was announced for the baths, resulting in an impending temporary closure, but more importantly a drop in the number of learners, as people waited for the new, redesigned pool to open instead of learning in the old baths. The answer was for Hannah, Lucy, Ruth, Sarah, Kate and Jenny to have lessons before the baths closed.

We enrolled the girls for a ten-week crash course of lessons, having decided that was the best way to ensure they were all proficient by the time the building closed for the winter works. I knew they were all going to take to the water differently, but we had to give it our best shot.

And we did. Straight after school, night after night, week after week, we made the swimming pool a second home.

Winnie, the swimming teacher, was absolutely brilliant, and with her personal attention the girls took to the water. As with most other things with my six girls, they progressed in different ways and at different speeds, some of them learning quicker than others, but together they enjoyed being in the pool environment. The more they swam, the better they got; some quickly learned the basics and even began climbing the various levels of proficiency; others would follow at their own pace. Each stage they completed was rewarded with a badge.

Adding to their enjoyment when we started, I made sure the girls each had their own colour costume and a special Disney towel; a different character for each of the girls. As they earned their badges, I sewed them on to their towels and as each week progressed metres were added to most of the girls' distances as they went from 100 to 500 to 1,000 metres, increasing the number of lengths they could swim.

The badges began to fill the girls' towels and soon there was a line of badges on all the towels . . . except one. Ruth just couldn't get it; as hard as she tried, she just could not do it and was lagging behind. Sometimes, I wondered whether or not it had been the traumatic episode at the caravan site pool that was the reason for her struggling to learn. She was as determined as the rest but it just wasn't happening for her — and the lower lip was starting to curl at the sight of all her sisters winning more and more badges. Jenny was strong and took to the water brilliantly; Lucy was just as good; and the others weren't far behind.

In the end Winnie, who was a fantastic teacher, ensured Ruth didn't get left behind. She had a couple of methods; some working on the body and some on the mind. The physical came in the shape of wings, floats and a long pole with a hook and a harness attached, which supported our enthusiastic but struggling daughter around her shoulders so that she wouldn't go under. The psychological was in the form of an award of a special badge of achievement when she finally managed to complete a breadth instead of a length of the pool. And as soon as the little Puffin badge was sewn on to her towel, Ruth was so pleased she swam and swam until she quickly caught up with the others. Together, over the ten weeks, they became more and more confident.

★ ★ ★

One evening, Graham and I were sitting watching the girls' lesson when Winnie casually threw what looked like a black brick into the deep end of the pool. The oblong shape was a prop used as a test of swimming proficiency; the idea being to mimic a rescue scenario. We didn't think the girls were ready for this yet, as it meant diving down and retrieving the brick without letting your feet touch the bottom. You had to keep both hands on the brick and move forward by leg power alone.

The girls were now taking a rest, sitting on the edge of the pool with droplets of water falling off eyebrows, noses and chins onto their wet costumes. Amid the odd involuntary shiver, one or two of the girls looked up at the sound of the splash, glanced at the ripples caused by the offending weight and then went back to thoughts ranging between 'Did Winnie really have to use the hook on me again?' to 'I can swim now — how much more of this do I need?' to 'I wonder what's for tea?'

Those thoughts were milling around the minds of only five of the girls. The sixth had something else entirely going on. Lucy had been watching Winnie and wondered what she was up to — because she had thrown the brick in without saying anything to the girls.

Suddenly, Lucy pushed herself into the water

and swam towards the deep end. She got close to the spot in the deep end where the ripples had almost vanished and in one smooth motion she raised herself slightly out of the water, bent forward and dived in, forcing her body to go below the surface until all we could see were her flipper-mimicking feet flapping forwards and backwards until they too were submerged below the surface.

For a second, I panicked. None of the girls had done anything like this; it felt far too advanced. But as I rose from my seat, Graham gently put his hand on my lap, reassuring me at the same time. He was confident Lucy not only knew what she was doing but was going to succeed.

Almost before I was back down in my seat, the black brick appeared, cupped between two little hands, in the same spot where the feet had vanished. Lucy's face then spluttered above the surface . . . but quickly beamed with the biggest smile. She had done it! She'd picked the weight up from the bottom of the pool and now held it triumphantly in the air, to the impressed cheers of all her sisters.

Yes, they could certainly swim now.

★　★　★

Swimming wasn't the only new skill demanded by the girls' childhoods. And it fell that much of the mechanical magic necessary to keep the girls mobile and a smile on their faces was Graham's department. Once he had set out on this particular road, he soon realised it was never-ending. There is not a great deal of difference between a dad holding his daughter as she rides her first bike and the same dad fifteen years later as he sits with his daughter after her first few driving lessons.

First there was the legend of Kate's skates. As with the swimming, one of the girls was always going to be last to learn any new thing they ventured — but even though that is what logic dictates and the competitive spirit between the girls was never ruthless, there were still different degrees of how much each was bothered about their progress — or lack thereof. Roller skating was no different. In that instance, it was Kate who couldn't do it. Invariably she would look as if someone had frozen the frame that pictured her on wheels as she stood stock still, not daring to push one foot in front of the other.

Worse was her awareness that, as much as she couldn't move, the other five were off and away, wind in their hair, winding their way along without a care in the world. Not that Kate thought all that, she was totally focused on not falling over, but that's how it was through my eyes. As it was with all the girls, I hated seeing any of them upset and I would always feel their crying cut deep inside me, even if the pain was tempered by the knowledge that, more often than not, whoever the last one was would eventually get the hang of it and succeed in the end.

But until then, the tears flowed as Kate watched her sisters whizz away to the distant ends of the driveway at the front of the house. She was worried she was going to fall over, worried she wasn't going to learn at all and worried the others were all going to be able to skate and she would be left behind.

Some of the girls quickly became quite accomplished and as each day passed and the skills of the others increased, Kate became more frustrated and in need of fatherly support. I would watch from the kitchen window while finishing the dishes as Graham would hold her and gently whisper into her ear, encouraging her time and again, never giving up until the day, with a face full of serious concentration, she finally mastered the art and skill that skating demands and slowly, with only the slightest of wobbles, wheeled from one side of the patio to the other.

Within days, any serious thought or worry about moving about with four plastic wheels attached to her feet disappeared as instinct set in and second nature released smiles of joy that beamed from Kate. They filtered, along with all those other moments, straight into my heart.

Once the girls had experienced the thrill of wheels under their feet, it wasn't long before bicycles were on their lists of objects of desire. A slightly more expensive hobby for the girls, but there was such equal enthusiasm that this was something we wanted them all to have at the same time. The bikes became birthday presents. Budgeting them into a celebration eased the purse a bit! As sensible as Graham and I tried to be in balancing the finances, the bicycle itself was just the beginning of the flow of pounds out the door. Convincing six excited children that the bikes for their birthday could only be ridden once Santa sent the stabilisers for Christmas wasn't going to work! Then there were all the extra safety measures to protect heads, arms, elbows and knees, all of which were at the mercy of both the wibbles and the wobbles of the learner cyclists.

The stabilisers were another minor nightmare for Graham, with nuts, bolts and washers slipping between oily fingers, flipping in the air and one or another disappearing just when he thought he had completed a set. As soon as he had finished one bike, there was another one to do and for a couple of days the garden looked like a production line.

No sooner were the bikes fit to go, some of the girls were off confidently on their own, while others had Graham bending over and holding them steady for days before they all were confident enough to ride alone.

After that, the bikes became part and parcel of the summer holidays when we went to the caravan. It was a lot of work to carry and transport so many cycles to the site, but the freedom and fun it gave the girls made it all worthwhile.

The girls each developed their own interests through their childhoods and, later, their teenage years. There were some things that they all wanted to do at the same time, like the roller skates and the bikes, but as each year went by they would find their own interests too. There were half a dozen fertile minds each dealing with new experiences of life, yet at the same time responding differently according to their individual personalities.

Hannah was endlessly absorbed in a book and loved writing and reading, which eventually developed into her own folder of poems. Lucy always had her mind on pets and a 'dog project' at school that seemed to go on forever. This was the catalyst that brought Peggy, our pet mongrel, into the family. For Ruth it was writing stories and running. Kate's creativity meant that there was always one painting or design being worked on, and she loved music. Jenny was very athletic throughout the childhood years and one of her great interests was swimming, at which she excelled, and Sarah was always content to be in the company of the others, and with her favourite book.

Whatever the next passion was, Graham and I would always try to make sure there was a fair and equal balance in catering for the girl's desires and dreams while also accommodating the rest of the family. Usually, it worked out fine.

And it was a sheer joy, as the girls grew and expressed themselves, to see how each was growing into her own person. We had long insisted that each girl was an individual. Now, as they chose their hobbies and interests themselves, they were showing the world that this was most definitely the case.

41

Parent-Teacher Evening

It was towards the end of term in the winter of 1994. Our six eleven-year-olds had almost completed their first term at high school and it was time to get a first progress report. Each girl had made her own journey through the usual subjects of mathematics, English, science, history and geography. Whether they were enjoying them or not was another matter. There were six different brains working away and some had settled into education better than others. The only way that Graham and I could know for sure what was going on, though, was through the tried-and-tested system that every school has to accompany the end-of-term reports and occasional letters to parents. It was the parents' evening at school.

★　★　★

The move to secondary school for the girls had gone without any major problems. It had been a slight concern because often it can be difficult to place one child in the school that you feel is right for the child and the family, and with six secondary places to be concerned about things may not have gone so smoothly. The only practical way from our point of view was for the girls to remain together at the same school. The idea of any of them being isolated away from their sisters was something Graham and I would have done anything to avoid. As it was, the junior school, St Georges, almost acted as a feeder school for Weatherhead High School, which also happened to be just up the road from our house, so it was really practical to have them there.

Dealing with the transition of the girls going to high school was no different from anything else. We were constantly working to a plan that had to be flexible enough to change as we went along. Although the school had guidelines and information we, like any parents, had our own set of unique circumstances. The pressure that each situation brought — whether buying new uniforms, paying for school trips or organising a new curriculum of schoolbooks — was, of course, compounded, organised six at once; in that, as usual, there was no older sister to hand anything down, so buying for one meant buying for six.

There was one less pressure to deal with when the girls began their journey through secondary school, though: no press and no cameras. Just before they started at the high school, we had some pictures taken outside Weatherhead with the girls all in a line, and they were published, but there was no great fuss or press call. And other than that, we avoided the media circus.

In fact, once the girls had settled into junior school, it was as if it was a watershed. Graham and I were acutely aware that over the next few years they would more than likely be better served by not having cameras involved in their school life. We did a couple of films when the girls were ten and twelve, but we insisted the school was out of bounds during term time. The balance had worked and as the girls prepared to start at Weatherhead, whatever else they might have been worried about, we at least knew that fighting a media scrum on their first day didn't need to be on the list.

There are moments we pass through in our lives that seem to act as a stepping stone to adulthood. The change of uniform from the junior school to secondary is one. Unlike the first time I prepared the girls for school, with their contrasting socks and individual books, this time they all dressed themselves. There was an impromptu fashion parade in our front room as the girls all lined up in their new uniforms.

I cast my gaze down the line of young women, barely able to believe my eyes. My mother's eye noticed that there were a couple of white collars on Kate and Lucy looking a little creased; and Hannah's and Ruth's ties needed straightening. But any attempt by Graham or me to help was met with an eleven-year-old's rebellious turn of the head and an insistence on self-correction. Now they were at the 'big' school, they were able to do these things for themselves. But Sarah was happy for the sleeves of her sweater to be turned over at the cuffs.

As I performed this simple act of motherhood, I instantly recalled myself at the girls' age, looking in the mirror in my bedroom at Rose Gardens and feeling proud in my new 'old' uniform that Mum had bought for me.

At the end of the line there was Jenny, our tallest schoolgirl, with a serious look that was hard to decipher. I wondered whether she was altogether happy about more of this school stuff; or maybe she was already thinking that no matter how new it was, school uniforms were not exactly the most fashionable clothes to wear. She did, though, look even taller and the corners of her mouth turned up, unable to resist a smile, when her dad told her and her sisters how beautiful and smart they all looked. She then let me straighten her tie, just as I had done when she was a five-year-old on her very first day at school.

As the new chapter in the girls' education began, tales continued to be told at the kitchen table, of daily life at school. One thing the girls had to adjust to was the increased size of the school body — containing plenty of new faces. The children they had gone through nursery and primary school with knew them well and any idea of 'celebrity' wasn't an issue — even less so for the girls, as they didn't know any different — but at big school they met fellow students who had only ever seen them on the TV or read about them in the paper before.

When they started at the high school, they noticed that if they happened to be all together or if there were a few of them with each other at breaktime, other pupils started counting them; older girls would, on seeing the girls at playtime, try to make sure they saw a 'full set'. They would go around the playground and see if they could count all of them. It didn't bother the girls very much, though. Something they found more amusing was one rumour at school that their autographs were on sale in the toilets for fifty pence; in later years, Lucy would always quip that if she'd known anything about that, she'd have charged a pound!

For the most part, the girls were more concerned with relating stories from their lessons. Time and time again there would be squeals of laughter round our kitchen as a caricature of a favourite or not-so-favourite teacher was set up and described by one of the girls for the benefit of the others. Who was the strictest and who was the kindest; which one's face had blushed a deep crimson in exasperation of a particularly popular classmate who was always winding up this particular teacher?

Whichever teacher they were talking about, there would always come a time at least once in every school year when Graham and I would come face to face with all these personalities. It was quite uncanny seeing how accurate some of our girls could be in sending them up!

That amusement aside, though, a parent-teacher evening was quite simply a nightmare. Graham always described them as the worst nights of his life! It may seem a little exaggerated, but this was no ordinary night for us. Firstly, it is difficult to think of any other experience we went through during the school years that was more embarrassing. It was like we were the laughing stock of the school, although it was all done good-naturedly. Having a large family is one thing, but even if you have a number of children at the same school, at least they are likely to be spread across different years and different parent-teacher evenings. We had no such luxury. This was one of those events that needed all the best forethought and planning to make sure we got something worthwhile out of the night.

In the winter of 1994, on this very first night of the parent-teacher evenings that we would be attending for the next five years, the blueprint for the way these events were to go was laid down. The evening would begin in the same way with fast food at the tea table, something like fish fingers and chips, and either my mum or Graham's mum would be seconded to be in the house while we were away. It wasn't like one of our normal nights out, as we didn't know what time we would be back.

That evening, there were a few noticeable differences in behaviour as the girls' awareness of our impending visit to their place of 'work' drew near. A couple of the girls were on their best behaviour at home and were helping to bring plates to the table. All seemed excited — or disturbed — by the knowledge that their private world was about to be invaded by their parents. For secondary school was much more private. Unlike at St Georges, where I had helped out on school trips and with cake bakes and school fêtes, Weatherhead required no such assistance. Other than the parent-teacher evenings, we barely walked through the school gates.

Now, we were about to be face to face with the

adults they knew so much better than we did. Over tea, Jenny and Lucy stressed the point that they had a distinct advantage compared to Graham and me on the matter of which teachers were the best ones to see and which were best to avoid.

'Well, really, Mum, there is no need to see any of my teachers.' Jenny was quite matter of fact.

'You don't want to get into any trouble . . . ' Hannah warned; she had assessed the situation and knew where her sister was going with the line of argument in the teatime teacher debate.

'No, Jenny is definitely right, Mum — and the same goes for my teachers too. You definitely don't need to go and see . . . ' Lucy had clearly gone through this plan with Jenny and they thought the art of persuasion might just succeed.

Other teachers' names were now brought up by Kate, Ruth, Sarah and Hannah, each of whom had their favourites. To show the girls my intention of avoiding bias and attempts at influence founded on unrepresentative scales of size, appearance, and degrees of how horrid or how strict any teacher may justifiably have been, I held up my notebook.

'Girls, listen.' Twelve eyes focused on the writing pad in my hand. 'I'll make a note of everything the teachers say about you all so I won't forget anything.' Not surprisingly, this didn't go down too well with Jenny and Lucy.

However, the truth was that the notebook was absolutely necessary. There was no way Graham and I were going to be able to remember so many comments in one night.

That first evening, we knew we were in for a long night. After all, even if only the basic subjects were covered, it meant that we had to sit through at least thirty discussions of how the girls were progressing. One notebook would barely be enough. We planned to get to the school right at the starting time of five o'clock, but feared we would still be there at ten o'clock when the school gates were due to clang shut.

At 4.45 p.m., we walked to the bottom of the path. As we went through the gate, I turned to close it and put the handle on its latch. I nudged Graham.

'I think I'm experiencing role reversal.' He had no idea what I meant. 'Just take a look at your daughters,' I said, pointing to the bay window of the television room.

They were all there, with my mum in the middle with the biggest smile, with one arm around Ruth and the other around Sarah to make sure they didn't fall off the chair. Hannah and Kate were leaning on the back of the settee with their noses pressed against the window and on either side of them, Jenny and Lucy were sending hand signals to us, as if to remind us of their earlier advice about who not to bother seeing. Mum's sense of humour touched the moment and they were all laughing.

It was our job to wave the girls off to school each day; not the other way around.

Just as they did each morning, we both obediently smiled and waved. And as he spoke from behind his teeth, Graham said, 'Fabulous, isn't it? If they only knew how much I am not looking forward to this.'

It wasn't a long walk, but there was a chill in the December air. Keeping close together to stay warm, with our coat collars up we walked arm in arm and we soon arrived. The entrance to the school grounds looked a little more imposing than usual and, almost without thinking, we both hesitated for just a single step before crossing into the grounds. The car park was full and we could see silhouettes of lots of people in the windows.

'You don't fancy a drink in the local instead?' Graham joked.

'I've got a feeling we'll need one by the time we're finished tonight,' I said.

Security and display lights illuminated the wonderful Georgian architecture of the main school building. Designed, no doubt, to issue a statement of authority and importance to the community, it was hard not to be impressed, if not intimidated. By the time we had made the short journey up the path, we felt like a couple of misbehaving pupils on our way to see the headmistress.

We entered through the doors of the school and, as with most of the other new parents, we then had to find out which teacher was where and who we would need to see. We followed the sound of the greatest number of voices, which was coming from the main assembly hall at the end of a long corridor. As we walked through the double doors into the room, it was difficult not to be impressed by the grandeur of the oak beams and panelling. There were a couple of nods of acknowledgement from one or two parents we knew, but there was also a distinct dip in the decibels as we entered, as if word had got around that we'd arrived, like trouble arriving at a saloon bar in a Hollywood Western. There was a dive for the desks to get in before us to see a teacher.

A friend who also had older children and was therefore an experienced veteran of the parent-teacher evening at the school, saw us looking a bit lost on our first night and came over. We clearly brought some joy to the proceedings — at least for him — because as he greeted us he was almost laughing.

'I'm glad I haven't got your job tonight!'

Others within hearing distance reacted as if he had just delivered the perfect one-liner. He was right, of course; there were a lot of meetings ahead of us, and the prospect felt like hard work.

During the evening, more than one smiling and knowing face said, 'How many more have you got to see?' Again, it wasn't difficult to detect the laughter. Another friend passing between appointments echoed Graham's earlier joke. 'You'll need a drink after this, won't you?'

'Yes, we will!' We had heard that, to add a little social flavour to the evening, some parents did pop to the nearby pub afterwards in order to relax and wind down, and we looked forward to eventually joining the others — when we had finally finished for the night.

There was an appointment system and you were only allowed so many minutes per child with each teacher. Well, those best-laid plans were laid to rest. As innocent as we were and as cooperative as we wanted to be, we completely brought things into disarray.

In some cases, the same teacher taught more than one of the girls which worked well for us, if not so well for the parents sitting in a queue behind us. Sometimes four, five, or even six of the girls were taught by the same teacher. The amount of taps on the shoulder that caused us to turn around, only to see a desperate face and a plea to allow them with only the one child to go in front were very regular.

There were always people behind us. Throughout those school years, there were two places in particular that people didn't want to get behind us; one was to see a teacher at parent-teacher evening and the other was at the till in the supermarket!

Somehow, we survived the evening. And when we eventually got home to the girls, it was, 'What did they say about me?' from six directions. And very deliberately and carefully, I dipped into my bag and brought out the notebook. By the time we'd got home, despite our best endeavours, we'd forgotten what they'd all said. Having seen at least five teachers per child, there was no way I could remember all the detail. So the notebook was a vital part of my preparation, and would continue to be for the next five years.

The funny thing was that whatever the teachers had to say about the subjects each of the girls were taking, no matter which teacher it was, they would all say the same thing: 'But she's a lovely girl!' As if anything else that had been said that may have been negative didn't really matter, and was made up for by the important underlying fact that the teacher did actually like the pupil.

And that was it. It felt as if we were always first in and last out. The pattern was set for the next few years. It was the nightmare night that produced some of the sweetest dreams when the girls collectively, or individually, were praised by one teacher or another.

There is a lot to be said for the joy you feel when teachers genuinely speak well of your children. So, although the parent-teacher nights were on the one hand not our favourite night out from a logistics point of view, they were nevertheless very satisfying — and filled us with pride.

42

Teenage Kicks

We believed our increasingly grown-up girls required increasingly grown-up experiences, so, for a couple of summers, Graham and I chose to holiday with the girls in Majorca. Travel was something that was being offered to us as a family to tie in with more media appearances, too.

When it was just Graham and me making the decision, early in the girls' childhoods, about whether or not to agree to the proposed documentaries, time and again we would wrestle with our thoughts on whether we were doing the right thing by the girls and whether it would have a positive or negative effect on them. But the fact was, there were only the two of us ultimately responsible to say yes or no when the girls were little, and it was our call alone.

Things changed once the girls began to express their own feelings regarding how comfortable they felt about life with the cameras around. As they grew up, it was now their choice. Each sister was given the opportunity to make herself heard and it was fundamental that each of the girls had an equally powerful voice. It meant, quite simply, that however good the opportunity or the reward of making a film, if any of the girls individually was not comfortable, then all would accept the veto.

The best feedback Graham and I ever had about the films from the girls not surprisingly came from our family chats around that most important piece of furniture — the family dinner table. I took comfort in the knowledge that little had changed since my earliest memories of the girls in highchairs, finding their way in the world and helping each other. Any media offers were always put to a vote, and no one ever fell out, no matter what the outcome.

In 1996, Phillip Schofield presented *Six Little Angels*, the first documentary since the girls had started school six years earlier, for ITV. The girls had grown up and changed a lot and did their own interviews for the first time with Phillip, who, with young daughters of his own at the time, knew exactly how to deal with them, ensuring they were all at ease throughout the filming.

When getting the girls to talk about each other, Kate, much to Phillip's amusement, said exactly the same thing about *all* her sisters — namely, that she would not want to change a thing about Sarah or Lucy or Hannah or Ruth or Jenny. And in a brilliant illustration of how we all retain our personality of youth, she said exactly the same thing twenty years later to describe Graham in a documentary made for the girls' thirtieth birthdays.

As part of that 1996 film, we returned to Malta, and I was asked to go back to the fertility temple in Gozo and sit on the same stone I'd sat on the year before I became pregnant with the girls. The documentaries, I'm sure, had both their good and bad points, but one of the very best was the opportunity they gave us to revisit significant moments in our lives. Sitting with the warm stone beneath me, I wondered if the childless Janet who had sat on that stone, so desperate with longing for motherhood, would ever have believed me if there was a way I could have told her that she would one day have six girls.

★ ★ ★

It would be simple merely to say the girls reacted this way or that to being filmed or photographed and perhaps it would be a lot easier to assess the impact the cameras had if it had just been the one event or one documentary. But as life has unfolded, it hasn't been that way at all — the world has watched the girls grow up and, with the exception of a couple of periods, the films have captured most of the landmark events and portrayed much of the thirty years of the girls' lives.

As they moved into their teenage years, we hit another watershed moment regarding the documentaries. There was a greater reluctance from the sisters to participate in any new film ideas at that time. It wasn't that they didn't particularly want to do them; I think rather they were sometimes just a little worried about the reaction of their school friends.

During those teenage years, I always got the feeling that they didn't want to do certain things because they didn't want to be in the limelight at school. Especially as they got older, if there was something we had been asked to do and it wasn't something cool, they didn't want to be seen doing it. I think the point is that sometimes they were embarrassed about doing certain things. They didn't want to appear on the television at that time because they didn't want to be different to anyone else.

There was one occasion when an opportunity arose for a new film when the girls were in their teens and, as always, we took it to the table to see how the girls felt. While some of the girls had a few reservations, they were all generally up for it as long as the others were also happy. But Ruth wasn't happy. She had arrived at a point where she didn't like being filmed and made her mind up that enough was enough.

Ruth was content in the decision she made and when she reflects now on that time, she believes she did the right thing then, because she felt that when they were teenagers the filming was a bit too intrusive.

She wasn't totally isolated in her feelings, either. Like millions of people around the world, Sarah will often be super-critical looking at her image on a photograph and say how much she doesn't like seeing herself on photos, although she says she doesn't particularly have a reason. It seems to me, though, that all the girls have become so used to cameras, with all the experience they have had, that they are really quite relaxed in front of a lens.

Along with Hannah and Kate, Sarah has a

quieter personality, so I think those three have naturally always shied away from being the centre of attention. I think they feel a little more relaxed when the attention is on all the sisters as a group.

Over those teenage years, along with documentaries, we turned down a number of media opportunities. There was always solidarity and support from their sisters when one didn't feel right about filming, which was always a good sign.

And it was also an age of discovery for the girls; a time when they were discovering themselves as they experienced the changes from childhood to adulthood. There could have been any number of reasons in the backs of their minds as to why it may not be good to do one thing or another. It made a lot of sense for the girls not to want to deal with some of those changes in front of 8 million people. There was always the fact of potential embarrassment; with that in mind, the decision not to be filmed or photographed was made easier.

★   ★   ★

After our trips to Majorca, we decided to return to Dinas Dinlle. It was one of the best decisions we made for the family. We'd expected disappointment when we told the girls we were heading back to the caravan, but the reaction was quite the opposite. They had loved the years we'd spent there, it was very much a part of their lives and they looked forward to going back.

There was both comfort and security in the familiarity, and most of the people who had been there on our first holiday were still sitting outside the same caravans.

The girls were growing up and expressing themselves as much in their zest for fun in life as in their competitive spirit. I think that when you have a large family you will always find, especially when the brothers or sisters are not too far apart in years, and even when they are, that there are those children who will either emulate or aspire to go further than their siblings. In many families there is an academic competitive spirit and while that wasn't a driving force in our family, as the girls grew up sport in particular was something at which they all equally excelled.

The girls were all particularly good at and loved playing both netball and rounders. It's not often the whole team can be made up of one group of sisters, but in our case that is exactly what happened. During our later years at the caravan site, a new tradition in the Walton family arose: the annual 'Rounders Challenge'. The attributes the girls had shown for winning in sport at school transferred easily from the schoolyard to the oval arena at the holiday compound, where they joined with their father and their Uncle Dave in a no-holds-barred contest. With both Graham and his brother never giving less than 100 per cent, it meant the games became serious challenges. Many of the other families joined in and on more than one occasion the matches went on long into the summer evenings.

On one hot summer night, the rounders game had been going on for even longer than usual. Whatever 'local rules' had been applied had not taken into consideration the evening meal, which had to be put back and put back again as the evening took on a serious tone. The fading light added to the tension. This game apparently was the 'Big One', the equivalent to the Cup Final at Wembley or the Yankees versus the Red Sox. There simply had to be an outcome to the game and there were some pretty mean and determined looks on the faces of both the boys, including the dads, and the girls, most of which were mine!

As the game progressed, there was nothing between the teams. Same amount of runs and the game was evenly balanced. By now the orange sun that had been shimmering on the distant line drawn between the sky and the sea had set and disappeared for the day, and the remnants of the fading light of the dusk only dimly lit the oval, with the aid of the lights that shone from inside all the caravans around the field through their large windows.

There was one more round to go, but with it becoming almost impossible to see, it looked as if that was it and it would be either postponement, a continuation the next day or a draw declared. Nobody wanted to see that happen.

The girls' team had one more chance to win the game. Ruth was the last of the girls to take the bat but it was clear by now that there was not enough light even to see the ball coming towards her, never mind for anyone to have a chance of catching it, if she was lucky enough to hit it.

'More light. We need more light!' The cry went round the field.

Graham and the other dads huddled together, a brief discussion took place, time out was called and each man went back towards his caravan. Within minutes, the whole field became as bright as though lit by the midday sun, as each of the spotlights from the roofs of the caravans and the headlights of the cars dramatically illuminated the Rounders Oval.

Play continued till the bitter end, when Ruth made a perfect swing with her bat and hit the ball out of sight, winning the game for her team, who cheered her all the way to the final base.

The spotlights lit up something else that was becoming increasingly apparent. Not for the first time during those teenage summers, the girls' athletic success was bringing them attention from a new breed of fans. Suddenly, boys who weren't in either team added to the numbers on the field. Well, they weren't quite on the field; they were spectators with a greater interest in the girls than the match. Throughout those summers, the girls' strikes were met with resounding cheers as the number of male admirers grew proportionally to the number of girls heading out to bat.

The girls were now full-on teenagers and quite grown up, so the attraction wasn't surprising. And the minute the boys on the caravan site reached seventeen (the interested parties tended to be a year or two older than my girls), they were driving — and the fact that they could drive meant it wasn't long before they were calling on the girls at home in Wallasey. All the boys from the site lived around the North-West of England, so driving to see the girls was a pretty cool thing for them to do.

The great thing for me and Graham, though, was that by the time the boys began coming to the house, a trust had long developed and been established. Many of the boys' families had been going to the site as long as we had, so everyone knew each other. Half the time they came to the house, the boys would have long chats with both Graham and me. It made the girls' first steps into romance a little easier to bear for us concerned parents.

And Graham and I were both sensible enough to realise that if we had made it difficult for the girls by stopping the boys coming to the house, there may well have been secret meetings or meetings in the street. And so, we decided early on that the best way was to have an open-house policy. Consequently, the baby clinic that had become a nursery and then an extension of a schoolroom became in the girls' teenage years something resembling a youth club.

Boyfriends weren't the only new accessory the girls acquired; when Graham felt they were old enough to have the responsibility of owning their own mobile phones, the girls each received one, with the thought that it was a good idea for them to be in contact with us all the time.

Graham quickly discovered, however, that he

was not at the top of their contacts list, not the only male they wanted to be in touch with by phone.

There is one day that stands out in my memory from this time. We were all in the house, moving from room to room with our various occupations. Graham passed by Lucy, who was on the phone to one of the boys from the caravan site. She was in the hall, lying down, kicking her legs in the air as if cycling and murmuring into her new phone, rapidly using up call minutes, so wrapped up in her conversation that she hardly noticed her dad going past. Half an hour later, he went by again.

'Are you still on that phone?'

This time, his teenage daughter heard him, gave him a wave, blew a kiss, melted his heart . . . and carried on murmuring.

An hour later, he came past again. Jenny, who was beginning the girls' new ritual — beauty preparations for going out — was now also lying down, near her sister. Her hair was fanned out flat on the floor around her head on a brightly coloured towel, like a peacock's feathers. Her assistant Hannah was ironing the strands with care. Lucy hadn't budged from her position on the phone.

I heard Graham's voice raising a tone. He'd given up with Lucy and was speaking to Jenny.

'What the heck are they talking about?'

'Oh, they hardly talk, Dad,' Jenny said, in a very matter-of-fact manner. 'They just listen to each other breathe!'

Though most of the boys who came to the

house knew the girls from the caravan site or school, and therefore knew their family background, as time went on some of the gentleman callers might come to the house without any pre-warning or even knowledge that the girl they knew had a sister, let alone five of them.

I remember one young man's visit in particular. The number of people who were at the house that day was, as always, on the high side. We'd had a manic day and there were loads of the girls' friends at the house. This chap was an only child and clearly not used to crowds in the home. He walked wide-eyed into the pandemonium. Later, when he described his first visit, he admitted to being totally bewildered and wondered what he was even doing in such a house.

Soon, though, the house was about to become just that little bit quieter, as the girls began to spread their wings and fly the nest. The time had come for a mother to say goodbye and wave her girls off into the world.

43

Leaving the Nest

The day the girls got their GCSE results was always going to be full of emotion. Six children in the same household all going through the same major public exams for the first time was unusual to say the least. Even the girls who hadn't been bothered with academia over the years, who couldn't wait to be leaving school, still showed enough interest in the upcoming day for me to notice their nervousness. I just wanted to make sure, as much as possible, that we were all there for each other to share in the inevitable ups and downs of the day.

It called for some advance thinking — as usual. We needed an agreement between all of us as to what we were going to do as a family on the day the results came out. I thought it was right that we should all be together.

It was clearly one of the occasions in their lives where there was no hiding from comparisons being drawn between the girls, whether that came from within the family or from friends or even others outside. The important thing, I kept saying to them in the weeks running up, was that whatever they achieved academically, the important thing was that they should be happy in whatever they decided to do after they were given the results. It wasn't so much what they got, but how they dealt with the success or the failure.

Graham and I had discussed it and our proposal was clear. We both thought — and the girls all agreed with our suggestion — that we should go to where the girls had experienced some of their happiest times: the caravan.

Lucy in particular confided in me a couple of times in the weeks leading up to the results. She was really dreading the day, mainly because, as she said herself, she sort of knew by then who was good at school and she had no aspirations of being an academic — she just knew that her results weren't going to be very good. She was similar to Jenny in that she struggled with revising and doing exams. She was worried because she felt that when she went up to school that day, people would be comparing results — and finding her lacking. I kept reassuring her and told her, as I did the others, not to worry. What will be is what is meant to be; and whatever it is, it will be for the best.

In the end, it did turn out to be a difficult day for Lucy, mainly because she thought that comparisons were being made and she thought everyone else was getting better marks. The girls overall achieved what they had individually expected to. But Lucy's sadness was brief because the plan worked perfectly. Immediately after they got the results, we took the girls straight off to the caravan. It was good for them just to get away and it took their minds off the results. By the time we got to the caravan, Lucy wasn't bothered about the exams; she just wanted to play rounders.

★ ★ ★

For all sixteen-year-olds, your exam results at that age are a watershed moment. All the girls now had decisions to make based on the results.

For Graham and me, it felt an extraordinary achievement to have arrived at this point — with all the girls getting on equally well, each sharing their ups and downs and supporting each other in different ways. Somehow sixteen or seventeen seemed so young for our children to begin to leave the family nest; breaking such strong ties made it even harder. But the summer had passed, and the results acted as a catalyst for our daughters to focus on their futures. The girls were making their own independent, life-changing decisions now and we simply watched with pride as they began to make their way in the world.

For many, the school years are the best years of their lives — people fondly reminisce and talk of how they would like to go back in time — but those thoughts were not for my youngest. Jenny couldn't wait to move on and leave those years behind. Changes in opportunities for higher education meant most of the girls were staying on to pursue one subject or another, but that wasn't what Jenny wanted to do; she didn't like school and simply wanted to do something that she *wanted* to do, something that she enjoyed doing. She had loved the family holidays in the sun on the island of Majorca, so she decided that she would apply to work as a children's rep in the Mediterranean.

Jenny would have gone through the interview process and indeed worked abroad alone. Lucy, however, who had no definite career plans but had, along with Jenny, taken courses in childcare, decided to join her sister in the application process at Manchester Airport. Her intention had only been to show some sisterly support but, to her surprise, after a full day of tests and form-filling, they were both offered the job.

It came as a bit of shock that all of a sudden two of the girls weren't going to be around the house and part of everyday life anymore. Graham and I both knew we were going to be worried about the welfare of two of our girls leaving home to work such a distance away, but I never realised the emptiness I would feel when we saw them off at the airport. Certainly the house was going to be a lot quieter without them. We were, though, pleased and even relieved that not only they were going together, but that they would be going somewhere familiar. For once they had arrived in Majorca and done their training in Magaluf, they then both worked in Alcúdia, near to where Graham and I had taken the girls on holiday.

The work was seasonal and so their empty bedrooms were a sad reminder of their absence only during the summer months. The first moves may have been made venturing away from home, but I made it a point to make sure that they, as with all the girls, knew there would always be a place for them to stay.

* * *

The move away from home for Jenny and Lucy resulted in four years of hard work and fun for my girls. Jenny's original independent streak and leadership skills would have seen her through by herself, but I did feel better knowing they had each other. And any worries I might have had that they may have been split up as the years passed proved unnecessary, as it never happened throughout the time they were working together. I wondered at the time whether the company was using common sense in keeping the girls together, but however it came about, for me it was good news.

And there was even more safety in numbers the year after the girls' GCSEs, when Ruth, who had stayed on in the school sixth form to do an advanced childcare course, joined her sisters. Her original plan was to get the qualification she needed to be able to look after children abroad.

Lucy now calls that time the best four years ever — and thinks everyone should do it! It was a job that suited their personalities perfectly. Each outgoing and strong, they found working every day on the holiday front-line with families a brilliant form of further education. While it may have been a very different environment compared to my early work experience, the same lessons were being learnt: it was all about people skills — just as Nanny Fox had made me realise. They were learning so much about life so quickly out in the real world. Each time they returned in the winter months, I could see them becoming more and more confident and independent.

That first job eventually led to ten years in Spain for Jenny; and, ultimately, to her meeting her partner. Today, she is no longer in Spain, but while all the other girls are either in their own properties nearby or at home, Jenny is the only one who lives some distance away, which makes family gatherings all the more special when she returns to the Wirral.

As for Lucy, it wasn't really her idea to become cabin crew, but that's what happened. An ex-boyfriend had casually suggested that it might be a good career for her; he'd simply said to her one day, 'Why don't you go into flying?' It was as much a surprise to her as it was to all of us, as it was something she'd never considered, but after searching the Internet for information and to see who was recruiting, a serious path was taken that led to an amazing job.

There were, though, a couple of bridges that Lucy had to cross before her career literally took off.

Firstly, exams at school hadn't been her favourite moments to remember. Becoming cabin crew demanded qualifying exams and annual ones thereafter, and she was worried they would dash her hopes, which were building up higher and higher the more she thought about flying as a career. We talked about it and the best advice I could give her was that if she wanted it badly enough, she should go for it and be positive.

Encouragement can be a powerful friend and Graham and I always provided it whenever we felt any of the girls needed or wanted our support. I only had to think back to the day I was told I was pregnant and had kept telling myself everything was going to be alright to know what a difference a positive outlook can make.

But, as a parent, words are one thing, but usually there is always a more physical contribution around the corner — or in this case at the end of the runway — required. After a show of absolute determination and persistence, Lucy succeeded in achieving her dream. She now found herself with her second bridge to cross. As the job was confirmed, now all she needed was the uniform . . .

One evening, not long after Lucy had been offered her position, we were preparing tea in the kitchen, which wasn't quite the palaver it used to be, as these days there were not so many hungry mouths to feed. Lucy entered, looking a little sheepish, which was usually a prelude to a big request. She was talking about the new job, but seemed to be skirting around the issue of her new uniform. It was a bit of a family talking point as we were all looking forward to seeing her fully geared up and ready to fly.

'Dad, is there any chance . . . ' Big sweet smile. ' . . . Any chance at all of a lift to get the uniform sorted?'

'Of course, sweetheart.' Graham knew this was

a time for doing what we could to help.

'You don't know where I've got to go yet . . . ?'

We had both assumed it would be the relatively local international airport at Manchester.

'What do you mean?'

'It's the other side of London. I've got to go to Gatwick.'

Six-hundred-mile round trip instead of sixty. But what are parents for?

I felt a silent gulp in my throat and glanced at Graham, who to his paternal credit didn't bat an eyelid and played the hero dad card perfectly.

'No problem! When do we go?'

But Lucy, thinking it was too much even for the dad who used to come out at what she would call 'stupid o'clock in the morning' to pick her and her sisters up when the clubs finished on a Saturday night, hadn't heard the reply. She was expecting to have to get the train and went on explaining.

'Well, I'd feel better if you were with me, and I don't know how long it's going to take and . . . '

'Dad said yes, Lucy!'

She was absolutely made up. A couple of weeks later, the three of us set off at the crack of dawn. The traffic was heavy and after almost five hours in the car we finally arrived, parked the car and prepared ourselves for the wait. Out came the plastic boxes, in which sandwiches were sealed in silver foil, protecting the flavour of favourite fillings of egg and tuna. Out came bags of crisps . . . but before Graham had answered the question, 'Plain or salt and vinegar?' the familiar clunk of the car door being opened from the outside put the provisions on hold. Lucy was back. The whole thing had taken five minutes! A 600-mile round trip just to try on a uniform!

But it was worth the effort and every mile. All round the world, people fly and receive rewards for collecting air miles — but 'child miles' are something for which you can never calculate the reward.

When Ruth moved on from working in Majorca, she travelled away from home quite extensively, taking jobs in hotel receptions and, for one season, as a nanny in a hotel in France, where the perks included ski passes. However, after an aborted attempt at the sport, during which she was almost stranded at the top of a mountain, she decided there and then that she preferred a sunny beach to a ski slope any day. She promptly removed her skis and walked all the way down the mountain, off to pursue her next vocation, of which she has had several.

Hannah was next to leave home. She had stayed on at school to do her A-levels and had pursued a more academic life than the others, but then she went on holiday with her sisters and decided, along with one of her friends who wanted to work abroad, to experience living and working in Spain for a time. Jenny by that time had friends who were able to find work for Hannah at a bar in Majorca, and she was off, one more chick flying the nest.

Sarah wasn't fond of school and as soon as she could, she found a job in administration while Kate went from school straight to university.

By the time Hannah returned to take her place at university, Lucy had been back and gone again; and Sarah had moved out. That meant only Kate was left in the house — but when she eventually acquired a flat of her own, Lucy came back once more!

Particularly in this day and age, I guess it was never going to be a straightforward situation that, at a certain age, all the girls would instantly move out of the family home at the same time. The way things have worked out, 'moving out' has been an indefinite part of life. Graham and I have become accustomed to that; it's still ongoing. Some of the girls have flown the nest, only to return a year or two later depending on their individual circumstances, relationships and work.

The one thing that was consistent with all the moving around was that Graham was busier than ever. Mainly because, every time one of the girls completed a purchase or a rental agreement on a new property, the first call was to Dad for painting and decorating!

Having the house to ourselves hasn't really happened yet, although there have been times occasionally when all the girls have been away at the same time.

I have been so used to the vibrancy the girls have brought to the family home, though, that on those occasions when they are all away, the house always feels just a little too quiet.

44

New Opportunities

Sometimes, I feel my life has unravelled like a string from one giant ball of wool. Certainly that could apply to my working life over the past twenty-five years. Because, yes — I have had a working life alongside bringing up the girls. As an apple doesn't fall far from a tree, I found not only were Nanny Fox's people skills the best way to deal with most things, but I also discovered new ways to use knitting and wool, as they became totally entwined with my work.

When the girls were born, Graham and I were really grateful for what the hospital had done for us, so as soon as we got home we made a donation to the neonatal unit. Once we had come through the insanely hectic first few years with our daughters, we began to find further ways to raise funds ourselves and, together with the help of Mum and Betty, we organised a few coffee evenings. I would encourage as many people as possible to come to the house in Wallasey, including family and friends and members of our branch of the Women's Institute. They all spread the word and, perhaps not surprisingly, the girls — who were by then four — were a big attraction. It only had to be mentioned that we were putting on a bring-and-buy sale or a coffee evening and we had a full house.

In April 1992, a new charity, The Newborn Appeal, was started, specifically to raise funds for neonatal units in Liverpool to buy equipment and fund research. The coordinator of the charity, Liz Nealey, asked us, along with other parents who'd had premature babies and benefited from the skill and services of Liverpool Maternity Hospital, to attend the launch.

I became friendly with Liz through that and my ongoing coffee evenings. But alongside the coffee evenings and being a mum, I had by that time also returned to work at the bank. It didn't take me long to realise that, because of my new uncertain schedule and the specific hours required at the bank, things were not working out. I left, but with the girls now at school I had plenty of time I was anxious to fill. So I rang Liz, told her of my banking experience and offered to help The Newborn Appeal voluntarily for a couple of hours a week, which eventually led to a part-time job.

In 1995, the new Liverpool Women's Hospital was being built and Liz was appointed as communications manager for that. Her new role left her job on the neonatal charity vacant, and the trustees of The Newborn Appeal asked me if I would be employed on a more permanent basis. The original target had been to raise half a million pounds, and when I took over the figure raised was standing at £300,000.

Money was being raised in different ways by all sorts of people who wanted to help. There were raffles and parents doing fundraising, but

371

on the other side of things I found myself having to go to events that although they gave us some publicity, weren't actually directly bringing in money. My practicality made me focus purely on the fundraising side of the appeal and I decided that even if the job was going to be short-term, I would relaunch.

Consequently, I changed the colours of the appeal to black and white, in line with introducing a new panda logo. One of the first and most effective things I did was to have little panda badges made and, with a lot of hard work and help from volunteers, we sold around 100,000. Fridge magnets, keyrings and other items followed, while collections for the appeal were also made at places like supermarkets and football matches.

More events followed. Each one had to be coordinated and carefully watched over; for not only is there the responsibility of running the appeal itself, there is always the caution required to ensure time and effort weren't wasted, for example that when expenses were created by advertising and other costs they didn't wipe out any gains. There were occasions, especially at craft fairs, where I had to encourage stallholders to participate but the experience and financial result simply weren't worth the effort.

Overall, The Newborn Appeal was growing each year and it wasn't long before targets were passed. That meant a growing amount of time spent working, but with the girls well settled into school life, the hours suited, plus the feeling of giving something back always made any extra effort beyond my salaried time absolutely worthwhile.

There was nothing new about the good deeds and kindness of people wishing to help the neonatal unit. For years knitwear had flowed into the unit, but with all the good intentions in the world, people still found it difficult to grasp the reality of the size of the babies that were cared for in the unit.

Sometimes the knitwear was too big and the unit would give these items to me to see if there was anything I could do with them at craft fairs to help raise money.

I quickly realised there was a gap in the market for these products, because every time we had a pop-up stall in the reception area of the hospital, all the knitwear sold out. It was an obvious next step to advertise for knitters and before I knew it there was a flood of applicants and volunteers ready with their needles to 'knit one, purl one'. The knitting element just got bigger and bigger and bigger and it was the key to The Newborn Appeal overall becoming so successful.

The knitting part of the fundraising became very much like a community knitting scheme. I would get phone calls from people from all walks of life and from groups who wanted to meet up and knit but had nowhere to donate the knitted garments. Sales of the baby cardigans, hats, booties and blankets were always good because of the high quality supplied by really good knitters. Today, we now have over 500 knitters annually sending in items from all over the country and also from abroad. It feels as if I have gone full circle from selling Mum's knitting on a market stall in Wales. Hats are the most common item knitted because, generally, anyone who knits can make a hat. As simple as a hat might be, whoever has taken the time and trouble to send something needs a response. The knitters are volunteers and I am not running a business, so every single time someone brings in some knitting I write them a letter of thanks.

As Hannah, Lucy, Ruth, Sarah, Kate and Jenny grew up, they became more aware of their mum's job and its significance. They got involved in events such as the Wirral Coastal Walk, which gave them the opportunity to find sponsors for each mile over a fifteen-mile distance. But most rewarding was when, as often as possible, Graham and I would bring them back to the neonatal unit to visit.

That has been one of the great benefits of the job: it's meant that we have all kept in touch with the staff at the hospital. We went to visit the unit with the girls for years, right up to when they were teenagers. There were always parents there who were sitting alongside an incubator all day and all night, week after week, not knowing what the future held. What was always clear, whoever was there, was that the experience of witnessing your newborn child being cared for is one of the most difficult things any parent can endure.

When we went and visited with the girls, for some parents it was almost like a form of therapy. Parents wanted to talk to us; it always felt appreciated and hopefully it gave them a boost.

I've noticed that, even when I'm not with the girls, or even in the unit, for example while I have been doing knitting stalls in the main reception of the hospital, people will come and tell me everything about their pregnancy, birth, and about any problems with their baby. I try to be as positive and reassuring as I can be, just as I was for myself all those years ago.

As part of the weekly routine of my work, I'll often find myself in one of the high-dependency units. When I see six incubators in a room and there is a different family by each one, even now, thirty years on, I think, *Oh my . . . when my girls were born, these would have all been used by them.*

So although, at times, the line between home life and work over the past twenty-five years has blurred, it has been for the best of reasons. When I finally retire, the figure raised will be over £2.5 million, much of it due to a niche for knitting that evolved from the simple act of knit one, purl one; that same pastime that caused the bell in my nan's shop in Neston to ring every time the door opened and someone came in for their wool.

And, speaking of wool, I somehow managed to pull it over Graham's eyes, or least twist him and it around my little finger, when I originally persuaded him to take on a new role for the WI.

My WI meetings used to be held at the same hotel where we had the reception after the girls' christening. During a drink with a couple of the others at the bar one evening after a meeting, an idea began to brew in my mind.

When I got home, Graham was sitting in the kitchen reading the back page of the evening paper.

'How was your meeting, luv?' he asked, as considerate as ever.

'Good. Very good. I'll put the kettle on, shall I, and make you a nice cup of tea?' I needed to try and get Graham into as positive a frame of mind as possible.

'Thanks — I was just about to make myself a drink. Everyone turn up?' Sometimes decisions and getting on with WI business took far too long if enough members didn't attend the meeting.

'Enough for a vote or two and a couple of resolutions.'

'Well, if anyone can sort out a couple of resolutions, you can.'

'Except for one little thing . . . ' I was now sounding a little sheepish; just like Lucy did when she wanted something, in fact.

He looked at me over the top of his reading glasses. I gave him a slightly awkward smile that he of course picked up on straight away.

'What is it, Jan?'

'Well . . . ' My hesitance was now highlighted, making Graham show concern. 'Well, the thing is the speaker has let us down for next week.'

'Oh, yes?'

The next bit had to come out quickly if it was going to be effective.

'Yes. And by the way I've put your name down

for next week as a replacement!'

'I can't do that; you must be joking.'

'Come on now, you can do it,' I said encouragingly. 'You've spoken well at all the big family functions and you've managed to make everyone laugh. You are good at it.'

'That's different. That's family.'

'Well, you're doing it.' My voice was carefree and breezy but had a recognisable tone: Graham knew I wasn't about to let him off the hook. 'So you'd better get writing something!'

In the end, of course, he did talk to the local WI branch — for twenty minutes. He was enjoying himself so much, in fact, that he could have talked for longer.

And what do you know? That acorn of a maiden talk grew and grew, until a couple of years later, I sat proudly in an audience of 3,000 women, laughing away at the WI convention in Bournemouth, as Graham entertained them all with one story after another of his experience of living with seven women.

I guess you could say that our family life has certainly been something to write home about.

45

Six Little Miracles

The kitchen table at Wallasey has always served as a source of inspiration to each of the girls in different ways throughout their lives. Even today, now that most of the girls have moved away from home, there is always a sense of excitement when all six manage to get together around it.

Graham and I encourage gatherings of the girls and their partners as often as possible. There has been many a Sunday over the last couple of years when brunches or buffets, each lasting for hours, have given Hannah, Lucy, Ruth, Sarah, Kate and Jenny the opportunity to catch up with each other's news.

Now our discussions around the table invariably include some memory of one of the unique experiences that the girls' lives in the occasional limelight has brought. Just recently, they were thrilled to fly to New York for their thirtieth birthday for an accompanying documentary; a film in which every sister chose to participate. For Lucy, who crosses the Atlantic as cabin crew more times than the others cross the River Mersey, it was a special treat for her to be a passenger pampered by other stewardesses. Following a surprise announcement by the plane's captain about 'the special birthday celebrations of the Walton sextuplets', the girls were given cake and champagne.

But our reminiscences might equally be about our trips to Japan or America, or Majorca during our daughters' childhoods. When I look at the girls today and wonder to myself how much all the attention has affected them, I feel more than ever that the experiences the media have brought to us have only served to enhance their lives. This incredible journey was always going to be an unusual one, whether or not the cameras had documented some of their most significant moments. The fact that they have been filmed and continue to be filmed today tells me that they are comfortable with the attention.

If Hannah, Lucy, Ruth, Sarah, Kate and Jenny hadn't done the documentaries, so many opportunities would have been missed. I actually believe they wouldn't be the confident and outgoing girls they are now, equally at home on the Wirral or on the Costa del Sol. It has brought them experience of travel to places we could never have afforded, and given them the opportunity of seeing and dealing with different cultures which has enriched their lives in so many ways.

As for the girls' opinions of it all, Jenny often says how she understands why people have been so interested in their story because they are the only all-girl sextuplets in the world. Sarah says that she and her sisters haven't known anything different, but she enjoys the fact that people take an interest and like to follow their progress. Her way of putting it is simple: 'This is all we've known.' Everyone's life is different and this

379

happens to be ours.

Similarly, Kate says, referring to the younger days, that she just thought it was normal to be filmed and that everybody in the world was filmed. She sees us, quite rightly, as a normal family, but does understand why the media attention happened.

The best thing of all, though, is that they all say the same about simply feeling normal. The extraordinary and unique life we have had that seems so unusual to many has to us been perfectly ordinary. First and foremost we are just a family: a mum and dad and six children, all of whom happen to be girls and all of whom happen to have been born together. 'Sextuplet' is a word the outside world uses as a label, but each of the girls sees herself as someone who just happens to have five sisters.

And those sisterly relationships are more important than ever to them all. The girls are always texting each other and at least once a day most of them are in communication using Twitter, WhatsApp or Facebook. It might be Kate rousing the troops, in her own quirky way taking a photo of her dinner and sending everyone the snapshot, to the amusement of her sisters; or Jenny might put a funny comment alongside an old family picture. But none of this modern technology, however good it may be for keeping people in touch, comes anywhere close to generating the pleasure the girls get from spending time together in each other's company. The love between them, the hugs and kisses that were so important as part of their growing up, are still there as they greet or say goodbye. The warmth between them all is as strong as it has ever been.

I regard these reunion times as special — a blessing. They also provide an opportunity to see how loving support and encouragement, something that once upon a time would be given only by Graham and me to each of our daughters individually, is now bestowed freely by each of the girls upon one another, as they inspire and help each other on their independent journeys.

I get a lot of comfort from seeing the values I have always tried to instil in the girls surfacing time and again. I might overhear a word of reassurance that Jenny may give to Kate — who, like my sister Alison, has always been a bit of a worrier, at least more than the others — and see Kate relax at her sister's encouragement. Or Ruth may proffer some practical advice to Sarah, or the other way around. It's a good feeling to know that their love and support for each other endures.

The sisters are all individual, expressing their own personalities in their own way. For me, that has been one of the greatest successes for Graham and me as parents-of-six: to encourage each child to be individual from day one. Today, the girls' chosen careers are as diverse and varied as their personalities. Every time we get together, the conversations reflect those differences.

Kate delights in sharing as much as possible about everything in her life with the others, embracing the special gift of having five sisters not just through zany texts and picture-sharing, but through talking to them and meeting up and going out with them as much as possible. Despite her apprehensive nature, she is not afraid to go out in the world, and her careful, serious side has seen her secure a very responsible job in human resources in a large organisation. The skills she has learnt at work have emerged in her personal life and she has become a confident central force of organisation between her sisters.

Jenny's independent nature, meanwhile, has now brought her the experience of managing her own business. She has shown creativity and talent in taking an idea and developing her own range of confectionery gifts. Having to deal with buyers, sellers, wholesalers and customers has given her an insight always helpful to the others.

Ruth has enjoyed a number of different vocations over the years but is now settled and enjoys her job as a personal assistant and receptionist in a nearby busy shopping centre.

Then there is Hannah, always ready with a considered and helpful piece of advice for her sisters, if needed. Hannah was the one who would always be around the table to help with homework, and it's perhaps no surprise that, in the end, she became a primary school teacher, working locally. She absolutely loves working with children and there seems to me to be a direct connection between her career choice and how comfortable she has always been with school life. She was the one out of the six who automatically took to her homework; it was never a bind or hardship to sit down after school and make sure it was all attended to before anything else. It was a different attitude and aptitude to her sisters', done out of interest and enthusiasm. I think that perhaps her love of education is the driving force behind a job that, for her, has been an ideal vocation.

Sarah likes to make a point of popping in at least once a week, if not more, just to make sure she is staying in touch. She knows, like the others do, that Graham and I will always have time for a cup of tea and a catch-up on all the news. Sarah has her own home close by, is happy working as an administrator in a medical centre and is planning for the future with her partner, hoping for a family of her own.

Every year, even now, Lucy will shut herself away and give all her attention to her annual cabin crew exams. She is totally focused when preparing for the test because she loves her work so much, enjoying the privileges it brings: travelling such great distances and getting the opportunity to see more of the world than she could ever have imagined.

But wherever in the world she may be at any one time, the same daily texts will be sent. Often she'll be in a hotel in Las Vegas or Cuba, having just arrived after a transatlantic flight, about to settle down to a midday meal — only to open a message from Kate with yet another picture of her sister's evening meal or a text from Ruth or Hannah seeking an opinion about a new dress or a pair of shoes.

Hardly a week goes by without me receiving a message from her in some far away, exotic location saying: 'This is the best job in the world!'

No matter how loud the chatter around the table gets, somehow everyone gives each other a platform to speak. Each girl is always fair with the others, listening and laughing as much as talking. It makes my heart swell to see them.

★　★　★

Over the years, I've learnt that, as a parent, you can only do your best. You find time and time again when you reflect that it really is a bit of luck if everything works out alright. Some might disagree and say it's all down to discipline and other such parenting things, but you can only do what you do as a parent because you think it's the best way.

When all the girls lived at home, every day was busy, hectic and chaotic, but they all understood the 'house rules' and the practical manner in which Graham and I always tried to run our home. When they were babies, if we hadn't been so organised, we would have had difficulty coping with doing six things at once at all times. Yet the irony was that because there was so much to do and to be done it never felt like there was time to do any planning, so I can only imagine we were both working on instinct much of the time. That never really changed as the demands of schooldays took over and then, each with their own social circles, friends became the centre of their world. Graham and I seemed forever on four wheels driving them here, dropping them there and delivering them to one place or another.

And things don't change, even now when four of the girls have left home and run their own lives with their own boyfriends and fiancés. Nothing changes for two main reasons. Firstly, when does any parent have a day go by without thinking at some point about the welfare of their children? When talking of the youngest offspring or when referring to a thirty-one-year-old youngest daughter, we still say 'she's the baby of the family'. These phrases are not far from the truth; the truth that while we all grow up, we are always our mother's children.

Secondly, all six daughters are in touch all the time. Whether it's to discuss a recipe Kate has just tried out and wants to share with me, or to advise Sarah on the colour scheme in her new lounge and which settee she should buy, or for some comfort if life is not running too smoothly. Though Hannah, Lucy, Ruth, Sarah, Kate and Jenny each have their own lives, not a day goes by without me having some sort of contact with each of the six girls. And at the end of each day, there always seems to be something else to say or do or share with one or another of them that I haven't quite had time to communicate.

And that is a state of being I realised would be constant almost as soon as they were born. For there is never going to be enough time in the day for me to give all the attention I instinctively want to give to each of my daughters. Something I had to learn when they were babies, and still study to this day, is how to be fair, and loving, and split my time and affection equally six ways. It was always important to me to make sure that the girls never had to wait to get my or Graham's attention; that they felt security and protection when something in their little lives went wrong; that they knew, even as we were helping their sisters, that our love for them was just as strong.

And I think we succeeded. I think from birth the girls knew we loved them just the same, and that we gave them each our full time and affection, whether they were first in line or in the middle or the last one over the line. A brilliant example of this was when the girls first started infant school. I remember it especially because the scene featured in one of the films we made. The director had asked us to go through the 'getting ready for school' routine. All we did was exactly what we normally did each morning, nothing different for the cameras.

The girls could barely contain their excitement for school each morning at that stage (it didn't last long . . .). They were so excited, they would parade on the landing outside their bedrooms in their very smart new uniforms. Once the vests, pants, blouses, skirts, socks and shoes had been sorted, the last item was usually the yellow-and-black tie that thankfully was of the pre-knotted type with elastic to go around the neck and keep it secure under the collars. Ties on, they were ready for the day.

It became, for a while during those early few weeks of school, before the novelty wore off, like an inspection at Horse Guards Parade and they would stand proudly in line with patent black shoes shining as brightly as their smiles. The girls would sometimes even stand in order of age.

'Hannah, you look very smart today.' I stroked the palm of my hand gently across her head. 'Now those ribbons look especially pretty, don't they?' As she beamed, her hand automatically shot up to move the tie I had just straightened.

'Look, Mummy!' Lucy pointed to her immaculate shoes that yesterday had arrived back home scuffed and muddy. I gave her a quick hug and kiss. 'They are perfect, Lucy. You'll have the shiniest shoes in school!'

'Kate's need cleaning!' Ruth shouted, as she came out of line and put her arms around me.

'Her shoes may need cleaning but she looks beautiful with her hair in such a long thick plait,' I said, as a worried Kate looked up from an anxious glance down at her shoes to catch my twinkling wink in her direction.

'Ruth Walton.' My tone moved into semi-strict. 'I think I would worry more about a missing clip and brushing your hair, young lady.'

A small soft children's brush suddenly appeared out of one of my pockets, together with a substitute clip and, within a shake of one of Sarah's pigtails, Ruth was ready for the day. My smile and kiss made her and next-in-line Sarah giggle.

As usual, I moved along from one to the next, detecting in the corner of my eye the next little one waiting her turn for the all-important hug and cuddle. Every morning, each of the girls' eyes and wriggling body movement was filled with the anticipation and excitement that only a

387

child has for a mother's love.

Standing patiently to attention at the end of the line, such was the reward for being the youngest, was Jenny. Rather than losing any of her enthusiasm — which would have been a perfectly understandable thing to do, having had to wait for five of her sisters to be attended to first — her excitement at the prospect of her 'turn' instead seemed to grow as I moved along the line and got closer and closer to my tallest daughter. By the time I arrived in front of her, she was bursting with pride.

All these years later, when I watch that particular moment, I can almost physically feel the love being shared on screen: the sharing of our emotions and my meticulous care for the girls' feelings, wanting none to feel slighted or abandoned or overlooked. When, at long last, I get to Jenny, she visibly braces herself to get ready for her pat on the shoulders or for my hand straightening her hair. She relaxes blissfully and contentedly into my touch when it comes, like a cat in sunshine; like each of her sisters has done before her.

The bond that is created between mother and child at birth, from the first moment you know a new life is growing inside you to the first time you hold your baby, is possibly the most powerful emotion any human being can experience. That bond for me, with each of my daughters, has grown stronger each year as they have passed so many milestones and anniversaries.

And, over the years, the same fundamental

feelings that arise from that bond have never gone away. Even in adulthood, children need the reassurance of a parent no matter how independent, successful or self-assured they may be. And I could not be prouder of my girls. For all they have achieved. For the wonderful women they are. For the fact that their feet are planted so firmly on the ground, despite the fame that has followed them from birth. I think they all have a mixture of my practicality and Graham's sense of humour. They never asked for fame, just as neither Graham nor I sought any limelight at the beginning. It is a great source of pride to us that they have come through more than thirty years of this worldwide attention, dealing with a life that began with odds of survival at 104-billion-to-one against, with such level-headedness and modesty.

Now that the girls have their own lives and relationships, people think that I must have plenty of time on my hands. I wish! Even on days off from working for The Newborn Appeal, things never seem to slow down. And the family is becoming even bigger. With engagements and now marriages on the horizon, those girls that have already chosen partners have chosen well; as the others I am sure will too. They now look to a future where they will find strength and success in building new families. That experience can only be enhanced with the unique and special sibling relationship that Hannah, Lucy, Ruth, Sarah, Kate and Jenny have with each other always there in the background.

What happened to us was probably the nearest

in this world that anyone can come to a miracle. I do know that I am lucky and for that luck I am grateful. I'm lucky to have met Graham, lucky that Sam Abdulla and his team were there together at the moment in my life when I needed their brilliant skill and dedication, and lucky to be blessed with six beautiful and accomplished daughters born together, each different and distinct in their own lives but identical in my heart.

At the end of the day, they will always be my six little miracles.

Epilogue

Tuesday, 7 October 2014
Focus. I needed to focus.

I had set off to work early but any plans of being extra prepared for what was going to be a special day were literally carpeted by an overturned lorry that lost its floor-covering contents.

Now I was at my desk, I kept telling myself to concentrate as I ploughed through the paperwork. I glanced across my office. A huge cuddly bear with a happy face waiting patiently for a new owner after the last raffle stared back at me, as if to say it's going to be a good day. But I had reason to be apprehensive. In many respects it was just another busy working day at the hospital, no different to the past twenty years, but today one of my girls was also in the Maternity Hospital and my thoughts were wandering back to the day they were all born.

Even though my little domain was right opposite the busy main reception desk, the solid wood door dulled any sound that dared to disturb my work. The only noise that I was aware of was the clicking of the buttons on the computer keyboard. There were letters of thanks to be written, minutes of the last trustees' meeting to type up and a hundred other chores, messages and little jobs that needed to be completed, responded to or organised.

I jumped as a sharp rap on the door broke the quiet. Opening the door revealed two happy familiar faces. Sarah and her partner Kieran hadn't stopped smiling for the seven or so months since they'd discovered Sarah was pregnant.

It had been a totally different experience than I had been through, beginning with her first scan at twelve weeks. I had gone to the hospital with them then, and as I'd patiently sat in the waiting room, I was surprised and delighted when Kieran's face appeared from behind the door of the scanning room and asked me to join them.

Even at that stage the images clearly outlined the embryonic new life — so different to the confusion I'd had in trying to see what Sam Abdulla and Illa had tried to show me. The atmosphere was also really calm compared to the mayhem of my first scan. As we watched, Kieran, with one hand in Sarah's, reached for my arm in a gentle act of kindness. The generations brought together for a moment.

The baby was breach and Sarah had been booked in for a Caesarean, having been told to be at the hospital at 7.30 this morning. They had now been told they were third on the list and there was a few hours until the operation. I called Graham, who hotfooted it to be with us, and for the next couple of hours we sat together in anticipation.

Alison had taken the day off work and, just as she had on the night of the birth of Sarah and her sisters, she sat staring at her phone, waiting for news. Five aunties-to-be, Hannah, Lucy,

Ruth, Kate and Jen, and all the other close members of both Sarah and Kieran's family, were all part of the group texts and call network, anxiously awaiting the arrival.

At 12.58 p.m. Jorgie Louise made her entrance upon the world's stage. Twenty minutes later, Graham and I, with new title 'Nanny Jan', were allowed into the recovery room to be with Sarah, Kieran and their beautiful newborn tiny wonder. Not so tiny! Jorgie weighed in at 7 lb 6½ oz and I reminded Sarah her little baby girl was equal in weight to three of her sisters when they were born.

Whether one child or six, to see a baby only moments old with a mop of hair, beautiful eyes and perfect features is the deepest feeling. To me, the creation of life will always be simply a miracle, and the beginning of a whole new story.

Acknowledgements

I have so much to be grateful for and so many people to thank as well as my fantastic husband Graham and his incredible sense of humour, which has shone through from the very beginning of our relationship.

We could not have managed without all the love, help, and total commitment given to us all from Nancy and Peter, my parents and Betty and John, Graham's parents and the patience and support from our close family and friends, especially my sister Alison.

Thanks to Sam Abdulla for being there for me when I needed him.

This book would not have been written without the long hours and expertise put in by my friend Robert Ettinger, who turned the many hours of interviews into this manuscript.

Also many thanks to family friend Philip Ettinger for his professional advice over the lifetime of our girls and the gallons of coffee and mountains of sandwiches consumed by us during the writing of this book.

Thanks also to Charlotte Cole at Ebury Press for her guidance.

Thanks to Hannah, Lucy, Ruth, Sarah, Kate and Jenny for being the gorgeous, wonderful, funny and inspirational daughters that they are.

And finally, thanks for the gift of our first granddaughter Jorgie Louise — I am probably biased but she is absolutely beautiful.

We do hope that you have enjoyed reading this large print book.

Did you know that all of our titles are available for purchase?

We publish a wide range of high quality large print books including:
Romances, Mysteries, Classics
General Fiction
Non Fiction and Westerns

Special interest titles available in large print are:
The Little Oxford Dictionary
Music Book
Song Book
Hymn Book
Service Book

Also available from us courtesy of Oxford University Press:
Young Readers' Dictionary
(large print edition)
Young Readers' Thesaurus
(large print edition)

For further information or a free brochure, please contact us at:
Ulverscroft Large Print Books Ltd.,
The Green, Bradgate Road, Anstey,
Leicester, LE7 7FU, England.
Tel: (00 44) 0116 236 4325
Fax: (00 44) 0116 234 0205

Other titles published by Ulverscroft:

THE LIFE AND LOVES OF A HE DEVIL

Graham Norton

From his varied career to his beloved dogs to Ireland, once a place that felt stifling but that now is home, Graham Norton shows how life isn't simply a series of dates and events: it is who and what we love. And so he tells of the men he has loved and lost; the booze that has flowed freely — sometimes with startling results; of his love affair with New York, and the divas who have awed him with their power and imperfections. Here, he shares an amazing variety of experiences, from the mundane (falling asleep on the night bus), to the grotesque (vomit-covered socks), to the sublime (floating down the river singing with Dolly Parton) — a plateful of life stories, along with a dollop of 'Graham Nortonness' on the side.

IN THE FAMILY WAY

Jane Robinson

Only a generation or two ago, illegitimacy was one of the most shameful things that could happen in a family. Today, babies' parents are as likely to be unmarried as married. This revolution in public opinion makes it easy to forget what it was like to give birth, or be born, out of wedlock in the years between the First World War and the dawn of the permissive age. In the Family Way tells secrets kept for entire lifetimes; in it we hear long-silent voices from the workhouse, the Magdalene Laundry, and the distant mother-and-baby home. Anonymous childhoods are recalled, spent in the care of Dr Barnardo or a child migration scheme halfway across the world. There are sorrowful stories — but also stories of hope, of triumph and the everyday strength of the human spirit.